BRIDGING MENTAL BOUNDARIES IN A
POSTCOLONIAL MICROCOSM

Bridging Mental Boundaries in a Postcolonial Microcosm

Identity and Development in Vanuatu

WILLIAM F. S. MILES

UNIVERSITY OF HAWAI'I PRESS

HONOLULU

Library of Congress Cataloging-in-Publication Data

Miles, William F. S.
  Bridging mental boundaries in a postcolonial microcosm : identity
and development in Vanuatu / William F.S. Miles.
      p.   cm.
  Includes bibliographical references and index.
  ISBN 0-8248-1979-9 (cloth : alk. paper). — ISBN 0-8248-2048-7
(paper : alk. paper)
  1. Vanuatu—History. 2. Postcolonialism—Vanuatu.
3. Nationalism—Vanuatu. 4. National characteristics, Vanuatuan.
I. Title.
DU760.M55   1998
995.95—dc21   98-9698
                                                                   CIP

Designed by inari

Buk ia igo long bigfala "wa" blong mi,
from we hemi bin tijim mi long rid fastaem.

This book is dedicated to my older brother Robert,
who first taught me how to read.

CONTENTS

List of Maps, Tables, and Figures

FIGURES

FOREWORD

It is a great pleasure to offer a few introductory words to Professor William Miles' *Bridging Mental Boundaries in a Postcolonial Microcosm*. The University of Hawai'i Press is to be congratulated for being in the forefront of recent academic publications regarding this most fascinating archipelago, following on Lamont Lindstrom's *Cargo Cult* (1993) and Joël Bonnemaison's *The Tree and the Canoe* (1994).

In spite of almost being wiped off the face of the earth—from an estimated precontact population of 600,000 down to as little as 40,000 in the late 1920s—the people of Vanuatu have bounced back with vigor and do not bear a grudge against the outside world. They are a very special people, and the country is the way the world should be: a myriad of interconnecting indigenous languages and cultures with intense respect for the material, physical, and spiritual world. The history of European contact nearly destroyed Vanuatu culture and, as Miles makes clear, newer, outside influences may yet try to do so. Yet, one has faith in the deep, philosophical wisdom of the Vanuatu people to choose what is really best for them and to reject those modern influences that they deem harmful for future generations.

I first met Bill Miles, his wife Loïza, and their children at the Second National Arts Festival of Vanuatu on Santo in June 1991, and we have kept in regular contact ever since. His pleasant personality, his fluency in English, French, and Bislama, and also the fact that he is American enabled him to pursue his studies throughout Vanuatu in 1991 and 1992 without facing the kinds of problems that a British or French researcher pursuing the same sort of "touchy topics" might have faced.

This book is not an anthropological study per se but is extremely relevant to those anthropologists, ethnologists, and historians interested in Vanuatu, to ni-Vanuatu themselves, and to those in the wider world interested in pre- and postcolonial history. It is also a "must" for those concerned with the reaction and interaction of two of the world's major international languages, English and French.

It may indeed be another generation before the so-called Anglo-phone/Francophone dispute in Vanuatu dies down. Time, ni-Vanuatu intelligence, and adaptability should eventually calm the periodically turbulent seas—if the outside world lets ni-Vanuatu alone to sort out their differences. In the meantime, holdover suspicions do cloud current politics. During 1996 and 1997, for instance, some ni-Vanuatu students were complaining virulently about disorganization and lack of opportunity in the Francophone side of the nation's educational system. Some ni-Vanuatu believe that internal divisions within the French embassy were almost purposely creating the problems, so as to send an indirect warning to Kanaks in New Caledonia—where a referendum on the French territory's political status has been scheduled for 1998—about the inadvisability of independence. Those of us who were in the country during the struggle for independence and recall the incoherence, antagonism, and factionalization both within and between the colonial and missionary camps can easily relate to these kinds of fears.

Since 1973 I have spent approximately seventeen years pursuing cultural and anthropological work in Vanuatu and I have found, of course, that Bislama was and is the most useful language in the country—neither French nor English are of much use in the more isolated, traditional areas of this stunning country. Bislama is a dynamic, developing language with magical, beautiful, and poetic qualities that can better convey the "real" Vanuatu than European languages, although it is not, of course, as deep and profound as the indigenous languages. Much of the value of *Bridging Mental Boundaries in a Postcolonial Microcosm* is that it conveys certain insights that formerly only one thoroughly familiar with Vanuatu's national language could obtain.

I once had a dream in Vanuatu (after a good kava session) in which important traditional and modern political ni-Vanuatu leaders invited English, Australian, New Zealand, and French diplomats and missionary representatives to a *kastom* reconciliation ceremony. In the first section of the ceremony the ni-Vanuatu leaders imposed a symbolic *kastom* fine upon the expatriate Anglophone and Francophone representatives for bringing their linguistic and cultural dissensions into the country. In the second part of the ceremony the ni-Vanuatu leaders presented these expatriates with ritual gifts that symbolized thanks to the early missionaries for introducing peace. In addition, the Vanuatu leaders offered gifts of thanks to England and France for giving the languages that enable Vanuatu to reach out to the world. Then a special kava was brought out and after all had drunk a few coconut shells of it, "evriwan i bin kam gud gudfala fren mo i bin gat gudfala rispekt mo andastanding" (they all became good friends, and there developed good respect and understanding).

Bill Miles' book may be a step in the right direction toward bridging these artificially induced mental boundaries. Let us hope so, for Vanuatu can teach the modern outside world about more things than the outside world can actually teach Vanuatu.

Kirk W. Huffman
Curator (National Museum),
Vanuatu Cultural Center
1977–1989

PREFACE: CHOOSING VANUATU

> When after two years of wandering and encamping in different places I
> came back . . . I found the same map of the New Hebrides which I had
> studied before going out there [in 1929]. It looked totally different. The
> names were enough to recall a picture of the different islands and what
> had happened on them.
>
> —Evelyn Cheesman,
> *Camping Adventures on Cannibal Islands*

I have often joked with friends and colleagues that the Condominium of
the New Hebrides was established in 1906 so that I might study it
eighty-five years later. For one who has specialized in the differences
between French and British modes of colonization, and particularly the
developmental implications of their respective decolonizations, Vanuatu,
as the South Pacific archipelago has been called since 1980, would seem
to represent the perfect case study. It is the only instance in the annals
of colonial history in which Great Britain and France have ruled jointly,
for an extended period of time, over the very same territory. As I had
already compared neighboring British and French colonies in the West
Indies, West Africa, and South Asia, it seemed paradigmatically perfect
to examine the one case in which both types of colonization existed side
by side within the very same territory, ruling the same indigenous people. *Et voilà:* Vanuatu!

It would be the height of solipsism and insensitivity to relegate an
entire nation's colonial past to the theoretizing fantasies of a social scientist. If I jokingly claim that the Condominium was prophetically conceived by French and British diplomats at the turn of the century for my
academic benefit, I dare to do so only because there is no satisfactory
answer to the converse question: For whose benefit *was* the Condominium created? Certainly not for the denizens of the eighty some-odd islands that were administratively grouped together for the first time and
remained stateless for seventy-four years. Certainly not for France,
which would have preferred out-and-out sovereignty for the islands, as
she had already acquired over nearby New Caledonia. Definitely not for
Great Britain, which had minimal interest in adding the New Hebrides
to her colonial custody but was pushed to do so by Australian
Francophobes. If the Condominium represented an administrative ab-

surdity, a colonial headache, and a human rights indignity, perhaps only a social scientist *can* extract some benefit, albeit conceptual, from it.

For all of its unique and idiosyncratic features, Vanuatu may be regarded as a microcosm of the colonial phenomenon. Not only did it experience the two major types of colonialism of the modern era, French and British colonialism, it did so in close proximity to each other, with intense rivalry, and over a long period of time. Thanks to its small size and young age as an independent state, Vanuatu is a theoretically compelling exemplar of the clash of contemporary colonialism and its repercussions for the age of independence. At the same time, the uniqueness of Melanesian culture highlights the role played by indigenous culture in shaping both colonial and postcolonial political realities. Understanding Vanuatu's experience in bridging mental boundaries enables us to better understand those challenges of decolonization, nationalism, identity, and development which face the Third World at large.

Geographical and linguistic features also impart to this South Pacific society quintessential attributes for comparative, and particularly developing society, politics. Spatial dispersal throughout an archipelago serviced by rudimentary transport and communication networks highlights the necessity of creating an interactive developmental infrastructure for achieving national identity. A multiplicity of languages, giving Vanuatu the highest language-per-capita ratio in the world, underlines the social challenges facing ethnically and culturally diverse states in their quest for national unity. In short, the classic challenges of nation building are here distilled within a topographically small territory.

Neither has Vanuatu been immune from the unfortunately familiar plagues of political fragmentation and ethnoregional secession. Although a secessionist rebellion spearheaded from the nation's largest island was effectively and definitely quashed at independence—thanks, not unusually, to foreign intervention—the scars of that revolt remain in the national psyche.

As a poor nation (in its Human Development Index of 1997, the United Nations ranked it 124th out of 175), dependent on foreign aid for its economic survival, Vanuatu well typifies the tension between national sovereignty and international dependency. Yet the long-standing weakness of central government has also perpetuated the venerable tradition of strong communitarian autonomy, a phenomenon which, when rediscovered by social science in the 1980s and 1990s, was studied under the rubric of "state–society" dynamics, "civil society," and "disengagement" theory. Vanuatu also shares many of the other problems facing developing nations: declining terms of trade for a small basket of primary export goods, subservience to profit-oriented transnational corporations, ecological stress, an ill-adapted educational system, growing crime, and the injection of religion into politics.

Nevertheless, Vanuatu is more than an exemplar of the developing world and its problems and more than a case of colonial division gone awry. The richness and distinctiveness of ni-Vanuatu society offer a vast resource for sociopolitical reflection and analysis into processes of state formation. It is a fascinating nation composed of many subcultures that nevertheless weave together a distinctive political entity whose name literally means "Land Eternal" or "Land That Stands Up."

In the course of writing this comparative and contextual history of the New Hebrides Condominium and Vanuatu independence, I witnessed the theoretical richness of the boundary paradigm progressively unfolding. Even though I knew that Vanuatu presented an exception to the colonial rule of partition, for a long time I remained conceptually wedded to boundaries in their formal, territorial, and juridical sense. When I eventually released myself from that more restrictive interpretation (thanks, in part, to a decade of marriage with a partner less literalist than I), new theoretical avenues of exploration opened. One of these paths brought me to that literature within political geography, an intellectually rich field well worth mining, which examines the cross-border interpenetration of national societies by global processes. This perspective does not nullify the existence or functionality of national boundaries, but rather emphasizes their porousness.

Another (border)line of inquiry applies notional, as opposed to national, boundaries of social separations occasioned by language, religion, gender, and nationalism—in short, the gamut of constructions that constitute human identity and distinguish communities from one another. Notional boundaries can encompass political divisions no less than national boundaries do, albeit in a less spatially rooted sense. As a political scientist returning to the classic literature on nationalism, I have also found the conceptual frameworks offered by social geography and cultural anthropology to be helpful in formulating a thesis which advances the use of notional boundaries. As Ron Crocombe has noted in the context of the Pacific writ large, "one cannot divorce one's meaningful localities and physical boundaries from one's genetic boundaries and kinship network, one's social boundaries of language(s) and culture(s) or the political boundaries of nation(s)."[1]

As one who is constitutionally wary of hyperbole, I do not use the boundary metaphor lightly. My primary use of the boundary concept in this book is still the political one, and I pray that it not be lost. There *was* a colonial partition in the New Hebrides, even if it was a mental boundary and not a formal territorial one. However attenuated, this mental boundary has persisted since formal decolonization. Other mental boundaries also persist, just as new ones are emerging. While the colonial mental boundary provides my point of departure, its dismantling, together with the emergence of newer types of boundaries, is the more exciting area of inquiry. Decolonization and development are impossible without the transcendence of mental boundaries.

Artificial boundaries are rampant not only in the history of colonialism but also in the architecture of academia. One of the first that I have tackled in my analyses of lingering colonial divisions has been that between academic disciplines. The very word "Vanuatu" often brings a smile to the lips of persons hearing it for the first time. Even among (non-Oceanic) colleagues the smile can convey a slightly patronizing attitude. Some academic disciplines regard small nations as amusing and consider remote populations—unless they turn violent—as insignificant or irrelevant. Among social scientists, it appears that only anthropologists do not need to be convinced of the importance of studying small societies: They intuitively grasp the theoretical richness such demographically marginal societies may yield, even with regard to such "big" issues as power and legitimacy.

To my brothers and sisters in political science, I therefore wish to underline the power complex that skews our discipline: the bias toward emphasizing, particularly with regard to nation-states, the large and the powerful. As a corollary to the Schumacher Principle (originally developed in the context of appropriate technology for the Third World), I submit that, even in the study of politics, small *is* beautiful. It certainly can be heuristically illuminating. Malyn Newitt and Helen Hintjens convincingly make this case in their aptly subtitled edited volume, *The Importance of Being Small*,[2] just as John Connell has in his long-standing work on island microstates.[3]

True, with rare exceptions small states yield little power. But in an era in which globalization transcends sovereignty, in which neighborhoods vie with nationhood, political processes and substate components have increasingly come to surpass formally bounded nation-states in importance. For the same reasons that the United Nations is beginning to disaggregate indices of development within nation-states (so as to compare cross-nationally, for instance, regional and gender discrepancies), so political and other social scientists must cease using juridical borders as our intellectual frontiers.

Time also constitutes a boundary, a marker of significance. In this book 1980 is such a boundary marker, separating the colonial entity of the New Hebrides from independent Vanuatu. Even though one of my theses is the lingering of colonial-era mental boundaries into independence, the historic significance of 1980 certainly warrants a commensurate semantic distinction. Unlike other writers who, intending to delegitimize colonialism and reinforce nationalism, use Vanuatu to describe the country even prior to independence (as some do with Zimbabwe, transformed from Rhodesia also in 1980, and others do with Palestine, even after Israel's independence and its takeover of the West Bank and Gaza Strip in 1967), I find it conceptually useful to refer to the New Hebrides while the Condominium still existed. This is in no way meant to diminish Vanuatu sovereignty or to minimize its national identity. It is merely misleading and anachronistic otherwise, in the same way that speaking of a United States of America before 1776 would be. Colonialism is better transcended by acknowledging its long-term impact rather than by repressing its terminology. Even if, as Alan Howard aptly notes in the context of identity in Oceania, there is an "obsession with boundaries in Western thought," it is more useful to understand how boundaries were introduced, how they functioned, and in what ways they persist, than to downplay their significance. The same holds true for colonial structures and processes more widely.

The year I commenced research in Vanuatu, 1991, was also a political milestone for Vanuatu. At the end of that year and near the completion of my fieldwork, political party turmoil and elections marked the end of Anglophone leadership of government and the beginning of coalition rule headed by a Francophone. The opportunity to return to Vanuatu a year later enabled me better to assess the wider significance of this major shift in Vanuatu politics.

Due to the recency of what I shall call condocolonialism and the bipolar political passions aroused in the aftermath to independence, conducting research into the impact of the Condominium on contemporary development in Vanuatu proved to be a politically delicate undertaking in and of itself. As I tacked between Francophones and Anglophones, Catholics and Protestants, Europeans and Melanesians, Australians and Australophobes, white settlers and black nationalists, religious missionaries and secular developmentalists, accredited diplomats and outer islanders, I often felt as if I personally was bridging mental boundaries as regularly as a commuter changes train stations. I cannot conceal that the experience was rather schizophrenic. Though geographically sprawling, Vanuatu is still a relatively small country, and the spatial proximity and overlap of the abovementioned communities, a historical consequence of a lack of territorial borders, only intensified my sense of schizophrenia. On more than one occasion I even had the hubris to think that only an American scholar who spoke French, was religiously sensitive but came from no locally implanted denomination, and was able and delighted to *storian* (chat in Bislama) about French and British colonialism around the globe could, given the multiple political snares created by Vanuatu's colonial and religious history, manage to pull off such research successfully. It was not, I believe, due to any cargo cultist weakness on my part that I publically reveled in my American *stamba* (roots, origin, being); but given the genuine affection among ni-Vanuatu for the United States, a deep and enduring legacy of America's role in the Pacific during World War II, I saw no reason to downplay that part of my identity which could only enhance my popularity among my ni-Vanuatu hosts. And where else could I turn my Uncle Hy Kramer into a war hero, by virtue of his otherwise unheralded combat experience in Papua New Guinea?

A few more words on methodology are in order, particularly since conducting research in Vanuatu was the most logistically challenging fieldwork experience I have ever had. From February until May 1991, from my base in Port Vila, I staged the first two of five separate trips to the outer islands: Aneityum/Tanna and Tongoa/Epi. Helpful staff at the Vila Cultural Centre, then headed by Jack Keitadi, provided me with the names and locations of field-workers and other pivotal informants throughout the archipelago, particularly those who could comment on the transition from Condominium to independence. A full list of interviewees, including expatriates and government officials, is appended at the end of this book. I am grateful to all who agreed to speak with me and assented to my recording their comments.

After three months in Vila, my family and I relocated (thanks to Captain David Samuel and the capable crew of the *Atchin Star*) to Luganville on the island of Santo. From Santo I traveled to Pentecost/Ambae/Maewo, Ambrym/Malakula, and, this time accompanied by Regional Development Planner Paul Laurin, to the Banks and Torres Islands. I can thus claim to have spanned in my fieldwork the proverbial breadth of Vanuatu "from Aneityum to Torres." Logistical reasons alone prevented me, regrettably, from visiting Erromango, Paama, Futuna, and Aniwa.

In addition to interviewing informants, during all these excursions (and also while on Efaté and Santo) I attended numerous primary and secondary school classes as well as Catholic and Protestant church services. In Vila and Luganville I also spent many hours at judicial proceedings in an attempt to understand the formal legal system and its relation to indigenous notions of conflict resolution. I was honored to be included among the trainees in the workshop for teachers in Burumba, Epi, sharing the misery of the "aquatically challenged" on board the rocky *Maratha*. These first six months in Vanuatu, preceded by a comparative reconnaissance tour of New Caledonia, were sponsored by the Fulbright Pacific Islands Research Program.

From a methodological perspective, this first research trip entailed frustrating trade-offs between in-depth participation in local community life and satisfactory territorial coverage of the pelagic polity. Geographic imperatives did necessitate some ethnographic sacrifice. Conversely, I did renounce some additional visits for wider social interaction. Despite these constraints, and disciplined by a comparative focus on Francophone vis-à-vis Anglophone communities, I believe I managed to gain a good empirical grounding in both Melanesian cultural life and European colonial legacies. I also came to appreciate that, under certain conditions, oral sources can be more informative and reliable than written ones (the "coconut wireless" has a long-standing reputation in the Pacific isles), and that transcriptions from radio can be as significant for research purposes as published sources.

It was only near the end of my departure from Vanuatu that I realized the full significance for my research of archival materials available at the Vila Cultural Centre and at the National Archives. A Northeastern University Research Scholarship and Development Fund grant allowed me to return a year later and complete this archival work, covering both Condominium and post-Condominium epochs, in the summer of 1992.

From Canadian volunteer and town planner John Mooney's home in Luganville, I staged my eye-opening, limb-numbing, and mind-bending four-day march across Espiritu Santo. It was during this second trip to the Pacific that I was also able to visit the University of the South Pacific, Fiji, and meet with my hospitable comrade-in-Francophonia, Eric Waddell.

A successful fieldwork experience required two things: first, that I learn the national language; and, second, that I familiarize myself with the intricacies of local society. For the first prerequisite I am indebted to Dr. Darrell Tryon, whose excellent audiocassette and grammatical manual made it possible for me, not only to easily converse in Bislama within two months of my arrival, but also, when called upon, to deliver speeches to local groups on the outer islands and to discuss my research over Radio Vanuatu. Regarding entrée into and empathy with Vanuatu society, I find myself in the company of many a foreign researcher who owes a great debt to Kirk Huffman, longtime *manples* and former director of the Cultural Centre, who combines phenomenal insight into Vanuatu life and culture with boundless humor, camaraderie, and generosity. Kirk's invaluable assistance extended to providing invaluable feedback on a draft of this book.

For understandable reasons, skepticism in Vanuatu about the value of academic research by foreigners ran deep in the 1980s and early 1990s. Appreciation for the potential value of my research agenda on the part of Vanuatu's then ambassador to the United Nations, Robert Van Lierop, proved crucial in obtaining governmental clearance for my project. My initial fieldwork in 1991 was carried out with the authorization of the Office of the Prime Minister, then under the stewardship of Father Walter Lini. Follow-up research in the summer of 1992 took place with the blessing of Father Walter's eventual successor, Prime Minister Maxime Carlot. During both stays I interviewed Serge Vohor who, as this book went to press, was serving as Vanuatu's fourth prime minister. I pray that the faith placed in me by all four of these men has been justified and that they will agree that this book does contribute, in however modest measure, to the process of development in Vanuatu and to a greater recognition of their underappreciated nation in the world at large.

The legendary Jimmy Stephens, one-time rebel leader but all-time prophetic figure, has since passed away. My two long meetings with "Jimmy," once on the eve of his release from prison in 1991 and then in Fanafo village a year later, will remain indelibly etched in my mind. Jimmy Stephens was a man whose personal struggle to straddle the boundary between the worlds of tradition and politics had tragic consequences. Although the written word was not his medium, I hope that this book does honor to his memory. I extend a similar posthumous salute to Chief Tuk of Tanna, who shared with me his hut, opened up his heart, and taught me how kava, that transcendental brew, ought always to be taken.

While the life paths and politics of President Jean-Marie Léyé, former President George Sokomanu, and the late president Fred

Timakata were all quite different, I express equal gratitude for the time and insights they shared with me. Similar thanks go to Chief Willie Bongmatur, former head of the National Council of Chiefs.

Tom Bakeo, in his capacity as head of the Directorate of Local Government, provided indispensable assistance in my travels to and understanding of the various local governments. To Jack Keitadi and Jacob Sam at the Cultural Centre, as well as to Miriam Bule of the Vanuatu National Library, I owe very much. Merilyn Tahi allowed me to share my findings at the Vanuatu Centre for International Relations, and I am thankful to her for that and more. Dr. Jean-Luc and Marie-Willie Bador extended me housing as well as hospitality, as did Marité Lemaire for my entire family in Vila and Lyn and Michael Mott in Sydney. Peace Corps Volunteers with whom this RPCV bonded are Tim Isaly and Kari Gould. For taking me through the interior of Espiritu Santo—an exhausting but elevating experience (spiritually as well as altitudinally)—I am eternally grateful to Henri Tamashiro.

Special thanks, *mille mercis,* and *tankyu tumas* go to: Simon Alazrah, Selwyn Arutangai, Billy Bakototo, John Baxterwright, Ken and Sandra Black, Peter Colmar, Georges Coulon, Tony and Easury Deamer, Derek Finlay, Max and Jenny Gerard, John and Joan Gosbell, Philippe and Verzella Guérin, Charles Louis le Guern, Gerald Haberkorn, Françoise and Dominique Henri, François Isave, Stuart and Liz Kinnear, George Kuse, Osman Dan Ladi, Allen Mahit, Jean-Paul and Brigitte Morin, Peter Morris, Pauline Najenmal, Dean and Cathy Polkinghorne, John Solomon, Bertrand Soucy, Serge Soufflé, Leo Tagaro, Jack and Michel Tronquet, Charles Vaudin d'Imecourt, Timothy and Mary Vocor, Françoise and Emmanuel Watt, David William, Barry Wrick, and Paul, Elisabeth, and Liliane Yaou. Colleagues who assisted me outside of Vanuatu include Robert Aldrich and John Connell in Australia, Eric Waddell in Fiji, Yves Pimont in New Caledonia, Jean-Michel Charpentier in France, the late Will Stober in the United Kingdom, and Joan Larcom and Lamont Lindstrom in the United States. I am also privileged to count among my lifelong, if long-distance, friends Jacques Gedéon-Louis. For transforming my rough visual ideas into attractive graphics, I am indebted to Terry Beadle at the Northeastern Media Production Lab and Danielle Hart, who helped design the cover motif and also to Tresja Denson, who worked long and hard on the index.

To the extent that my research in Vanuatu was a success, it is due mostly to the forbearance of my wife, Loïza Nellec-Miles, who regularly overcame her deep anxiety when I left her and our children Arielle and

Sammy, then three years and one year old, heading for the outer islands by way of *kéké* (her Martiniquan Creole way of saying "puny and dubious flying craft"). Her fears, alas, were not unfounded, as the tragic crash that took the lives of eight passengers and pilot on Santo on July 25, 1991—the very day Vanair accommodated me with a special landing on Ambrym—proved. Readers who are not family members will therefore forgive me if I take this opportunity to commit to publication my promise to her: no more research projects in archipelagos!

Research is not friendship, however, and my sentiment for the people of Vanuatu, to whom I owe a great debt, remains unflagging. Although my contribution to the actual betterment of your society may be minimal, my commitment is not. In these pages I have aimed to raise consciousness about your country's strength, resiliency, and dignity. It is in this spirit that I hope you will accept this book.

The introductory chapter fleshes out the boundary paradigm and provides a summary of Vanuatu's geography, history, and politics. In chapter 1 I recount the evolution of the Condominium and expose those mental boundaries and rivalries which persist in its wake. I also coin the term "condocolonialism," distinguishing it from the more classical modes of colonialism that were practiced elsewhere in the Pacific and throughout the colonial world. In chapters 2 and 3, I examine the mental boundaries that nationalism and religion have erected. Chapter 4 examines long-standing linguistic boundaries, while chapter 5 explores emerging boundaries in space, time, law, economics, gender and race. In the concluding chapter I aim to resituate Vanuatu in a reconfigured Pacific and even wider processes of globalization.

Boundaries, Juridical and Mental

[D]espite the "acceleration of history," one cannot expect the partitions in the minds of people to shift quickly. . . . The real partitions, those which are the most stable and the least flexible, are in the minds of men.

—Jean Gottmann,
The Significance of Territory

[I]n the oceanic isles of the New Hebrides . . . wild wings are happily untrammelled by political boundaries.

—A. J. Marshall,
The Black Musketeers

Were it not for the clear demarcations imparted by international boundaries, we would all have a hard time making sense of the world. Boundaries impose merciful limits on our finite capacities to understand the global jigsaw puzzle into which our planet is divided. Bombarded from infancy with unfiltered stimuli, faced with the need to learn the essentials of survival, content to pursue the pleasures of life when granted the privilege, we narrow our cognitive range to that political space which is of greatest importance to us. Astronauts may enjoy the occasional luxury of perceiving Earth as a unified, undifferentiated mass, but most of us terrestrians choose one country (usually the one where we have been born and raised) and focus our hard-pressed attention on it. In school we may be forced to learn about other nations; a few of us devote our lives to studying them. But whether student or scholar we are limited in the amount of social reality, in the form of separate nations and societies, we can reasonably assimilate. Boundaries simplify the task. They enable us to choose, and thereby limit, the countries we wish to read and learn about.[1] Boundaries, by establishing manageable cognitive limits, paradoxically broaden our horizons.

In conceptually setting nations off from one another, boundaries also facilitate the task of comparison. Since each country has its own history and specificities, we can compare ostensibly similar ones and still expect to find interesting differences between them. This is all the more so when we examine neighboring nations with similar geographical, ethnic, cultural, religious, and linguistic features. Contrasting Canada with the United States, say, or Argentina with Chile, is likely to yield more fruit than comparing Canada with Argentina or the United States with Chile. In my own research agenda I have relied upon boundaries (geographical as well as juridical) to differentiate adjacent territories under French and British tutelage.

But boundaries are confining, too, not just spatially but also conceptually. Scholars who make a career out of comparative politics are generally tracked into concentrating on one or two countries or a geographical region. Thus, we have specialists on Europe, Latin America, Africa, or China, each group holding onto its self-contained paradigms. More unfortunately, we lose sight of the overarching insights that can be found in unique national and regional contexts, for only with difficulty do they meet the test of generalizability.

Psychiatrists and clinical psychologists have also acknowledged the problematic implications of boundaries. On an individual scale, compulsive border crossing has been recognized as a personality disorder, that of the "peripatetic paranoid."[2] From a larger, psychohistorical plane it has been hypothesized that

> with the advance of civilizations, human beings have on the whole become more obsessive and compulsive, so that a rigid system of compartmentalization (drawing precise maps with national borders) has been imposed on geography, politics, diplomacy. . . . Behind such rigidity lies the fear of loss of boundaries, that is the fear of loss of the self and nonbeing. . . . It is clear that the emotional meaning of one's country's borders, unconsciously, is fused with that of one's own boundaries. To give up territory . . . is to some a great narcissistic loss and injury. . . .[3]

Whether rooted in pathology or politics, boundaries have become an intrinsic component of the human condition.

The most notorious boundaries, which continue to condition our own spatial maps of the world, are those which emerged as a result of colonial partition in the Third World. In Latin America, and particularly in the Caribbean, Spanish, Portuguese, Dutch, French, British, and American sovereignties created a cultural hodgepodge within a dominantly hispanophone zone. Africa was carved up principally between

France and Great Britain, with Portugal, the Netherlands, Germany, Italy, and Spain playing secondary roles on the continent. In Asia, Britain created India and Pakistan, France commanded Indochina, and jointly they dismembered the Ottoman Empire; China, meanwhile, maintained a nominal independence while enduring de facto European and American hegemony. And in the Pacific, Great Britain and France (the former seconded by Australia), followed by Japan and the United States, have all created distinct spheres of influence, with the Netherlands putting its stamp on Indonesia.

Throughout most of the Third World, territorial division imparted distinct monocolonial patterns. Partitioned peoples were subject to a single colonizer, at least at any given time. Even when defeated European powers relinquished colonial possessions to their rivals (as Germany did to France, Belgium, and Great Britain as a result of World War I), the successor mandate holders enjoyed unrivaled political sovereignty. In those few instances in which colonial territories were administered by more than one metropolitan power—such as in Cameroon, shared by Britain and France—internal territorial boundaries clearly demarcated one colonial sphere from the other. Language, education, administration, law, and economy all followed the monocolonial model: different colony, different model. Partition was not just a matter of space, therefore, but of mind. And where the colonial enterprise entailed a missionary component, there was also partitioning of souls.

After independence, the inheritors of colonial boundaries conserved these territorial divisions. There are exceptions, of course: Bangladesh refused to stick with Pakistan, Eritrea withdrew from Ethiopia, Mayotte left the Comoro Islands. But, for the most part, colonial divisions have remained in place. So have the mental boundaries.

Decolonization does not necessitate the dismantling of international boundaries; but it does require the bridging of mental ones. Regional organizations throughout the Third World—the Association of Southeast Asian Nations (ASEAN), the Organization of African Unity (OAU), the Caribbean Community (CARICOM)—have all tried to overcome the differences of member nations arising from inherited colonial and, of course, authentically national divisions. The record of such organizations has been mixed, in part because colonial legacies have been so strong. But the imperative of transcending historically fostered divisions remains as keen as ever. Regional, and indeed global, reconciliation of externally stoked cleavages is an imperative if the world is to enter the twenty-first century with a modicum of peace.

VANUATU MICROCOSM

There is one small, understudied society upon which history has conferred the onerous distinction of embodying this challenge of global decolonization. Only one nation experienced throughout its entire pre-independence tutelage the tug of competing hegemonies to which the colonial world at large was subjected. Only one country faces as its domestic challenge the surmounting of multicolonial divisions faced by the Third World in general. This is the South Pacific Republic of Vanuatu, formerly known as the New Hebrides, which alone in the annals of history experienced simultaneous and coextensive territorial domination by two foreign powers, France and Great Britain, throughout its colonial past. As Vanuatu, which achieved independence in 1980, comes to grips with the political, cultural, linguistic, religious, and psychological divisions induced by nearly a century of dual colonial rule, those concerned with the healing of wider imperial ruptures may wish to take note. For the otherwise quixotic goal of harmonizing, not just reconciling, foreign-fed but deep-seated differences between national and political cultures is precisely what Vanuatu confronts—alone—on a practical, day-to-day basis. So do Germany, Vietnam, and Yemen, nations once physically partitioned whose psychological reunification has proven more difficult than their territorial reintegration.[4]

Mental boundaries imposed and internalized during the colonial era, though dissipating, persist beyond formal decolonization. At the same time, new mental boundaries of more indigenous origin are gradually erected in their place. While these two observations, which constitute the major thesis of this book, emerge most directly from my experience in Vanuatu, they are also consistent with my previous findings on colonial partitions in Africa,[5] the Caribbean,[6] and French India.[7] They can also be fruitfully applied, I contend, to the developing world at large.

The way in which indigenous cultures have adapted to colonialism, modernization, and development is also a major theme in the unfolding story of the South. Vanuatu, such as the colonial powers configured her, has been endowed with an extraordinary degree of indigenous cultural richness and diversity. Colonial divisions were superimposed there, as throughout the world, upon once thriving, evolving, and dynamic cultures whose beliefs and practices were often repugnant to Western values and norms. Vanuatu provides a very instructive case of the evolution of indigenous culture under diverse colonial experiences, as well as of the more general interaction between culture and colonialism. It also typifies the "miniaturization" of the international community, as microstates and ministates, many no less pluralistic for their diminutiveness, have come to constitute a sizable portion of the post–World War II membership of the United Nations.[8]

As an archipelago within a region of island-nations, Vanuatu serves as a useful reminder, particularly for natives of landmass or continental nations, of how fluid transnational boundaries can be. Social scientists otherwise sensitive to the fragility of international borders, but who overlook island-nation and insular regions, tend to take boundary determinacy (the ways in which boundaries are drawn) as distinguished from boundary stability (the maintenance of given boundaries) for granted. This is not only a question of defining maritime borders but formulating conceptual ones. For boundary drawing is not only a question of legal and diplomatic convention but of mental mapping. "Unlike nations, where the unit concerned is usually precise, there are many definitions of the Pacific region. Each definition is based on different boundary markers."[9]

One of the most critical components of mental boundary formation and fusion is language. Modes of communication can facilitate intergroup understanding or seriously impede it. Carol Eastman recapitulates this important point when she writes that "language either demarks ethnic boundaries or transcends them."[10] In Vanuatu both processes are at work: Official languages (English, French) demarcate boundaries, national language (Bislama) transcends them. But the experience of Vanuatu also shows that the mental boundaries which stem from language differences may be nonethnically based. Whereas language has usually been subsumed within studies of ethnicity, the experience of Vanuatu demonstrates the need to consider language as an independent variable in group-identity construction and differentiation.[11] Vanuatu highlights the transformational power of language, independent of ethnicity, to crystallize group identity. By so doing, it underscores the dynamism and malleability of group-identity formation.

Fredrik Barth demonstrated in his pioneering study how ethnic groups erect social boundaries to preserve their collective identity.[12] A. I. Asiwaju[13] and Peter Sahlins[14] have shown how new identities arise from ethnic boundary partition. By substituting nonethnic linguistic affiliation for ethnicity, the case of Vanuatu thus helps advance a theory of the interrelationship between boundaries and identity. Collective constructions of self, even when externally superimposed, persist even when such political imperatives as decolonization and independence dictate otherwise. At the same time, recognition of national boundaries is essential to the construction of new national identities. While identity gives rise to boundaries, boundaries also create identities.

BOUNDARIES IN LAW AND METAPHOR

One could challenge my conceptual framework on the grounds that it misleadingly uses the term "boundary" in two separate ways—one juridical and determinate, the other social and abstract. How can the boundaries of cartographers and diplomats be compared to those of ethnographers and theoreticians? Such an objection can be overcome if there is consensus that the very notion of the boundary is undergoing metamorphosis. Even international boundaries that were once believed to seal, separate, divide, and partition are now recognized to be fragile, permeable, porous, and circumventable. "Hard" notions of the boundary are giving way to softer, more realistic ones; a linear demarcation is, after all, "a political 'perversion' . . . a political and geographical paradox [that] camouflages a zone as a line."[15] Alternately, juridical boundaries, if they are to have any force or meaning, must themselves be anchored in the mind. They must possess (funda)mental underpinnings and evoke commonly shared expectations. Otherwise, they are merely, as the saying goes, lines in the sand (or sea). To appreciate political development in Vanuatu and throughout the Third World sufficiently, academics and politicians alike must bridge their own mental boundaries *about* mental boundaries.

Vanuatu presents numerous examples of the need for a more supple understanding of boundary matters. A principal impetus for the indigenous political struggle against European economic and political hegemony—land disputes—really concerned differing Melanesian and Western notions about the method and meaning of boundary delineation. European landowners and jurists applied formal rules of land registration, based on paper agreements and written titles, that demarked fixed points, reified imaginary lines, and divided contiguous property. Indigenous landholders countered that, even if their forefathers had granted access and usage rights, Melanesian land is ultimately communal and cannot be alienated. The rigid, definitive, cleaving borders of the European worldview does not exist in that of the Melanesian.[16] Even when demanding that territorial demarcations be made to protect indigenous land claims, Nagriamel, land protection activists on Santo, Vanuatu's largest island, opted, not for clear-cut boundary markers, but rather for "a kind of frontier" or recognized "zones of influence" between their land and European terrains. Nagriamel's most physical boundary limits were symbolic ones: gate barriers at the entrance of their village to demonstrate clearly to abutting European plantations the existence of an autonomous, indigenous entity.[17]

Legal, institutional, and mental influences from a century of European dominance translate into continuing problems of land boundary definition even after the accession to independence. Indeed, the continuation of land disputes, both between government and customary landowners but particularly among customary landowners themselves, is seen as the major obstacle impeding Vanuatu's development.[18] This is not an isolated Melanesian problem, however. The clash over Western and indigenous notions of boundary reification and land alienation also continues to be a source of conflict in Africa (particularly in the former settler colonies of Kenya, Zimbabwe, and South Africa), Australia (with the Aborigines), and both Americas (reservation tribes in the United States and Canada, Amerindians in the Amazonian rain forest). Land and boundary disputes may be particularly pronounced in Vanuatu, but they are far from unique to it.

POLITICAL GEOGRAPHY AND COGNITIVE MAPPING

If Einstein revealed the relativity of time and space in the twentieth century, one may credit Friedrich Ratzel with demonstrating the interrelationship between space and politics at the end of the nineteenth.[19] Ratzel (1844-1904), considered the father of political geography, drew attention to the territorial dimensions of state life and growth using a quasi-biological model. Sir Halford Mackinder (1861-1947), applying geography to military analysis, helped found geostrategy as a school of thought. As long as political power was viewed as a derivative of national territory, geopolitics was an important field of study and a concern of military strategists. Though geopolitics waned as a discrete academic field after World War II (in large part due to the predominance of air force and other transterritorial projections of power), inquiries into the relationship between geography and politics—political geography— were never completely abandoned. Indeed, in recent years, spurred in part both by the breakup of the Soviet Union and by the territorial challenges raised by globalization, political geography has enjoyed a renaissance of sorts.

Although it initially narrowed the scope of analysis to the individual, developmental psychology, as pioneered by Piaget, also revived general interest in spatial learning and perception. This spawned the paradigm of cognitive maps and cognitive mapping.[20] Cognitive mapping refers to the ways in which information about the spatial environment is collected, processed, remembered, and used. Cognitive maps are the products of this process. They reflect an "organized representation of some part of the spatial environment" and are often individualized.[21] But patterns of cognitive mapping can also be culturally specific.

The political relevance of cognitive mapping resides in the identification of certain, often distant, territory with one's own. The expression "motherland," for all its emotiveness, obscures commonsense knowledge that maternity can hardly be dispersed in equal measure over enormous distances and include multitudes of offspring. Cognitive mapping nevertheless allows Texans to place Alaska and Hawaii within their mental national map, just as Welshmen may so situate the Falkland Islands and the Rock of Gibralter within theirs. It is relevant that these distant appendages of the "motherland" are insular, often desolate, and sparsely inhabited: Though theories of nationalism often downplay this reality, cognitive identification is often more with territory than with inhabitants. It is irrelevant that mental mastery of one's nation's geography may in fact be distorted, fuzzy, and inaccurate; the Texan is likely to be more ignorant of relatively nearby Chiapas in Mexico, and the Welshman, despite the Chunnel, bewildered by place names in Normandy across the Channel. European integration or *non* in France, where geography remains an essential part of primary education, it will be a long time before the Parisian knows Luxembourg as well as she does more distant Provence. Geographers have measured how international borders act as "invisible landscapes," shaping mental images and warping "information fields."[22]

Let us consider Vanuatu, a Y-shaped archipelago in Melanesia[23] encompassing eighty-three islands (sea level permitting) approximately 1,500 kilometers northeast of Australia, between 166 and 171 degrees east longitude and 13 and 21 degrees south latitude (see Map 1). Fewer than a dozen of these islands (Efate, Santo, Pentecost, Tanna, Malakula, Ambae, Ambrym, Epi, Malo, Tongoa, Maewo) had a 1989 population greater than two thousand, the entire nation (excluding fewer than 3,500 resident aliens)[24] numbering 140,000 (see Table 1). More important in terms of political geography is the distance separating Aneityum in the south from Hiu, tip of the Torres group, in the north: 850 kilometers (530 miles). While Aneityum is closer to Grande Terre (New

Table 1 Population of Vanuatu, 1989
Resident Citizens Only

Island, Island Group, or Local Govt. Region	Population
Efate (of which Port Vila = 16,827)	28,133
Santo (of which Luganville = 6,659, Malo Island = 2,862)	25,144
Tanna	19,789
Malakula	19,222
Pentecost	11,298
Ambae	8,548
Ambrym	7,170
Banks Islands (of which Vanua Lava = 1,336, Gaua = 1,279, Mota Lava = 1,044)	5,502
Shepherds (of which Tongoa = 2,501)	3,965
Epi	3,611
Maewo	2,354
Paama	1,695
Erromango	1,253
Aneityum	543
Torres Islands	457
Futuna	430
Aniwa	361
Total	139,475

Source: Derived from data in Table B3, *Vanuatu National Population Census 1989*, p. 66.

Caledonia) and Hiu to Santa Cruz (the Solomons), the evolving cognitive map of ni-Vanuatu (the people of Vanuatu) includes imaginary lines separating islands of Vanuatu from neighboring ones of New Caledonia, the Solomons, and the Fiji Islands. (Inclusion of the uninhabited Mathew and Hunter islands, also claimed by the French as part of New Caledonia, is the most internationally controversial aspect of the Vanuatu mental map.)

Mentally bridging the physical barriers of the ocean to imagine a discrete island ensemble is particularly challenging for a people who, unlike their long-distance seafaring counterparts in Micronesia and Polynesia, are not particularly aquaphile. (For the purposes of this discussion, we may momentarily ignore the land barriers—nearly impassible mountain ranges—which also continue to physically separate communities on several of Vanuatu's major islands.) Beyond the general problem of legitimizing colonial boundaries and territorial amalgamations fol-

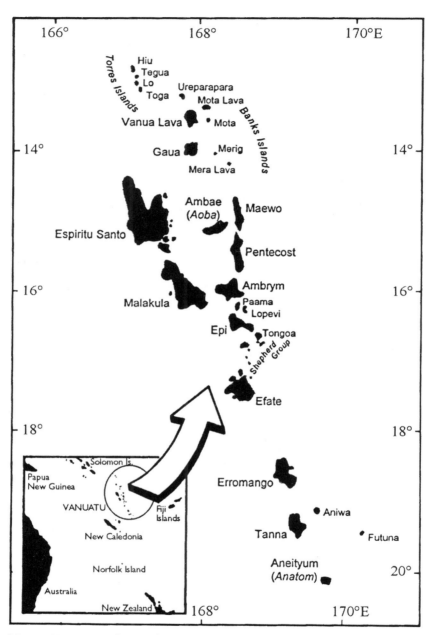

Map 1. Vanuatu in the Pacific

lowing decolonization, maintaining national unity under conditions of contested unipelagism (the fact of belonging to a single archipelago) is a particular challenge, as witnessed by insular separatism in Indonesia (with East Timor), Antigua (with Barbuda), and the Comoros (with Mayotte). Vanuatu also experienced an independence crisis of contested unipelagism during the Santo secessionist rebellion.

To illustrate the political significance of cognitive mapping for archipelagos, it is useful to contrast the islands of Vanuatu with those of the West Indies. Whereas the happenstance of Pacific colonialism created a single administrative entity (albeit with two colonial powers) out of the New Hebrides, Caribbean colonialism gave way, despite some attempt at confederation, to a political splintering of comparably small islands, particularly in the Lesser Antilles (see Map 2). West Indians, accordingly, do not view themselves as belonging to a territorial whole or unifying archipelago but rather to separate island nations and cultures (for example, Montserrat, Grenada, Dominica, Guadeloupe). Insularity is entrenched; "Caribbean consciousness" is more elite ideology than lived reality. Cognitive distance between Malakula and Aneityum is accordingly much less than that between Martinique and Antigua, even though inhabitants of the first pair of islands rarely travel to each other's islands, and trade, communication, and transportation networks are much more developed in the Caribbean than in Vanuatu.

Whereas one archipelago—the former New Hebrides—is thus seen to constitute an island ensemble, another—the Lesser Antilles—remains a vague geographical designation. This is because territorial groupings have no intrinsic meaning; they are human constructs, something of the mind. "Human societies create territory out of meaningless space for they partition space and use it . . . [P]eople . . . impute meaning to and gain meaning from territory."[25] National identity, moreover, requires a "territorial ideology," the fusing of spatial knowledge with nationalistic conviction.[26] Space is politics, politics is space.

Whereas continental peoples view oceans as empty areas of limitation and separation, island peoples see them as central and interconnecting. "For most people, the South Pacific is a blank area on their cognitive map of the world, a vast blue-shaded expanse with very little whatness in a large chunk of 'nowhereness.'"[27] Sea does not divide landmasses for the Pacific islander, it links them.

For instance, to the Puluwat sailing is essential. It is the basis of social structure and life-style, a fount of myth, an outlet for the curious and adventurous, and a source of prestige, ambition, and self-worth.

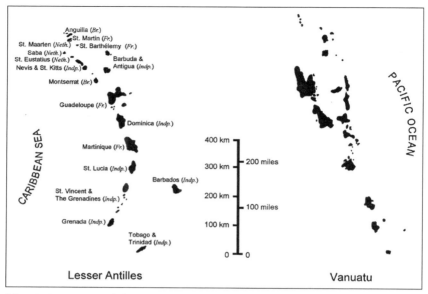

Map 2. Vanuatu and the Lesser Antilles

Long-distance sailing as practiced by the Puluwat requires a disciplined memorization of the star course, without which the oceanic journey would result in disaster. Cognitive mapping accordingly conditions the Puluwat worldview. "In their eyes, the ocean is a safe highway, which *connects*, not separates, the islands. It is not an amorphous mass of water, but a well-known, mentally charted landscape that can be crossed with safety."[28]

Analysis of the mental geography of the coastal people of Tanna also reveals the psychosocial significance of cognitive mapping in Vanuatu and, by extension, Melanesia. Though not undertaking the hazardous long-distance voyages characteristic of the Puluwat, the canoe people of Vanuatu share with them a fluid notion of space. By paddling along the networks of space separating communities, spaces that encapsulate human relationships, Melanesians reconnect places that had been ripped apart in prehistorical time. The "tree"—the individual, vertically rooted in the ground—connects with the "canoe"—the group, mobile, horizontal, and wandering. Lines along the water are not empty of land and meaning but rather are "pathways of alliance." Routes connect roots. In insular space, the partition of peoples is not, as it is understood in continental Africa, the result of colonialism; it is a legacy of cosmology.

"Space in traditional Melanesian society is not perceived by its divisions, nor by its limits, but by relations along the route." Melanesian communities live within a network society and reticulated space. They are "not groups enclosed by some 'frontier,' but networks of little local societies in relatively constant communication one with the other, according to their proximity."[29] Even if the metaphor of the tree and the canoe forms the traditional basis of Melanesian identity, its vertical and historical rootedness must be horizontalized and fast-forwarded, we shall see, if Vanuatu national identity itself is to become meaningful.

A PARADIGM OF BOUNDARY PERMEABILITY

One of the ideological predicaments for late-twentieth-century societies intent on achieving national liberation and protecting national sovereignty is that they have come to political age precisely when international boundaries have lost much of their familiar functionality. Global networks of economy, communications, and environmental and security interdependence render the old notion of national boundaries as barriers or screens virtually anachronistic.[30] "Boundaries are more accurately seen as porous membranes, transmitting a wide range of external forces to domestic society and allowing outside agents either deliberately or inadvertently to exercise influence over internal politics and economics."[31] For countries that have long equated decolonization and development with national sovereignty, the new reality of global interdependence and boundary penetrability can be disorienting.

A paradigm of boundary permeability is nevertheless more hopeful than the theory of dependency, with which it shares certain features. Both boundary permeability and dependency theory allow that smaller and economically weaker nations in the international community will be disproportionately subject to the influence of larger and stronger states. Yet while dependency theory, for the sake of ideological consistency, often leads policymakers down the futile road of protectionism and autarky, the boundary permeability paradigm relativizes and undemonizes the reality of mitigated sovereignty, economic and otherwise. With dependency theory, national liberation is never really achieved, for imbalanced economic relationships lock former colonies into a state of protracted neocolonialism. Boundary permeability recognizes that no state can hermetically seal its borders, for they are now so easily breached electronically and notionally, as well as economically and physically.

In having simultaneously experienced both British and French colonial systems, quickly followed by Australasian and Pacific Rim (particularly Japanese) foreign influence, Vanuatu epitomizes this paradigm. Familiar notions of political liberation and economic dependency inspired its national leaders to struggle for independence; yet Vanuatu was decolonized precisely when, on a global level, boundary permeability had rendered "national sovereignty" a precarious, almost archaic, concept. Development for Vanuatu, along with all other young states, requires successful adaptation to the new reality of boundary permeability, even as fostering national consciousness and achieving national unity remain legitimate and essential goals. Financial globalization, economic integration, and luxury tourism all converge in this remote archipelago—once associated with cannibalism and missionizing—and which now provides offshore banking, flag-of-convenience, and cruise-ship travel services for corporate clients and private consumers throughout the region and the globe. One need not embrace a full-blown world-systems approach to political geography[32] to appreciate how the reality of insular and "peripheral" Vanuatu contradicts older notions of boundary division and national autonomy.

A BRIEF HISTORY

Despite their dark skin (which, following the Greek term for black—*melas*—gave rise to the name Melanesia) and curly hair, the indigenous inhabitants of the New Hebrides archipelago are neither ethnically nor historically related to Africa.[33] Rather, they are believed to have migrated from southeastern Asia three thousand years ago. Dugout canoes carried families and domestic animals—including pigs, which have remained a focus of indigenous Melanesian culture, economy, and ritual[34]—over great distances and under perilous conditions. Just why so many descendents of such valiant seafarers retreated into the tropical forests and shunned the sea—thereby creating a long-standing cleavage between mountain dwellers and coastal inhabitants—remains a mystery. It is clear, however, that most of Melanesian society in the New Hebrides evolved along small-scale, clan-based, and factional-riven lines.

Little is known of precontact history in the Vanuatu islands. The largest one, Espiritu Santo (or just Santo), was sighted and named by the Spanish explorer Fernandez de Quiros in 1606, as the South Pacific entered the general European "Age of Discovery." De Quiros thought he had discovered the southern continent, a logical fiction that European scientists thought necessary to "balance" the weight of the land in the northern hemisphere. One hundred and sixty-two years later, a French-

Santo hillsman.

man, Louis Antoine de Bougainville, returned with de Quiros' plans and named two more islands: Pentecost and Aurora. The religious name of Pentecost has stuck, but Aurora—so named for its discovery at dawn—is now called Maewo. However, the honor of naming most of Vanuatu's islands went to Captain James Cook, the Yorkshireman who in 1774 was the first European to set foot on Malakula and Erromango. The other major islands were called Efate, Tanna, Ambrym, Ambae (immortalized by James Michener as "Bali Hai"), and Aneityum. Although they bear no resemblance whatsoever to Scotland, Captain Cook called the whole cluster of islands the New Hebrides.

The sheer act of naming the whole group imparted a novel cogni-

Rural Melanesian habitation.

tive unity to these islands. In indigenous terms, the Banks group of islands to the north (Vanua Lava, Gaua, Mera Lava, Mota, and Ureparapara), named by Captain Bligh of the *Bounty* after the botanist Joseph Banks, have more in common with Santa Cruz than they do with Tanna and Aneityum. (This is also true of the smaller Torres islands of Hiu, Tegua, Lo, and Toga, latterly named after Luis vaes Torres, Quiros' second-in-command). But Santa Cruz has been lumped together with the Solomons, and so is part of another nation entirely.

Traders, Missionaries, Blackbirding

Whereas the early explorers of Europe came, baptized the islands, and left, their successors thought that they had found a treasure chest in the islands. Seamen plied the seas of the South Pacific for whales. They also discovered that sea slugs—valued in China as an aphrodisiac—were abundant in the waters of the New Hebrides. On the island of Aneityum, sandlewood—a fragrant, delicate tree—grew wild. Traders established themselves on Aneityum and elsewhere, setting up as sandalwood-sailor intermediaries and introducing the indigenous islanders to the manufactured goods of Europe. It was the trader network which brought a cash economy to the New Hebrides.

Sea slugs and sandalwood were not the only material attractions the

New Hebrides held for Europeans. With the expansion of the sugar plantations in Queensland, Australia, New Hebridean men were looked to as a source of cheap labor. Thus began the blackbirding period. New Hebrideans were encouraged to sign up for agricultural work in Australia, Fiji, and New Caledonia for years at a time, in a kind of indentured servant arrangement. But when voluntary recruitment did not fulfill manpower requirements, blackbirders took to involuntary recruitment. A number of islanders were kidnapped, by outright coercion or under false pretences, to work in the fields of Australia. In practice, blackbirding often differed little from slavery, with one important exception: Most islanders were eventually repatriated. Along with their meager savings, New Hebrideans returned home with a new language: Bislama, a kind of simplified or "pidgin" English that enabled Melanesians to communicate with each other throughout the archipelago.

Not all white men came to Melanesia for profit: Some came to save souls. Christian missionaries looked upon the so-called natives as heathens and pagans who needed to be introduced to Jesus Christ for their own salvation. The earliest missionaries were not all welcomed with open arms. Some, such as John Williams who arrived at Erromango, were killed and probably eaten: Cannibalism was still common throughout Melanesia in the nineteenth century. But others, such as Bishop George Selwyn of New Zealand, John Geddie of Canada, and Father Emmanuel Rougier of France, were more successful and set up mission stations, many of which remain to this day.

Missionaries were often at odds with each other, particularly when they represented different versions of the Faith. Protestant missionaries, particularly Anglicans and Presbyterians, both feared and despised their Roman Catholic counterparts. Missionaries, often the sole white people on certain islands, could go for years without speaking to each other, especially if they were of different Christian faiths. An unofficial demarcation evolved: Anglican missions could have the Northern Islands to themselves, Presbyterians would focus on the central ones, and Catholics would concentrate on Santo, Malakula, and Efate. The division was not watertight, though, so religious competition permeated the entire archipelago. On islands such as Pentecost and Tanna, the competition was particularly intense.

Overlying the religious rivalry was a national one. While most Protestants hailed from the British Empire (particularly Australia and New Zealand), Catholic missionaries were generally French. In the late nineteenth century, both Great Britain and France coveted overseas territory, and Melanesia did not escape the imperial hunger of European superpowers. France already had a colony in nearby New Caledonia, whose claim to infamy was a penal settlement. The Société Française des Nouvelles Hébrides (SFNH), successor to the Compagnie Calédonienne des Nouvelles Hébrides, a real-estate company backed by the French government but really animated by John Higgenson, a naturalized French, English-baiting Irishman, bought and claimed huge, uncharted tracts of New Hebridean land under rather dubious pretenses. British, Australian, but mostly French settlers built coconut plantations for the production of copra, which was useful as an oil extract. Later they also moved into cattle ranching. France was eager for outright colonization to consolidate these landholdings and to protect its settlers.

Great Britain, on the other hand, had already staked its claim to Fiji and the Solomon Islands and was less eager to intervene on behalf of the English-speaking private companies that were conducting business in the islands. But pressure for British intervention came from Australia, itself a British possession. Australians did not appreciate having one French *bagne* (penal settlement) already in their backyard, with the possibility of ex-convicts taking over islands even closer! That most of the former convicts were, at least nominally, Catholic only deepened the predominantly Anglican Australian anxiety.

So Great Britain and France came to an unusual arrangement in the New Hebrides. Both powers would exercise custodianship over the entire archipelago. Each would have its own police force, judicial system, medical services, and school system. In cases of legal conflict there would be a joint court composed of a French and a British judge but presided over by a Spanish jurist—in honor of the original "discoverer," Ferdinand de Quiros. Britain and France would be jointly in control; the inhabitants of the islands, in contrast, were left completely stateless. This unique colonial arrangement, conceived in 1906 and formalized in 1914, became known as the Anglo-French Condominium of the New Hebrides. We shall examine the institutions and operations of the Condominium in more detail in the following chapter. For the moment, it is merely necessary to stress that there was never any question of officially partitioning the archipelago into explicitly French and British zones or islands. Even though Port Vila took on a greater French than English accent (reversed after independence), this was on account of the greater number of Frenchmen than Englishmen or Australians living in and around the capital. Similarly, the French-owned plantations around Luganville (Santo) also gave the New Hebrides' second-largest town its decidedly French flavor. The implantation of schools and religious missions also imparted Anglophone or Francophone stamps to given areas. But such settlement patterns stemmed from geographical randomness, not national demarcation: Sovereignty was shared, not divided.

World War II

Until World War II, the New Hebrides remained a relatively sleepy colonial backwater for both Britain and France. But Japanese expansion in the 1940s suddenly thrust them into the heart of the Pacific war. Over a hundred thousand American GIs were posted to the island of Santo, whence they battled in Guadalcanal and elsewhere in the Solomon Islands and New Guinea.

Although the New Hebrides were spared the physical trauma of war (the only fatality on Santo caused by Japanese bombing was a cow), the social and economic impact of the American military presence was considerable. Luganville on Santo, until then a small outpost accessible only by steamer, was transformed almost overnight into a GI city with an elaborate transportation and communications infrastructure. The distinctive mark of World War II military architecture—the Quonset hut— still dots the town.

More important, the sudden influx of goods and men changed New Hebrideans' perceptions of the world. Material hardware that literally fell from the sky (thanks to the U.S. Air Force) kindled some and bolstered other cargo cults, quasi-religious movements inspired by gifts sent from heaven. Other New Hebrideans, without viewing the Americans as mythic saviors or godlike figures, were nevertheless impressed by the American spirit of backslapping amiability. This was in sharp contrast to the colonial, plantation, and missionary mold of whites they had experienced up to that point. Particularly impressive was the sight of black GIs in uniform performing military tasks as full-scale soldiers.

Although the Americans physically evacuated the New Hebrides, they left two important legacies behind: a taste for material goods and a flirtation with freedom. Though the Condominium arrangement would continue to insulate the New Hebrides from the spirit of decolonization that was soon to sweep the Third World, the seeds of independence were planted. In response to the changing international environment, a renewed rivalry would emerge there. This time, however, it would not pit only the British against the French but New Hebrideans against each other.

Struggle for Independence

In the half-century of Condominium rule, Christianity vanquished much of traditional Melanesian culture. Not only were tribal warfare, cannibalism, and infanticide outlawed (if not entirely eliminated), but some of the more puritan Protestant sects banned drumming, singing, dancing, and the consumption of kava, a liquid narcotic associated with Melanesian ritual. Though some villagers in mountain hilltops still donned penis wrappers and grass skirts, most islanders came to dress in Mother Hubbards and shirts and trousers. But if conversion could change external behavior, it could not guarantee political complacency.

Beginning in the 1960s, two major types of resistance to the colonial rule of the Condominium emerged. The first was led by Jimmy Stephens (Stevens or Steven), the unschooled but inspirational Santo-bred grandson of a Scottish seaman and a Tongan princess whose formative years included working as a tractor driver for American GIs during World War II. Although the original goal of Stephens and his followers was to reclaim land appropriated by white settlers and companies, particularly on the island of Santo, his popularity stemmed more from his image as colonial opponent than as land reformer per se.[35] Stephens' movement, Nagriamel, acted in the name of *kastom*, traditional Melanesian values and customs, upon which Christianity and colonialism had dangerously encroached. Chief among these traditional values was the sanctity of the land. From Stephens' headquarters at Vanafo (or Fanafo) on Espiritu Santo, Nagriamel gained followers on other islands; on Tanna, local rebels coordinated with Nagriamel plans to mount an organized resistance to the independence engineered from above. Most Nagriamel followers were rural traditionalists who responded to Jimmy Stephen's call for cultural and economic autonomy.

The second type of resistance movement also appealed to *kastom*, but within a broader, more politically cosmopolitan framework. This was the nationalist movement headed by Father Walter Lini, an English-speaking Anglican priest from the island of Pentecost. Divinity training abroad had exposed Father Walter to anticolonial thinking throughout the Pacific and stimulated him to work for political independence along the same lines that colonies elsewhere in the world were achieving. Lini's religious background led him to a version of liberation theology that linked spiritual freedom to political independence for the oppressed. At the same time, his was a culturally progressive Protestantism that celebrated Melanesian *kastom* as a manifestation of spirituality compatible with the basic doctrines of Christianity.

Jimmy Stephens, founder of Nagriamel.

Father Lini's organization spoke the modern language of nationalism and had wider appeal than Jimmy Stephens' Santo-centered, traditionalism-grounded movement. The British, who were reconciled to the inevitability of independence for their far-flung colonies, were tacitly sympathetic toward Lini and his Vanua'aku Pati (Party). He was, after all, an Anglican and an Anglophone. The French, whose postwar foreign policy did not embrace decolonization, were determined to oppose Lini, his British supporters, and all advocates of independence.

So the French turned to Jimmy Stephens as a counterweight to Lini's nationalist party. Although Stephens' original targets included French landowners on Santo, he accepted French government support.

The author with Father Walter Lini, first prime minister of Vanuatu.

After all, he too was suspicious of the party of the English-speaking pastor and could use all the outside help he could muster. Stephens even embraced American real-estate speculators and libertarian entrepreneurs whose promises for a rich Vemarana, as they all called Stephen's imaginary kingdom, were dazzling.

The French had other constituencies to counter the nationalist threat of Walter Lini and his Anglophile Vanua'aku Pati (VP). French planters and their mixed-blood relations—the *métis*—were also wary of the, as they saw it, Anglophone rabble-rousers. The settlers and *métis* in turn enlisted New Hebridean Francophones, the Melanesians who had been educated either in Catholic mission or French government schools; for Father Lini's hostility to colonialism was not only more vociferous when directed at the French than at the British, but seemed to include the suppression of French education in postindependence Vanuatu. The Francophones—which in the New Hebrides context included all persons who identified with the French-speaking camp even if they themselves could not actually speak the language—united under the banner of the Union of Moderate Parties (UMP). A prominent UMP leader was Maxime Carlot, a *métis* who had worked for the French administration.

Nationalist ferment and Anglophone–Francophone friction intensi-

Maxime Carlot Korman, first UMP prime minister.

fied throughout the 1970s. Father Lini's Vanua'aku Party refused to recognize the Condominium and instead set up its own government throughout the archipelago. Elections were held and boycotted. Clashes between Anglophones and Francophones became frequent, even after the creation of a government of national unity. Some Francophones vowed not to acquiesce to an independent government headed by Anglophones of the Vanua'aku Party. Jimmy Stephens declared secession and was joined by a number of Francophones.[36] Whether the French resident commissioner, Jean-Jacques Robert, encouraged the rebellion remains a point of contention.[37]

Reluctantly, France agreed with its British partners to disband the Condominium and to grant independence. A constitutional conference in 1979 designed a unicameral legislature headed by a prime minister elected by secret parliamentary ballot and technically overseen by a president selected by an electoral college. The constitution also stipulated that both English and French be official languages and that Bislama also serve as national language. On July 30, 1980, Vanuatu was declared an independent state and Father Walter Lini became its first prime minister. Troops from Papua New Guinea, with Australian logistical support, were called in to crush the Santo rebellion. Jimmy Stephens was sentenced to fourteen and a half years in prison for "mutiny." Vanuatu, heir to the New Hebrides, survived the transition to independence. A republic had succeeded the Condominium.

Post-Condominium Politics

Under Walter Lini and the Vanua'aku Pati, Vanuatu's first decade of independence was characterized by ideological boldness, confrontational foreign relations, and domestic partisan rivalries. Building on *kastom* as an instrument of nation building, Lini elaborated a doctrine of "Melanesian socialism" characterized by communalism, sharing, and humanism.[38] France, while remaining a major supplier of foreign aid, was kept at arm's length on account of lingering resentment over its role in the Santo rebellion and its continuing "colonialism" in nearby New Caledonia. Indeed, during his tenure Lini expelled three French ambassadors. To thank Castro for his support for New Hebridean independence at the United Nations in the early 1970s, diplomatic relations with Cuba were established in 1983. Even Libya's attempts to project a Pacific profile at first received a positive response in Vila, and formal relations were fleetingly established with Tripoli in the mid-1980s. Diplomacy with the Soviet Union, paving the way for a fishing agreement in 1987, was also intensified. Combined with its accession to the regional nuclear-free movement, these actions tested Vanuatu's relations with the United States. At the same time, rapprochement with Australia and New Zealand generally proceeded apace as these Oceanic powers came to supplant Vanuatu's erstwhile European sovereigns, Britain and France.

Remarkably, given its dualistic colonial legacy, contested independence, political infighting, extreme geocultural pluralism, and economic underdevelopment, Vanuatu maintained a democratic system of governance. In its first post-Condominium election in 1983, the VP maintained a majority of 24 of 39 seats, with the main opposition UMP gaining 12. (In run-up elections to independence in 1979, the VP had won 26 seats.) Four years later, with the size of parliament increased to 46 seats, the VP under Lini in 1987 gained 26 to the UMP's 19 seats. In terms of popular vote, however, the VP share dipped to under 50 percent, while the UMP's rose from 33 to 42 percent.

Throughout the 1980s Prime Minister Lini faced constant conflict with the UMP, sporadic criticism from President Sokomanu, and brewing disaffection from one-time VP ally Barak Sope. Sope's populist leadership over a landownership issue sparked riots in Vila in 1988, prompting his dismissal from the cabinet, his expulsion from the party, and his ejection (along with four other VP renegades) from the parliament. Eighteen members of the UMP boycotted parliament out of solidarity with the Sope group and were also ousted. While the Melanesian Progressive Party parliamentarians (as Sope's group reestablished themselves) were reinstated under constitutional grounds, the UMP members remained banished.

Shortly after the (uncontested) by-elections for the vacant UMP seats, President Sokomanu formally dissolved parliament and swore in Sope as head of a transitional government. In due course Prime Minister Lini had Barak Sope, President Sokomanu, and Maxime Carlot (member of the ephemeral transitional government) under arrest. Carlot and Sope, convicted of mutiny, seditious conspiracy, and the taking of unlawful oaths, were sentenced to five years' imprisonment; Sokomanu (replaced as president by Fred Timakata) was sentenced to six years in prison for incitement to mutiny, seditious conspiracy, and administering an unlawful oath. On appeal, however, all convictions were overturned, the appeals court in 1989 citing trial court error and insufficient evidence.

By the time of Vanuatu's first-decade anniversary in 1990, Lini's grip on his party and nation was seriously beginning to lessen. A stroke in 1987 had physically weakened him and attempts to reestablish command with an authoritarian leadership style were backfiring politically. Lini's accumulation of ministerial portfolios, his seemingly arbitrary firing of cabinet members, antagonism toward key members of the judiciary, and alleged interference with the press and radio all worked against him. So did revelations of unseemly ties to a local Vietnamese businessman and an expatriate American entrepreneur. In the summer of 1991, party rivals voted to replace Lini with Donald Kalpokas as president of the Vanua'aku Party. Lini, together with VP loyalists, consequently formed his own National United Party (NUP). Just as the VP could not prosper without Lini, neither could Lini thrive without it. In elections at the end of 1991, with seven parties contesting and the NUP and VP as vociferous rivals, the UMP, after a decade of leading the opposition, emerged with a plurality of 19 seats; VP and NUP split with 10 each. UMP formed a coalition government with Lini's NUP and Maxime Carlot became Vanuatu's first Francophone prime minister. Carlot added the traditional name Korman, to become Prime Minister Maxime Carlot Korman. Carlot Korman's deputy prime minister was Sethy Regenvanu, a longtime Lini associate and cofounder of the NUP.

While stressing the need to redress (and not avenge) the imbalance that a decade of alleged anti-Francophone discrimination had created, Prime Minister Carlot emphasized "moderation" in his policies. Under Carlot Korman, Vanuatu reversed its unequivocal support for the Kanak National Liberation Front in New Caledonia, its systematic enmity toward France, its flirting with radical regimes, and its openly anti-American nuclear-free Pacific stance. Ideologically, the socialist bent to Lini's Melanesian path of development was replaced by a more free-market, openly capitalistic policy. Reconciliation with the former secessionists— begun under Lini when, shortly before losing power, he released Jimmy Stephens from prison—proceeded even more strongly, with compensation extended to those Francophones who had fled Santo.

Carlot Korman's coalition survived the defection of Walter Lini in 1993, thanks to those NUP members who refused to follow the lead of their party president and remained with the Korman government. They subsequently formed the People's Democratic Party (PDP). The UMP-PDP coalition comprised 26 seats.

In 1995 a Unity Front (UF) alliance, joining the Vanua'aku Pati under Donald Kalpokas, the MPP under Barak Sope, and Tanunion under (Francophone) Vincent Boulekone, took 20 seats in parliamentary elections. Walter Lini's NUP gained 9 seats, while the UMP dipped to 17. Even more problematic for the UMP was the factional cleavage that divided the ruling party into camps led by Prime Minister Carlot Korman and UMP President Serge Vohor, also a Francophone and Carlot Korman's original minister of foreign affairs. (Three smaller groups of candidates, Independents, Nagriamel, and Fren Melanesia, captured four seats among them. Neither the PDP nor four new parties—Independent Front, Women in Politics, Labour Party, and the Christian Independent Group—managed to secure any representation.)

As in 1991, a coalition between the UMP and NUP emerged to form the government of Vanuatu. Once again, a Francophone was elected prime minister and an Anglophone deputy prime minister. This time, however, Serge Vohor was prime minister (Maxime Carlot Korman becoming parliamentary speaker) and Walter Lini his deputy. After only 48 days as prime minister, however, Vohor resigned when six UMP parliamentarians joined the UF in a motion of no confidence. In February 1996, Maxime Carlot Korman temporarily regained his post as prime minister of Vanuatu, losing it once more to Serge Vohor in September. Democracy in Vanuatu soon thereafter came under its greatest threat ever when, on October 12, 1996, members of the nation's paramilitary Vanuatu Mobile Force (VMF), disgruntled over a pay dispute, abducted President Jean-Marie Léyé and acting Prime Minister Barak Sope. Although Léyé and Sope were soon released, government fears that the brief mutiny was actually prelude to a full-fledged coup d'état impelled it to order the arrest of a good portion of the VMF. This

Serge Vohor (UMP prime minister, 1995–1998).

was accomplished in November by the general police under the direction of Walter Lini, Vohor's new minister of justice.

Elections in 1998 were held under the shadow of a state of emergency (the result of riots in Port Vila over governmental financial improprieties) and were accompanied by an unusually low turnout rate. Donald Kalpokas, who had briefly held office as prime minister in 1991, succeeded in regaining that post as his VP captured 18 parliamentary seats and subsequently entered into coalition with Walter Lini's NUP (11 seats). UMP—no longer with Carlot Korman, who had split off to form the Vanuatu Republican Party (VRP)—netted 12 seats, and no Francophones were included in the VP/NUP government. Barak Sope's MPP gained 6 seats, the remaining 5 going to John Frum candidates, Independents, and the VRP. Walter Lini again became deputy prime minister.

Despite the evidence of increasing intralinguistic factionalization, cross-cutting partisan cleavages, and coalitional fluidity in the post-Condominium era, outside observers have persisted in viewing Vanuatu politics almost exclusively through the preindependence lenses of a bicommunal, European-language–based structure.[39] The dualistic model is tempting, for it is historically consistent, paradigmatically tidy, and intuitively accessible. It does, however, underrate the indigenous essence of the Vanuatu polity as well as the significant transformation in Vanuatu politics and identity since independence. Strategies for development, foreign policy, and patronage politics have come to play a larger role in shaping Vanuatu politics than whether Anglophones are besting Francophones or vice versa. While the Anglophone–Francophone dichotomy *is* important for understanding contemporary Vanuatu politics, it is an incomplete paradigm. As I have argued elsewhere, "[w]ith independence, politics in Vanuatu have come to reflect indigenous interests, cleavages and factionalisation more than colonial preoccupations: francophone-anglophone rivalry is no longer the nation's paramount political issue."[40] Discerning the new mental boundaries that are gradually taking the place of the older ones is essential to understanding Vanuatu's present and future. While part of this conceptual challenge is to appreciate the re-Melanesianization of Vanuatu politics, the other is to apprehend the ways in which development and globalization are transforming Vanuatu society.

For Vanuatu, the key to understanding how colonial rivalries translated into mental boundaries in the first place is the Condominium. It is to this peculiar system, formally abolished but perniciously lingering in postcolonial posterity, that we shall now turn.

CHAPTER 1

Mental Rivalries and Condocolonialism

Between peoples with temperaments as dissimilar as the French and the English [the Condominium] was doomed to disaster from the beginning. There is a complete lack of that sympathetic co-operation so essential in such an obviously exacting enterprise; neither trusts the other for a minute.
—A. J. Marshall, *The Black Musketeers*

The experiment has always been and will always be a failure, until such time as Frenchmen are no longer French and Britishers no longer English.
—Tom Harrisson, *Savage Civilisation*

The British and French were like two wild dogs, fighting for a bone between them—and we were the bone. . . . Each pulled the other in a different direction. They didn't work together. I tried to straighten them out. . . . There are Black Frenchmen, there are Black Englishmen, but there aren't Black *kastom* men.

—Jimmy Stephens, interview, August 1991

The Condominium which governed—or neglected—the New Hebrides for so long, and whose stamp is still very much felt in contemporary Vanuatu, has had no dearth of detractors. It has been the butt of some very acerbic, but also literary, thrusts. Edward Jacomb invoked Cato and Carthage in 1914 (*"Delendum est Condominium"* [It must be destroyed]), excoriating the Condominium as an "experiment . . . based on a negation of all previous political experience."[1] Mocking the tricephalous (British, French, and Spanish), character of the Condominium's highest judicial tribunal, the Joint Court, Jacomb later wrote a play entitled the *Joy Court* (1929). Writing under the pen name Asterisk, Robert Fletcher parodied the archipelago as *Isles of Illusion* (1923). Native organization compares favorably with colonial administration in *Savage Civilisation* (1937), in which Harrisson characterizes the Condominium as a "bastard" and the Joint Court as "pure musical comedy."[2] Marshall (1937) castigated the Condominium as "a tragic compromise

. . . the most insane and disastrous experiment in the history of modern colonial enterprise . . . a completely asinine arrangement."[3] Administrators privately joked that the Condominium institutionalized a *mésentente cordiale.*[4]

Contemporary commentators have been no more charitable. In the title of his independence-issue book, Vanuatu's first prime minister, Father Walter Lini (1980), invokes the old farago of Condominium as "Pandemonium." Jeremy MacClancy, playing on the official designation "sphere of joint influence," recasts this unique colonial arrangement as "a system of joint neglect";[5] his concise history is aptly entitled *To Kill a Bird with Two Stones.* Critically engaged writers, such as Grace Molisa, Nikenike Vurobaravu, and Howard Van Trease, have been more disparaging minus the humorous quips: "the Anglo-French Condominium . . . was so inefficient and cumbersome. . . . The Vanuatu people were neither consulted in its establishment nor involved in its operation."[6] Even the most objective of analyses admits that the Condominium "assumed its form by a series of accidents and through patching together a variety of institutions separately created and never intended to work with each other. . . . The [b]asic constitution of the Condominium . . . was a patchwork of ambiguous compromises formulated by amateurs."[7] To appreciate fully the mental boundaries bequeathed to *ni-Vanuatu,* we need to assess the historical, cultural, and institutional peculiarities of this one condominium.

CONDOMINIA OF NOTE AND A WEST AFRICAN COUNTERPART

Arguably the longest-lasting condominium in recorded history is that of Andorra, wedged in the eastern Pyrenees between France and Spain. In 1278 Andorra was placed under the joint suzerainty of a Spanish bishop and a French nobleman. With the suppression of the monarchy, the head of state has come to assume French responsibility for Andorra. Communications and educational services are provided by both Spanish and French governments. Faisans Island in the Bidassoa River is also, as it has been since 1856, a French-Spanish condominium.

From 1816 until 1919 a Prussian-Belgian condominium prevailed over Moresnet, until it was annexed to Belgium. Sakhalin Island, jointly administered by Japan and Russia, functioned as a condominium for two decades beginning in 1855. Two of the (uninhabited) Phoenix Islands of the former Gilbert and Ellice Pacific islands group, Kanton and

Enderbury, were under joint British and U.S. administration from 1939 until 1979, when they were joined to the new nation of Kiribati. Several maritime areas have been declared to be de jure condominia, including the Bay of Fonseca, which abuts Nicaragua, Honduras, and El Salvador.

As a colonial construction, the Anglo-Egyptian Condominium over the Sudan rivals that of the New Hebrides in historical notoriety. Established in 1899 as the outcome of continental-cum-colonial conquest, Egypt was empowered to select, subject to British ratification, the governor-general to administer Anglo-Egyptian Sudan. In actuality Egypt was less than an equal partner in the operations of this condominium, and British officials, mostly military, effectively administered the territory. The Anglo-Egyptian Condominium officially ended in 1955, the year preceding Sudanese independence.

Although Cameroon was never a Condominium per se, its physical territorial partition into British and French zones, with eventual reunification under Francophone dominance, provides a relevant contrast with Vanuatu. An extremely multilingual society whose topographical and cultural features contribute to its reputation as the microcosm of Africa, Cameroon was divided into two separate territories in 1916, a result of Germany's defeat during World War I. Under separate mandates extended by the League of Nations and later endorsed by the United Nations, France administered eastern Cameroon, an area ten times as large as that of the British-controlled western Cameroons. French Cameroon was more populous than the British Cameroons, too, four times so by the time of independence in 1960.

By merging the two parts of the country, first through a federal structure in 1961 and then into a unitary state in 1972, independent Cameroon came closer to the New Hebridean Condominium model where divisions were linguistic rather than territorial, more a matter of mind and tongue than of land and borders. Writing in 1967, Edwin Ardener observed that "Contacts between people from the two states tended to be expressed in terms of 'English' and 'French' stereotypes" and quoted M. Manga's depiction of these differences: Francophone Cameroonians were "sophisticated, talkative, artistic, passionate, and witty," while his Anglophone countrymen were "sportsmanlike, reserved, trade-loving, conventional, intelligent . . . courteous, honest, extremely nationalistic, and humourless."[8] Nearly twenty years later, geolinguistic associations still lingered, much in the way that Luganville and Port Vila were viewed as "French" in the New Hebrides: in ambience, yes, but not officially.

Even a quarter-century after [Cameroon's] independence, an excursion
westward along the coast from Douala to Victoria is like a voyage
across the English Channel. . . . Political discussions take place on one
side at sidewalk cafés, on the other in pubs. . . . The nature of the
roads, the uniforms of the police, the music, even the mannerisms of the
people change once one has crossed the undemarcated cultural and linguistic frontier.[9]

Only in the New Hebrides was a condominium imposed over an
inhabited territory that, notwithstanding the existence of local political
structures and chiefly hierarchies, did not constitute a preexisting, internationally recognized legal entity. Here, the Condominium both created
a geopolitical unity out of an archipelago and mitigated that unity by
fomenting colonial rivalries.

GENESIS AND STRUCTURE OF THE CONDOMINIUM

"The manner in which both Great Britain and France became involved
in the New Hebrides is so bizarre as to suggest that history took a
cynical revenge on European expansionism."[10] While traders in sandalwood and laborers exercised influence in the archipelago from the 1840s
on, to be joined shortly thereafter by other European and Australian
missionaries and plantation settlers, the French and British governments
themselves waited nearly half a century before attempting to extend any
formal jurisdiction over the islands. As both subjects of Britain and
citizens of France initiated settlement on their own, some joint method
of official Anglo-French protection, supervision, and control seemed appropriate. It was France that consistently took the initiative in proposing
such formal arrangements, beginning with the *entente commune* of
1886. The *entente commune* called for joint Anglo-French policing,
supplanting parallel military intervention, to protect Europeans in the
archipelago. Britain counterproposed a common naval agency which,
negotiated as the Convention of November 16, 1887, became the precursor to the Condominium: the Joint Naval Commission.

Constituted of French and British officers of their respective navies,
the Joint Naval Commission ostensibly provided for the maintenance of
law and order on behalf of their respective nationals residing in the New
Hebrides archipelago. Although it was erected exclusively for the benefit
of European residents, not for the indigenous islanders, it was the settlers who criticized the Joint Naval Commission for its remoteness,

inefficiency, and ultimate irrelevance. So as to improve the workability of the commission, and within the context of the emerging "Entente Cordiale,"[11] in 1904 the two sides produced a joint declaration which, once officialized by the Convention of 1906, constituted the cornerstone of the Condominium. Remarks by Britain's representative on the occasion of the Convention's proclamation in Port Vila reveal the naïveté and paternalism that were to plague the Condominium thenceforth:

> We meet today to make history. We are, today, starting a remarkable and absolutely new experiment in the joint yet separate administration by two great Powers on one area. . . . Henceforward Frenchmen and Englishmen will live intermingled, each enjoying the benefit of the laws of his own nation and . . . both joining together to rule the natives of these islands.[12]

Although the Convention promulgated the overarching principle of the Condominium—the establishment of a "sphere of joint influence"— the arrangement was no more successful than the Naval Commission in settling property, legal, and administrative conflicts that arose among the British, French, and Australian persons and companies which continued to converge on the islands. The major innovation of the 1906 Convention over the 1887 Joint National Commission was a common court for legal matters not unilaterally justiciable by either national system. But the Joint Court was notoriously corrupt and comical (how could the Spanish, French, and British judges communicate with each other?) and the other joint agencies did not function much better.

Thus was spawned the Protocol of 1914, which, once ratified in 1922, formed the effective constitutional basis of the Condominium until Vanuatu's independence in 1980.[13] The Protocol confirmed a tripartite division of governance over the New Hebrides: a British national administration, a French national administration, and a joint Anglo-French Condominium administration. When referring to the administrative system prevailing in the New Hebrides, one must therefore distinguish between the Condominium as an institutional arrangement, under whose aegis three separate governments operated, and the Condominium per se, the jointly constituted organ of governance. To illustrate the distinction, French and British officers of the Condominium, though taken on by and answering to their respective Resident Commissioners, were not part of their respective national administrations—a situation which gave rise, incidentally, to grievances over pay and benefits inequity. The Resident Commissioners themselves, on the other hand, were part of both their respective national and the Condominium structures.

The Residencies

Each of the national administrations, or Residencies, was in principle headed by a High Commissioner. In the case of Britain, this was the Honiara (Solomon Islands) -based British High Commissioner in the Western Pacific; for France, the governor in Nouméa (New Caledonia). In fact, authority was delegated to their respective Resident Commissioners in Port Vila. The British Residency was eventually established on Iririki island, across from but clearly within watchful eyeshot of the French Residency on the heights of Vila. For administrative purposes the archipelago was divided into four districts, jointly (or competitively) governed by pairs of District Agents: an F.D.A. (French District Agent) and a B.D.A. (British District Agent).

Each Residency maintained jurisdiction over its nationals, French law applying to French citizens and British law to British subjects. Nationals from other countries, whether permanently residing in the New Hebrides or just passing through, were obliged to opt for either national jurisdiction within one month of their arrival. (Because French administration of justice was known to be relatively lax, particularly regarding labor infractions,[14] even Anglophone expatriates opted for French "protection.") Native New Hebrideans, belonging to neither national community or jurisdiction (as in "normal" colonies), were effectively stateless and subject, depending on what other parties were involved, to either French, British, or "joint" (i.e., Condominium) justice.[15]

Each Residency, then, maintained its own legal system, used a different currency, issued a different set of postage stamps, and employed separate standards of weights and measures. Each also set up its own health service, educational system, and police force (commonly referred to as "militia"). Although the French and British corps were theoretically merged into a single New Hebridean Constabulary in 1923, its members were still appointed by and ultimately answered to their respective Resident Commissioners. As a result, the two forces actually continued to operate separately. A policeman recruited by the British, for instance, had no authority to arrest someone for breaking French law (though of course he could report it to his counterparts.) Whether or not the two police corps enjoyed mutual powers of arrest over persons under each other's jurisdiction (Britain said yes, France said no) complicated police work for as long as the Condominium endured.[16]

The Condominium Administration

Joint services, even if staffed by British and French (with later some native New Hebridean) personnel, were set up exclusively by the Condominium administration. Every service headed by a Frenchman had a British second-in-command, and vice versa. In certain departments the top posting was reserved by nationality (for example, the Condominium treasurer was always British and the auditor French). Condominium agencies were responsible for communications (postal and telegraph systems, weather services); land and water infrastructure (roads, bridges, ports, harbors, buoys, marine lighting); agriculture, livestock, and conservation; land survey and registration; customs and treasury; public health (in addition to the national public health services); finance and management of the administrative districts; and non-national administration of justice (the Joint Court, Native Courts, joint native prisons). An official gazette was also published by the Condominium.

Unlike the case with the national administrations, each locally headed by a Resident Commissioner, there was no separate executive body charged with overseeing the overall operation of the Condominium administration. The Resident Commissioners acting in concert were ultimately responsible for the functioning of the Condominium, but they, as we have seen, were primarily answerable to Paris or London. At the district level, good governance depended on the extent and quality of collaboration between B.D.A. and F.D.A., and this, more often than not, depended on the personal chemistry of the two. The same could be said for the Resident Commissioners.

It would be facetious to refer to the Joint Court as the crowning glory of the Condominium: "farcical," "bizarre," "comical" are the adjectives more generally applied to this experiment in judicial multinationalism. Originally, the Joint Court was established to settle disputes arising from conflicting land claims between and among European settlers and landholding companies. In principle it was also designed to protect native laborers from exploitation. In actuality, it mainly served the forces of inertia, leaving virtually unfettered freedom to private-sector interests. Because of the important role it played throughout the Condominial era—indeed, the Joint Court was the Condominium's centerpiece of embarrassment—a few more words on its structure are in order.

According to the Convention and the Protocol, a three-member panel consisting of a British national judge, a French one, and a Spanish president were supposed to constitute the Joint Court. From its formation until 1934 the Count of Buena Esperanza—remembered more for hardness of hearing than for blindness of justice—presided. At one time the multinational stamp of the court's operations peaked with the presence of a Dutch registrar and a Spanish public prosecutor. When the Count of Buena Esperanza's successor, Bosch-Barrett, retired just before World War II, it was decided that until a suitable replacement could be found (France's strained relations with the Franco government was the obstacle), the remaining French and British judges would continue their deliberations anyway, postponing those judgments whenever in disagreement until the reposting of their Spanish colleague. Since, to paraphrase O'Connell,[17] the Spanish Court president was "temporarily" absent for four decades, showing little sign of return, the French and British judges were constrained to compromise. When not serving on the Joint Court, they presided over their national courts.

Whereas the French considered *les Nouvelles Hébrides* to be French territory, even if shared, the British made no such claims. Notions of the unity and indivisibility of the French Republic run deep and still include overseas possessions, even those only partially controlled. Overseas dependencies for Britain were never regarded as British soil in the same way. Technically, the island group was a "foreign territory under Her Majesty's jurisdiction," the equivalent of a protected territory but not a British possession. Accordingly, the New Hebrides were never thought of as British in the same way that *les Hébrides* were considered, even imperfectly, French.

It is amazing to see in retrospect how little provision was made for native New Hebrideans by the legal structures of the Condominium. Their statelessness and, in consequence, their electoral disenfranchisement was only one side of their predicament, the political side. Economically, by falling outside the range of national administrations and legal protections, New Hebrideans were denied a whole range of commercial and administrative possibilities. They could not form companies, enter into contracts with each other, or register their boats. Indeed, not until 1967 was a mechanism put into place to register their births, deaths, and marriages! Though the Joint Court provided for a native advocate, hardly ever did customary landholding claims prevail over settler ones. It was assumed that "native law" would pertain to most disputes among islanders, but a lack of codification nullified the practical application of this assumption. Regulations that as late as the early 1960s prohibited "natives" from purchasing alcoholic beverages illustrate the paternalism of the legal regime.

With no fewer than three governments exercising powers over them, the sparsely populated New Hebrides may appear to have been overgoverned. In fact, a lack of financial commitment and a paralyzing intra-European rivalry meant that, ultimately, New Hebrideans were underadministered. To a large extent, Western-established governance was irrelevant to Melanesian society.

Nevertheless, when political parties emerged and independence loomed, local schisms coalesced along bipolar lines.

CONDOCOLONIALISM

The distinctive process of imperial rivalry in the New Hebrides, externally imposed but indigenously internalized, justifies the introduction of a term specific to it. For even if Vanuatu did experience a kind of colonialism, the administrative framework of the Condominium created a rather special variant of it. I therefore offer the term "condocolonialism" to designate the peculiar form of European rule that prevailed over the New Hebrides from the establishment of the Condominium in 1906 to its formal abolition in 1980.

Whereas "Condominium" refers to the administrative *structure* of joint British and French rule, "condocolonialism" denotes the *process* of divided and divisive domination. Condocolonialism differs from classical colonialism in five respects: (1) foreign rule is extended and maintained over an overseas possession as much to counter and irritate an imperial rival as to benefit the mother country per se; (2) infrastructural development is limited and targeted, lest the benefits of such investments accrue to the rival partner; (3) the subjects of such rule (the condocolonialized) are neither repressed by a metropolitan power nor assimilated into a metropolitan model but rather are induced to join one side against the other; (4) the condocolonized learn to play off the imperial powers against each other, often to further local interests and pursue indigenous politics; and (5) imperial rivalries are reproduced and internalized by the condocolonized, giving rise to political cleavages that outlast the accession to independence and perpetuate exploitative attitudes toward the institution of government.

Even though classic colonialism sowed the seeds for postcolonial rivalry by heightening ethnic cleavages and creating new rivalries, it did so within an indigenous social framework. Tensions between Hutus and Tutsis were aggravated by Belgian colonialism, just as Ibohood, a precursor to the Biafran war of secession, emerged only during British rule in Nigeria. Hutu, Tutsi, and Ibo nevertheless remain African categories of identity. Likewise, Hindus and Muslims had peacefully cohabited in the subcontinent until Britain proposed an Indo-Pakistani partition. The ensuing frictions, however regrettable, are Asian, not European, in essence.

Condocolonialism, in contrast, superimposes competitive identities along nonindigenous lines. French versus English, not Aneityumese versus Mota, constitutes the linguistic cleavage. Catholicism or Protestantism, not cannibalism or baptism, becomes the defining ritual of choice. Even in a weakly linked archipelago, allegiance to island holds less significance than affinity with European overlord.

CONDOCOLONIAL MINDSETS

Condominial rule did not create differences in colonial attitudes but rather crystallized and institutionalized them. Early commentators could not fathom how French and British could cohabitate, much less coadminister, the same territory. Anglo-Saxon and Gallic mentalities were seen as inherently incompatible in terms of colonial aims as well as methods. Edward Jacomb was persistently struck by the "general lack of colonising genius" exhibited by the French:

> The Frenchman passes his life in agitating for new favours. . . . Frenchmen are too fond of politics. It is one of their national failings. One of the first things which is done in a nascent French Colony is to found a local newspaper, and given the excitable, impulsive Gallic temperament, it soon becomes filled with columns of mingled abuse and scandal.[18]

Another failing of the colonial French, according to Jacomb, was their "instinctive attitude, which govern[ed] all relations . . . with native races": "He regards them as little removed from the beasts of the field. . . . [I]n addition to the scorn which a Frenchman instinctively feels for a native there seems to be a strain of sheer cruelty in Latin blood, which likes to inflict suffering on weaker creatures from mere wantonness."[19]

Marshall echoes this view: "Rather than as a subject to be taught and understood, [the French] regard even the tamest Kanaka as a wild animal to be held in gravest suspicion."[20]

Such comments are perhaps more reflective of a certain British animus toward the French than an accurate commentary on the French national character. The rivalry between co-Europeans was intense and overshadowed the possibility of any ennobling colonial partnership. For all the invective he heaped on the French for their dealings with "the natives," Jacomb himself was no egalitarian:

> [Melanesians] taken as a whole . . . represent one of the lowest rungs in the ladder of the human race. . . . They can best be described as children. All of them, even the oldest men and women, are merely children in character and disposition. They have the same faults and the same virtues. They are in general honest as the sun, save in matters of food; they are happy in temperament, but subject to sudden fits of anger or sulking; they forget injuries as easily as they forget kindnesses; they are constitutionally lazy, but they are good workers while the mood lasts; they are however fickle and soon need new interest to amuse them; they are cruel unconsciously and kind intuitively; they are intensely imitative.[21]

Paternalism pervaded British thinking throughout the colonial empire. The New Hebrides were no exception.

Needless to say, the French of the New Hebrides had their own unflattering views of the British. John Higginson, the Irish Anglophobe turned French Pacific land procurer, acquired as much of the New Hebrides as he could, no less to stymie the British as to aggrandize France. "England won't fire cannons for the New Hebrides," he mused at the turn of the century. "She'll be satisfied to conquer by commerce. With her, business begins with the Bible and finishes with a bill."[22] It was only after Higginson realized that "the best colonial agents of the Australians in the New Hebrides [were] the Presbyterian" pastors did he cajole the undersecretary for colonies to support his idea of opposing each "English missionary with a French [one]." Selfless and spartan French Catholic Marists were needed, in Higginson's and other Frenchmen's view, to offset the shrewd and profit-seeking Anglophone Protestant missionaries.

Decades later, Pierre Benoit, member of the French Academy and author of the novel *Erromango,* picked up on this theme after reading a book by the Englishman Robert Cust ("for should we not know what our enemies are thinking?"). Cust had written: "the French priest practices the art of preaching everywhere not the religion of Christ but the religion of France." Benoit turned the tables thus: "It is not for me to rise against the vulgarity of the first of these assertions, but with what energetic alacrity shall I embrace the second! In Africa, in the Near East, in China, in Korea, today in the archipelagos of Oceania, everywhere have I observed its rigorous exactitude."[23]

Elsewhere Benoit extols the French "navigators of genius" who first gave France her headstart in the New Hebrides and compares Anglo-French tax contributions to the Condominium government to "prove that our supremacy is now recognized, accepted by our rivals."[24] He even intimates that the architecture of the two powers' headquarters—the French Residency blending into residential Vila, the British Residency isolated and ugly on its offshore perch on Iririki island—reveals the aloofness and intrusiveness of the English in the New Hebrides. But perhaps most evocative, through its personalization of the antipathy, is this passage:

> The predecessor of the current British resident, deceased in Port Vila through a bizarre accident, left among his papers a note in which he expressed his wish not to be interred in a land fatalistically destined to become French. Good Englishman that he was, he requested the rippling shroud of the sea which, one well knows, is a thing of the Empire. They did their best to respect his wish. But the boatmen in charge of the lugubrious ceremony, badly trained or too much in a hurry, let the corpse go before exceeding the limits of the territorial waters. Should the Hebrides one day become ours it shall be in French soil that this man, whose lucidity merited a better recompense, will, in spite of himself, rest.[25]

One will not find in French writings a more enlightened view of the Melanesians than those expressed above by Jacomb. Because French planters were more numerous than British and Australian ones, and their regulations (such as the ban on grog selling) less vigorously enforced, Frenchmen had the greater reputation for drinking and philandering with "the natives." It is indeed from French-Melanesian unions that most mixed-blood New Hebrideans were spawned. For someone like Jimmy Stephens, it counted that, while the French recognized and educated their *métis,* the English treated their half-castes as outcasts.[26]

It would be unfair to leave the impression that virulent Anglo-Gallic antipathy and European racism persisted until the end of the Condominium, however. Settlers and officials of the 1960s and 1970s would be hard-pressed to recognize as their own the prejudices commonly expressed in the 1920s and 1930s. Education had indeed transformed mentalities, of Europeans as well as Melanesians. By the 1970s the differences separating the British and French stemmed less from "innate" national character than from perceived strategic interest: Whereas the United Kingdom was resigned to liquidating its colonial encumbrances, France was anxious to maintain an overseas presence. Of course, these differing foreign-policy objectives reflected long-standing distinctions in political culture and colonial philosophy. Self-serving as it may have been, France's linguistic and cultural "generosity" made it more difficult to sever affective ties with her overseas wards than Britain's contrasting aloofness did. While the expression and explanation of Anglo–Gallic differences in the New Hebrides evolved significantly from the early days of the Condominium, the duelling in colonial mindsets persisted throughout. Some of the nuances in this evolution may have been lost on the Melanesian subjects of the Condominium; the fact of intra-European rivalry, however, was not.

THREE, TWO, OR ONE?: CONDOMINIUM VERSUS
TUFALA GAVMAN

The Condominium per se was joint administration by French and British "partners," alongside whom operated two separate national administrations. Three systems of government thus operated simultaneously under the auspices of the Anglo-French Protocol. It is not surprising that, given its inherently complicated and convoluted structure, the New Hebrideans themselves understood the structure of government during the Condominium in starkly different terms than did the Europeans.

Tufala gavman—literally, "government[s] of the two [fellows]"—is the indigenous New Hebridean term for the Condominium. The Bislama expression aptly captures both the ambiguity and the duality of governance as experienced by the condocolonized. Linguistically, it is unclear whether *tufala gavman* denotes one government composed of two sets of rulers or two separate governments existing side by side. (Pluralization in Bislama requires a nominal or adjectival qualifier; there is no plural form of nouns themselves.) For the native New Hebridean, such a distinction was in any case irrelevant. What counted was that there were two kinds of *waetman* (white man): *man Franis* or *man wiwi* (man [saying] *"oui oui"*) and *man Inglan,* who ostensibly were in charge but who consistently bickered between themselves. Whatever the setup in European theory, the Melanesian point of view was condocolonial dualism. Though dualism per se was not alien to indigenous Pacific cultures, the extension of a particular form of it, over a recombined cluster of islands, was.

Unlike in West Africa, where partitioned borderlanders concur on the sharply divergent styles of French and British rule,[27] Melanesian islanders of the former Condominium retain irreconcilable and partisan views of the colonial difference. Even when in agreement on the rightness of independence, depending on their familial, religious, linguistic, village, and political ties, ni-Vanuatu provide either pro-British or pro-French versions of the colonial experience. The intensity and specificity of the condocolonial narrative varies dramatically according to degree of personal exposure to the Condominium: In the highlands of Santo and in the remote Torres islands, for instance, informants expressed to me a relatively vague appreciation of the difference between the two powers. This is most likely due to the relative aloofness and weakness of all official European administration during the Condominium, a system that only latterly made any attempt to extend itself into rural communities and transform outer island life.

Compared with the partitioned African experience, moreover, where folktales and songs about long-dead colonial administrators (still remembered by their native nicknames) thrive,[28] there are remarkably few reminiscences in Vanuatu about the *waetman* who administered the local districts. Notable exceptions to this rule include Mr. Wilkes, the infamous B.D.A. of Tanna, and Oscar Newman of Malakula. That Newman should be considered a colonial "ruler" of Malakula is revealing, for, though he was a plantation owner and occupied no official administrative position, he is acknowledged as having been the true power king of the district.

Colonial comparisons could also be of the crudely pocketbook variety. Officers of the French national administration, for instance, were employed by the French national civil service, thereby enjoying generous benefits associated with overseas posting. (A similar situation still prevails in overseas departments and territories.) Officials of the British Residency, on the other hand, were not part of the British civil service but were "locally" employed by the British Commission of the Western Pacific. Pay and benefits were not as high. Such differences in remuneration were exaggerated at the level of New Hebridean employees in the respective national services and contributed to corresponding feelings of envy and haughtiness between Anglophones and Francophones.

But who was an Anglophone? Who was a Francophone? Although in most contexts these terms are linguistic referents, in the Vanuatu of today, no less than in the New Hebrides of yesteryear, "Anglophone" and "Francophone" refer, above all, to correlations of affinity and identification. An Anglophone did not necessarily speak English, nor a Francophone French. An Anglophone might be someone whose great-uncle had been employed by the British national service. A woman became Francophone by virtue of marrying a man who had spent a year or two in a French school. Generally, though, the most important criterion was religious affiliation and schooling: Those who attended Catholic mass were Francophone; being "schooled" into Anglicanism or Presbyterianism sufficed for being Anglophone. Never mind that actual linguistic competency in either French or English might be nil. Anglophone/Francophone identity, particularly outside of Port Vila and Luganville, was largely communal and spatial: Entire villages were Anglophone or Francophone, depending on which type of religious mission or school was implanted closest. And Anglophone villages could exist cheek-by-jowl with Francophone ones.

Depending on which side of the Anglophone–Francophone mental boundary one stands, one can reconstruct two diametrical histories of the New Hebrides and Vanuatu. This, in composite form, is how they go.[29]

The Anglophone Version

"Both British and French took control over the islands of the New Hebrides, but only the French came to stay for good. That's why they built their schools in brick, because they never intended to leave. They were land-hungry, stealing our ground and violating land agreements. They held on to us as tight as a man holding an umbrella in the rain. British people came to make money, too, but not by taking over our lands and turning them into plantations. The French even poisoned blacks to get them to work on their plantations and would whip them once they were there! Only after the war, because they feared America, did they stop this. Unlike the British, who are quiet, the French would yell at you if you wanted to speak to them and interrupted what they were doing.

"In punishment, the French were much more severe than the British. They'd side only with the Whiteman in court and their fines would be higher and prison terms longer. The French would drink and fight. They encouraged our own people to drink and fight, too, and then would throw them into prison. British justice was straight. It was on account of the French that we almost drowned in the Condominium hole.

"France tried to turn the people of Vanuatu into little Frenchmen, so that they would not oppose French rule. They did this by preaching Catholicism. How many ni-Vanuatu became Catholic priests? Hardly any. In religion, the Blackman was taught to just obey the Whiteman. We, in contrast, had our own elders, pastors, and preachers. Our Bible and our prayers have long been in Bislama, a language we can understand. Each of us prays directly. But with the French, the *père* holds the book and does the praying. There's no clear thinking for the people. Their eyes are not open.

"French schooling was another way to brainwash the Blackman. Sure, they would have prettier buildings. Yes, they would give free room and board. True, the families paid nothing for their schooling. But they gave up their minds and their dignity to the French.

"Together, the French and British divided the Vanuatu people with their Condominium. But the British finally saw the light and eventually agreed to give us our independence. They prepared our leaders. They taught us self-reliance. They realized that 'the child had grown, was beginning to shave, and so was old enough to take a wife.'[30] The French resisted and therefore so did the Francophones. France wanted to stay on forever—just like in New Caledonia, which has yet to become free. They helped the rebels in Santo and, when that failed, tried to subvert Vanuatu independence with their ambassadors. That's why they had to be thrown out, so we could achieve our freedom and independence.

"Things are certainly better with independence. We own our land again. There are more roads being built, better communications, more development. You can see airports on islands that didn't have any. There are medical facilities, water storage tanks. There is better schooling than before."

The Francophone Version

"Vanuatu is a small country. In the past, we needed help to progress. The French gave us the best opportunity to do that. They let us have their language, their education—the real one, not like what the Anglophones wound up with. When Anglophones went to school they *thought* they were learning English but they really didn't; they were given 'broken' English instead. They learned some Bible, maybe, but never received the same instruction that English children did. Catholic school education was always more serious, more rigorous. In public schools, too, we had teachers come all the way from France. Teachers in Anglophone schools weren't so strong in English language to begin with. The French would teach practical things, like mechanics and carpentry. 'Gospel is good for heaven, for the afterlife,' they'd say, 'but you also have to learn how to succeed in this world.' England didn't want to spend the money to really educate our people. France was willing and did so because the French liked us as people.

"You could see the difference in how they lived here. Frenchmen would chat with blacks, eat with them, even marry their women. But the English—they didn't want to mix with blacks at all. They were stingy with their food. Why, they'd give one can of fish for three persons to divide and then just barely enough rice to go with it! You lacked for nothing with the Frenchman. If you asked for something—a fishnet, say—they'd give it to you right away. But the English would take their time and never get around to delivering on their promise.

"Yes, the English were as slow as the French were quick. But in one respect the English were impatient—to go away and leave us to our own devices. At first they wanted to conquer the people, expand on our land, and convert us. But when they'd had enough, they just upped and left. They never really cared for us and so were happy to leave. But the French did like us and that's why they were sad to have to go. Before leaving they paid us better than the English did. They were generous and didn't interfere in our *kastom*.

"We weren't against becoming independent. We just didn't want to be rushed into it before the country was ready—particularly by Anglophones unqualified to rule an independent government. We needed a few years more to prepare, that was all. France was ready to help, but England didn't care about our future. The British never really cared for anything but their own profit. They liked us only for our work, not out of friendship.

"Things did get worse after independence under the Anglophones, not only for us but for the economy as a whole. They didn't have the experience or qualifications to run things. Look at the educational level of the people running the country after independence—primary. Ministers of religion, with no administrative experience.

"We are for independence now—we are all ni-Vanuatu. The past is the past. But it was unjust how we were treated after independence, and it's too bad how the country has been run. We have to make up for all that now."

Anglophones and Francophones came to hold such views regardless of their level of education and direct exposure to the Condominium. But the key institutional mechanism in the transference of mental rivalries was education. Schools constituted the condocolonial battlefield, and primary schools were the frontlines.

EDUCATIONAL RIVALRIES

Largely on account of a basic reticence to invest in territory shared with a rival, neither the British nor the French government established a school system until long after World War II. Prior to then, Western education in the archipelago was provided by missionary groups. Protestant denominations greatly outnumbered Catholic missions, imparting an Anglophone advantage within this church-sponsored, loosely organized educational "system." There were four reasons for Protestant-Anglophone dominance over Catholic-Francophone education.

First, the various Protestant movements succeeded in implanting themselves earlier, and more extensively, than their Catholic counterparts. Second, they enjoyed greater material support from their sponsoring metropolitan institutions than the Roman Catholic Church provided. (This may have been at least partly doctrinally deliberate, given a more ascetic and spartan, if not semimonkish, streak in the predominantly Marist Order present.)[31] Third was a geographic consideration: While the Protestants could be replenished and renewed fairly easily by relatively close benefactors in Australia and New Zealand, the Catholic missionaries were separated by half the globe from their mentors in France. (Succor from missions in New Caledonia only partly mitigated their isolation.) Fourth, and perhaps most telling, strict lay–clerical separation within the French polity meant that the Catholic missionaries operated without the official assistance of French officialdom. The British and Australian governments, in comparison, were considerably more supportive of their missionary nationals.[32] The mix of these factors meant that, as of 1960, British outnumbered French enrollments four to one.[33] Though informal zones of linguistic influence existed, never was there any official territorial division on the basis of language.

In 1959 a new British Education Service began to standardize the disparate denominational primary schools where English was the medium of instruction.[34] A primary-level curriculum adapted specifically to the New Hebrides was developed and put into use in 1968. The churches nevertheless retained overall ownership, and locally educated graduates still undertook virtually all instruction. It was not until 1973, in response to a concerted French government program of school expansion, that the British Residency took full control of the entire network of Anglophone missionary schools.[35]

British government control did not dramatically change the nature of missionary schooling, however. For most youngsters primary education remained relatively brief (three or four years) and rudimentary. Few pupils were selected to further their education and the vast majority remained in their villages. Jean-Michel Charpentier identifies four important consequences: (1) conducted within a familiar, Melanesian environment, the lessons in English were superficial and easily forgotten; (2) reading and writing levels of graduates were minimal; (3) the quasi-exclusive use of religious texts in the hands of church teachers inculcated a "narrow religious conservatism"; and (4) alienation or deracination from indigenous Melanesian culture and language was minimal.[36]

Most secondary schools retained their denominational character: Presbyterian at Onesua High School on Efate, Anglican at Vureas Secondary School on Ambae, Church of Christ at Ranwadi on Pentecost. Formal teacher training began in 1962 with the establishment of the Kawenu Teacher Training College, which merged with the British Secondary School in 1977 to become Malapoa College. Prevocational courses (e.g., agriculture, woodwork, home economics, commerce, technical drawing) reflected a British penchant for pragmatic schooling.

At the same time that British education officers were put in place to enlarge and improve the educational infrastructure, their colleagues in the Colonial Office were considering a withdrawal from the New Hebrides. As a whole the British favored the extension of English, but language per se was not viewed as a device to undermine independence. A more desirable outcome was an independent *and* Anglophone government in charge. English-speaking New Hebrideans had come to the same conclusion.

For France, independence for the New Hebrides was anathema. Yet from a linguistic standpoint France was seriously outnumbered. Catholics, and therefore Francophones, were in the minority; decades of more rigorous missionizing on the part of the Protestants had seen to that. In consequence France looked to *l'école,* the school, one of her proudest institutions and a traditional pillar of colonial policy. A calculus had been made: Mastery of the French language would translate into loyalty to the French state; the more Francophones, the more loyalty. Unlike its policy in colonial Africa, the thrust of French educational policy in the New Hebrides was to produce as many Francophones as possible, not to cultivate a select group of indigenes who could assure high-level administrative responsibility of their own. Few resources would be spared in the campaign to convince unlettered Melanesian parents of the virtues of Francophonie, the extended family of French language and culture.

It is worth noting that promoting French language and education was employed as a strategy in the New Hebrides long after the classical doctrines of *mission civilisatrice* and *assimilation* had been supplanted in France by contemporary norms of decolonization and self-determination. This is why Francophonie in preindependence Vanuatu was so strongly perceived as catering to strictly partisan aims. By the late 1970s, portraying the extension of Francophonie as an exercise in cultural elevation was no longer tenable, not when pitted against internationally accepted standards of Third World solidarity and liberation theology. With Francophonie promoted so baldly for partisan purposes before independence, the case for its postindependence retention on purely *cultural* grounds required great ingenuity and generosity of spirit.

From France's perspective, the critical element was time. If the momentum of an expanding French education could be maintained, then the majority of the new generation of New Hebridean youth would be Francophone and thus, it was assumed, Francophile. Independence under such circumstances would not be so traumatic to France or detrimental to French interests. "Premature" independence in 1980, however, still implied an Anglophone political dominance. In his memoirs, the French delegate Robert Delauney put it plainly:

> We accepted the principle of independence, of course. Our African experiences had demonstrated that, in countries where our political, economic, and especially linguistic influence could not be challenged, it was perfectly possible to establish amicable and constructive relations preserving reciprocal interests intelligently understood. . . . In the New Hebrides . . . we needed ten more years to mold a complete generation of young Melanesians so that French influence would equal, if not exceed, British influence.[37]

To pursue these goals, the French ministry of national education began assuming financial and administrative responsibility for Francophone public schools in 1968 and for parochial ones in 1973: Politics aside, personnel and supply scarcities in the Catholic Mission helped to overcome the old clerical–lay divide in French education.

Both the number of public schools and Francophone pupils boomed throughout this period, continuing into the 1970s. In twelve years (1960–1972) the percentage of Francophone schoolchildren practically doubled and, by independence, had achieved virtual parity with the Anglophones (48.9 percent to 51.1 percent; see Figure 1).[38] Had the

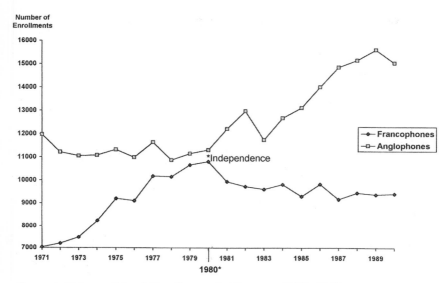

Figure 1. Primary School Enrollments in Vanuatu, 1971–1990

average growth rate of the five years prior to the 1979–1980 peak (1.3 percent) been continued, the very next year the numerical balance would have swung to the Francophone side.

Fifteen new schools, with a capacity of over one thousand pupils, sprang up almost overnight, from a preceding base of four rural primary and one urban secondary schools. Whereas Anglophone schools were often made out of cane, bamboo, and thatch, Francophone ones were prefabricated structures of glass, cement, and panel. Many of these schools were built next to older, established Anglophone ones. In the remote Anglican stronghold of the Banks islands this took the extravagant form of installing an illuminated water fountain on the grounds of the school on Vanua Lava.

Secondary-level schooling reflected a similar numerical trend though on a smaller scale. In the decade preceding independence (1970–1980), the share of Francophone enrollments went from 40 percent to exact parity with Anglophone ones (see Figure 2). This Francophone momentum was halted at independence, a decade after which secondary school enrollment fell back even below the 1970 level.

France pulled few financial stops in building schools and sending teachers—many in lieu of military service—to staff them. By 1976 French educational expenditures exceeded that of the British more than fivefold;[39] and ten times as many expatriate teachers were sent from

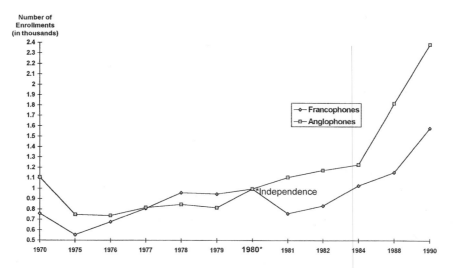

Figure 2. Secondary School Enrollments in Vanuatu, 1970–1990

France than from Britain. Overall, almost one-third (30 percent) of teachers in New Hebridean French-language primary schools were themselves French while fewer than 4 percent of those in English-medium schools were British. Salaries could be double in the French compared with British schools.[40] Compensation by the missionaries, most of whom were Anglophone, was even less.

Nearly five times as many (local) teachers in English medium schools had no formal training compared with French medium teachers. Teacher training was conducted, beginning in 1964, at the French-medium primary school on rue Colardeau and lasted one year. It was open to students who had completed four years of study at the French lycée.

Whereas tuition payments were required for entry into New Hebridean British schools even at the primary level, admission to French schools was absolutely free for primary, secondary, and postsecondary school. Francophone pupils also enjoyed free meals and transport, an attractive consideration for relatively poorer New Hebridean families. Whether it was due to French money or the Cartesian method, as measured by standard pedagogic criteria the Francophone quality of instruction surpassed the Anglophone.[41]

Large numbers of native French cadres, generous educational budgets, and rigorous methods of instruction in parochial as well as state schools succeeded in creating a critical mass of Francophone, and generally Francophile, Melanesians. Although more New Hebrideans passed through the nominally English-speaking mission schools, here literacy and numeracy were secondary to theology.

Tertiary education, on the other hand, remained an Anglophone affair. Only the few Francophones who passed the French national baccalaureate could go to Paris for university. In addition to the United Kingdom, Anglophones had university options in Fiji, Papua New Guinea, Australia, and New Zealand.

RESPONSES TO EDUCATIONAL RIVALRY

Ni-Vanuatu were not passive spectators to condocolonial school rivalry. As had often been the case throughout the Condominium, local communities exploited the intra-European competition for their own benefit. France could build schools and provide free tuition, board, transportation, and clothing, but in a society that generally functioned by barter rather than donation this was not sufficient to "buy" enrollments. Other reasons for acceding to French schooling included: an affinity among *kastom* movement members toward an alternative, non-Christianizing system; appreciation that French schools were willing to accept pupils who had dropped out or been expelled from Anglophone ones; recognition that the French would pay higher wages to local support staff; increased prestige for the chief who could bring a school into his community and thereby "put it on the map"; an opportunity to neutralize the influence of any local pastor seen to favor a rival village's chief; and a desire to punish any local British administrator thought to prefer a competing village (in which case the Anglophone school would be closed and a Francophone one opened in its place). The combination of motives for endorsing the establishment of a Francophone school was different in every case: "it would be vain to seek general reasons valid for the establishment of all the [French] schools, too many historical, social and individual factors being at the origin of each [one]."[42] Latter-day condocolonial rivalry strongly diluted the traditional correlation between Francophonie and Catholicism: ni-Vanuatu youngsters named Jimmy, Joe, Michael, Bob, Jay, Tommy, Janet, and Rick (as per the Francophone Arep school roster on Vanua Lava in the Banks) are not likely to have been baptized in a South Pacific Catholic church.

The critical point is that the duplication of school facilities stemmed not solely from British–French rivalry but also from indigenous rivalries, conflicts, and jealousies between neighboring villages. The

Condominium did not superimpose cleavages among otherwise cooper-
ative, mutually supportive Melanesian communities; rival Melanesian
groups used the bait of dangling resources to further their own interests
vis-à-vis each other. Condocolonial rivalry may have aggravated traditional conflicts on the local level, and indeed enlarged the scale of such
competition (from valley to island to archipelago) along bipolar lines,
but it did not create local divisions ex nihilo.

THE PREJUDICES OF PEDAGOGY

Francophones and Anglophones differed not only in the languages they
learned but in the subject matter they studied. These gave rise to varying
standards of achievement and different levels of confidence. Anglophone
schools, missionary and British-state, used learning materials more
closely geared to the South Pacific context that were written for non-native English-speakers. In Francophone schools the texts came from
France and followed the national ministry of education's curriculum. If
French education was Eurocentric, Anglophone schooling was Oce-
anocentric. A deductive, Cartesian educational method competed with a
more basic and pragmatic Anglo-Saxon program. Melanesians emerged
from the two school systems not only speaking different European languages but trained to think and reason in different ways. This superim-
position of dissimilar thought patterns within the same national community created a cognitive wedge deeper than the one recognized in the
simple linguistic cleavage between English- and French-speaker. It is
here, in the deceptively benevolent setting of the schoolroom, that
Vanuatu's mental boundaries were most deeply encoded, lesson by lesson, class by class.

Anglophones were trained in what Jean-Michel Charpentier calls a
"pyramidal elitist system."[43] Those who made it to the endpoint of the
curriculum (which usually entailed final training in other Pacific territories) firmly believed that they had achieved a superior level of education.
Highly self-confident, smug with religious pieties reinforced throughout
their training, Anglophone graduates depreciated both those who had
not equivalent training and those who had gone to French school. Radio
broadcasts by returning, graduated heroes were common on the Anglophone side. Charpentier claims that such confidence building was part
of British strategy to stimulate and legitimize calls for New Hebridean
self-determination.[44]

Initially, ni-Vanuatu in French schools retained the self-effacement and shyness characteristic of all Melanesian youngsters entrusted into European hands. For a long time they remained awed by their teachers and self-conscious about their lack of knowledge. Unyielding standards and inflexible curricula did little to alleviate this complex. Nor did the French have parallel political reasons to encourage assertiveness among their wards. In the educational context, religious faith decreasingly correlated with a sense of superiority: Mission schools had progressively diminished the religious component of their curricula, and French-state schools were secular from the outset.

Only later, in the workplace, did Melanesians educated by the French discover that the condescension of those educated in English was unwarranted. They found that their abilities were as high, if not higher, than those of their Anglophone counterparts. Demystification gave way to denigration. Francophones dismissed and undercut Anglophone self-confidence in terms of British paternalism: *Olgeta i switim Anglophone nomo,* they might say in Bislama ("They merely 'sweeten' the Anglophones"), employing *switim* in the pejorative sense of insincere flattery.[45] In the end, Anglophones and Francophones bludgeoned each other equally with their respective prejudices, though they wielded different ideological axes. Self-confident, freedom-loving Anglophones mocked the meek, French-aping Francophone graduates who feared political independence and rupture from the colonial umbilical cord. Prudent Francophone survivors of the more stringent testing grounds of *l'école française* disdained the more numerous Anglophone bullies who muddled through a broken version of English to demand responsibilities they were incapable of fulfilling. Although softened somewhat in the decade following independence, the older generation of schooled ni-Vanuatu still carry some form of these pedagogic prejudices with them today.

Views of Anglophones Toward Francophone Education

Only with difficulty do older, educated Anglophones accept the legitimacy and authenticity of the Francophone experience in Vanuatu. For them, Francophonie is an alien cultural expression imposed wholesale on duped or greedy fellow islanders. They reject that it was introduced for any but political reasons: to create a native class favorable toward the continued French presence in the archipelago. Francophones were brainwashed, according to Anglophones, into little Melanesian Frenchmen incapable of thinking independently or acting contrary to the bidding of their schoolteachers and masters. They are inauthentic mimics, bought off by the lure of free meals, free transport, and free education.

In exchange for accepting the gilded gifts of French education, they surrendered their dignity as freedom-loving ni-Vanuatu. Though Francophones know they have lost the battle for political autonomy and now profess allegiance to the Vanuatu state, they remain suspect as true nationalists and retain narrowly parochial political interests.

Rarely do prominent Anglophones articulate this view publicly, at least outside of their own circles. Anglophone politicians would be even more loath to admit it, too, lest it revive old wounds. But such views were expressed in interviews with Anglophones throughout the archipelago and reflect a persistent, if underreported, anti-Francophone prejudice.

> Because everything was free [on the French side] they had no discipline. They avoided community work. . . . Chiefs found a lack of cooperation from those coming out of French schools. . . . They demanded payment for village work. To build the schools, dig the toilets they would be paid, provided with food. . . . [The British proceeded] on a help your-self basis—you want it, come and do it. (Arep School [Banks Group] headmaster)

> French teachers have had the impression of being French, so we must give them the sense of being ni-Vanuatu. . . . In meetings, French teachers keep quiet and at a distance. Decisions are made by Anglophones. Perhaps this is because French teachers were spoon fed in the past. (Headmaster, Louiapeng-Ienaula bilingual primary school, Tanna)

> Colonial thinking is still there. . . . The French system is too advanced. (Regional Education Officer, Eastern Region)

Still, most Anglophones accept the utility of Vanuatu remaining a bilingual state. As long as economic opportunities are enhanced by possessing a second European language, so much the better. Tourism, trade with New Caledonia, and the prospects for subsidized higher education in the French Pacific (and France itself) justify the retention of French-language education. Such views are revealing in their own acquired, colonial way: They apply the Anglo-Saxon criteria of pragmatism and utilitarianism even in assessing the traditional rival.

Views of Francophones toward Anglophone Education

Educated Francophones still look down upon their Anglophone counterparts with ill-disguised disdain. They are smug in their conviction that their education, more rigorous than the Anglophones', is superior. It was not they who became pale imitations of their colonial masters so much as the Anglophones who unthinkingly swallowed the politicized dogma of their pastors. "In the Francophone school I developed a critical spirit and mentality. That's what counts for me. *Et je peux dire merde ou non!* [I can tell anyone off if I want to]." This same Francophone, the first ni-Vanuatu primary school teacher in the French public sector, goes on to claim:

> If I say that I am proud to be Francophone, it's because I seek out ques-
> tions and I can answer them, whereas I don't see this among the Anglo-
> phones. I don't want to underestimate them, but among these people,
> at times, one would say that they are robots. No critical spirit, just
> "Yes, Sir!"

A headmaster (and one-time policeman) on the island of Malakula, who schooled for six years in New Caledonia, distinguishes the ephemeral and flimsy structure of Anglophone schools with the more solid, durable Francophone ones: "French schools are built with strong materials. They last!" (The same holds true for prisons: "French prisons are the ones still most in use. Prisoners escape from the British-built ones.") Architecture is emblematic of the enduring and practical nature of French education: "The French teach you how to drive, how to get about on a motorcycle, how to turn on a turbine, how to use the lawnmower."

Anglophones are jealous and relatively incompetent: "They've begun to steal French methods of teaching. . . . One Francophone technical adviser does the work of two Anglophone ones." And Francophones are much more likely to understand English (even if they cannot easily speak it) than Anglophones are to understand French: "There are no secrets kept from us. *We* can make the secrets."

Writing on the eve of independence, Jean-Michel Charpentier noted: "More than an organized official bilingualism, what we have are two international languages juxtaposed, without any relationship between them. The current 'bilingualism' which the New Hebrides experiences, on account of its bicephalous character and lack of single orientation, is more a factor of division than enrichment."[46] Today the challenge to Vanuatu policymakers is to recoup a comparative advantage out of what previously had been a condocolonial handicap—to wit, to exploit the nation's legacy of being the only bilingual, Anglophone-Francophone polity in the South Pacific.

RIVAL MENTALITIES AND GENERATIONAL BOUNDARIES

From the beginning of the Condominium until its liquidation, ambivalence overlay the relationship between its French and British partners. By its very nature the Condominium represented a peaceful compromise between two rival powers over terra incognita. Each party had a different reason for implanting itself—France to expand its Pacific colonial empire, Britain to reassure its Australian protectorate—with corresponding levels of commitment (higher for the French than for the British). Neither side was happy to share the archipelago with the other, but resorting to force to establish exclusive control was out of the question. Solidarity during the two great crises of the twentieth century reinforced Anglo-French ties in general (during the Second World War the French Resident Commissioner, Sautot, unequivocally supported de Gaulle and shipped pro-Vichy compatriots off to Indochina) and the Protocol, imperfect as it was, held. At the local level, many British and French coadministrators also developed a common colonial solidarity based on shared isolation, ethnocentrism, and ennui.

And yet that old European tug-of-war between French and British did persist, even transplanted to the Pacific. Had the question of independence for the New Hebrides not revived dormant patterns of conflict, Anglo-French rivalry probably would have remained at the level of good-natured teasing, spiked only by minor institutional nuisances and occasional mutual jabs at national pride. Contemporary French–British relations on the social level might be likened to what anthropologists call "joking cousins": an enculturated pattern of mildly derisive bantering that maintains social boundaries and identities without impeding friendly and even intimate relationships. But the thorny issue of decolonization—favored by the British, eschewed by the French—reignited what I have elsewhere called, based on extensive archival readings of French Residency monthly reports *(synthèses mensuelles)* of the 1960s and the 1970s, anachronistic antagonisms.[47]

Disagreements over decolonization both stemmed from and were intensified by diametrically opposed colonial philosophies. French policy overseas was imbued with the spirit of a civilizing mission, of extending the benefits of French culture, language, and education to less evolved civilizations and thereby joining them within a global French fraternity. British colonialism made fewer pretenses of turning "natives" into Englishmen, valuing the colonies almost exclusively in terms of the material advantages they brought to the mother country. Whereas the preferred French model of decolonization was fuller administrative integration within *la République,* alternatively called *assimilation* and then *départementalisation,* decolonization for the British entailed the much simpler prospect of granting outright independence. In reality, of course, French colonial paternalism did not entirely exclude racism, any more than British segregationism prevented the emergence of Black Englishmen and, as referred to in the context of Barbados, Afro-Saxons. Nor has colonial theory precluded the continuing existence of colonies within the British sphere and nondepartmental dependencies (territorial collectivities and overseas territories, with constitutional rights of secession) in the French camp. Still, the overall distinction between French and British modes of colonialism and decolonization holds, as can be clearly seen among partitioned continental peoples of Africa and insular indigenes in the Caribbean and Pacific.

Retention of mental rivalry is largely generational. Many of the educated elite, those ni-Vanuatu whose formative years were spent within the framework of the Condominium and who internalized the Anglophone–Francophone rivalries it engendered, remain locked into reflexive negative stereotypes of the linguistic Other. It is up to the rising and future generations to put aside the superimposed anti-Anglophone and anti-Francophone prejudices still held by so many of their elders. Beyond ministerial speeches, beyond civics education, beyond liberation theology, beyond national arts festivals, Vanuatu requires the passage of at least another generation before the mental boundaries inculcated by condocolonialism can be effectively dismantled. Time is a necessary element in the formation of Vanuatu national unity. Not until at least 2020 will there be a transformed cadre of ni-Vanuatu leaders for whom the Condominium, with all its divisive dualism, will be no more than a lesson in history.

Had the British and French succeeded in creating an irreparable chasm between competing Melanesian camps of Anglophones and Francophones, the Vanuatu nation would have been doomed. In actuality, while Britain and France, in tandem with their missionary counterparts, did create distinctive groups of Anglophone and Francophone elites, Westernization of the Melanesian populace constituted a thin coating to an otherwise multilayered polity. Condocolonialism may have exploited indigenous rivalries along Anglophone–Francophone lines but it never supplanted Melanesian essence with European identities. Indigenous practice, belief, and tradition, even where weakened and atrophied, had kept the Melanesian heart beating during generations of condocolonialism. Nationhood in Vanuatu would entail the grafting of the condocolonial infrastructure onto an indigenous, albeit evolving, foundation. But first this foundation needed a name and a movement. Thus emerged *kastom*.

Nationalism, *Kastom,* and Other Boundaries of Identity

[S]tates have used their force to create cultural diversity, and [also] to create cultural uniformity. This has made the state the most powerful cultural force in the modern world and the most schizophrenic.

—Immanuel Wallerstein, "The National and the Universal"

Here is one important thing to remember. You are a ni-Vanuatu, a citizen of Vanuatu. Try not to think of yourself as someone who comes from Santo or Tanna, Epi or Aniwa or one of the other islands. Instead think of yourself as a ni-Vanuatu and use [Bislama], your national language.

—*The Story of Our Islands, Part II. The People and Government. An Environmental Studies Handbook for the Teachers and Children in Senior Primary Schools in Vanuatu*

Painted with the broadest strokes, the evolution of nationalism in the New Hebrides mirrors that of struggles for independence elsewhere in the Third World. A cluster of peoples that a century before may have had only the remotest glimmer of solidarity—indeed, who may frequently have been at war with each other—now found themselves united in opposition to some colonial power. This sense of unity was both natural and contrived: It was natural in that colonial political structures, and often a colonial language, institutionalized economic exchange, regular communications, and general interactions among discrete sets of colonial subjects; but it was contrived in that colonized elites, invariably educated and therefore Westernized, had to channel such emerging commonalities into a voluntaristic sense of national identity. From there the goal was statehood. The model of nationalism, and indeed its legitimiz-

Viewing Independence Day celebrations.

ing force, was the European nation-state itself. Imparting this political ideal to the less acculturated masses constituted a major challenge. In multiethnic colonies, this nationalizing challenge has continued since independence.[1]

This, on one level, was the experience of the New Hebrides, where hyperinsularity and local warfare negated precontact national unity. Prior to and even during most of the colonial era, island populations had minimal mutual contact. In the south, Aneityum and Aniwa islanders had little truck with each other, much less reason to canoe to the northern islands of Gaua in the Banks or Hiu in the Torres. Even when coastal inhabitants of adjacent islands did interact with each other, as those of southern Pentecost and northern Ambrym, they usually had no communication with groups on the other side or in the interior of their own islands. And what contact they did have was not especially peaceful: On Malakula and Santo, localized intra-island warfare, which often resulted in the eating of the enemy, was particularly renowned.[2] It is therefore not surprising that neighboring communities rarely agreed on a name for the island they shared, much less on a transpelagic cosmology. In the absence of any overarching myth of common descent and glorious history, which Walker Connor asserts is necessary for nationhood,[3] some transcendent common culture has had to be created, constructed, or, as Benedict Anderson would put it, "imagined."[4]

Even though the condocolonial administration increased geographical awareness of the outer islands (particularly in Efate and Santo, whence northern and southern islands were administered), in the late 1960s and 1970s nationalist leaders still needed to overcome geographical dispersion, religious rivalry, and parochial identities to create a sense of New Hebridean nationalism. Along with Bislama, *kastom*—a common denominator of indigenous customs, rituals, and practices with which all islanders could broadly identify—was chosen as the means to achieving this unity. Because the church infrastructure often overshadowed the colonial one, political and religious leadership, particularly from within the Anglican and Presbyterian hierarchies, overlapped.

What distinguished the Vanuatu nationalist struggle was the nature of the Condominium. On account of the dualistic nature of New Hebridean colonialism and the bifurcated loyalties that intracolonial rivalry engendered, the nationalist struggle became uniquely divisive. Unlike in Algeria or Ireland, it did not pit loyalists to the colonial regime against revolutionaries for independence, but rather split indigenous communities according to religious, linguistic, and condocolonial affinities. Nationalism in Vanuatu still entails overcoming those divisions which brewed during the condominial era and boiled over in the pre-independence period.

History has shown that nationalism is easiest to achieve where colonial domination has been strongest. Independence insurgencies—in Algeria, India, and Vietnam, for example—nationalized[5] populations in ways that did not occur in Mali, Nepal, or Kuwait. Island colonies were usually powerless to wrest sovereignty from colonial powers, which partly explains why insular nationalism has been so problematic. Both in the Caribbean and the Pacific, islands became independent when the colonial power (usually Great Britain) so decided; when a monocolonial power (usually France) has chosen otherwise, nationalism and independence have been forestalled. Though questions of economic viability are often invoked, these political reasons explain why the greatest number of nonindependent territories today are islands.

As Eric Hobswawm acutely observes, in his influential analysis of nationalism, "we cannot assume that for most people national identification—when it exists—excludes or is always or ever superior to, the remainder of the set of identifications which constitute the social being. In fact, it is always combined with identifications of another kind, even when it is felt to be superior to them."[6] The identifications which ni-Vanuatu possess are manifold and changing in saliency. These include religion (and denomination), language (indigenous and official), island of origin, and, more embryonically, wider region (qua Melanesia). Nationalism is a relatively recent addition to the psyche of many islanders in Vanuatu, and its ongoing formation is fascinating to observe.

Hobswawm also stresses the importance and difficulty of knowing how the masses react to the nationalist program (the "view from below"). But Hobswawm wrote as a historian and his main concern was with Europe. New nation-states, such as Vanuatu, give us the opportunity to examine expressions of nationalism more carefully, even though their contemporaneity precludes descriptive closure.[7] Anthony D. Smith bestows conceptual freedom upon this endeavor by showing how studies of ethnicity and ethnic identity, formerly the preserve of anthropologists and sociologists, have been legitimately appropriated by historians and, we might add, political scientists.[8]

Adapting and expanding the insight of Fredrik Barth, who tied the persistence of group identity and culture to "ethnic boundary maintenance," we can thus usefully begin to view nationalism as a dual-process boundary marker. On one level, nationalism is a separationist phenomenon, marking off one people and one identity from another, often the colonized from the colonizer. At the same time it is an inclusive identity marker, conferring national unity on all citizens within its literal, territorial boundaries. In its unobtrusive way, Vanuatu reveals how the separationist process of boundary drawing—formal decolonization—is more easily accomplished than the integrative one—the formation of national identity. Alas, Vanuatu is not alone in experiencing this borderline discrepancy.

CONDOCOLONIAL IDENTITIES

The Condominium's peculiar nature complexified colonial loyalties. As native New Hebrideans were not subjects of either Britain or France, neither colonial power could directly inculcate an ideology of "mother country." Anglophone New Hebrideans were not raised to revere the queen any more than Francophones were bound to protect the French Republic. National holidays of both countries were celebrated, but New Hebridean guests were involved more as observers than participants. Assimilation, association, direct rule, indirect rule—condominial reality precluded the application of any of these classical doctrines of colonial rule.

Depending on level of education and exposure to Residency representatives, New Hebrideans nevertheless identified with one or the other condominial parties. This was not a matter of political identification — for there was no question of acquiring French or British citizenship — so much as stylistic interpretations colored by local circumstances. Religion and language were relevant but not determinative. Thus, in addition to the ordinary equation C(atholic) + F(rancophone) = P(ro-French), diverse non-Catholic, non-Francophones such as Chief Tuk of Tanna and Jimmy Stephens of Santo both came to identify with France over Britain, even though the former glorified Prince Philip of Windsor as a semidivine, *man Tanna* in exile, and the latter began his political career by opposing the holdings of French planters and the Société Française des Nouvelles Hébrides. (Chief Tuk and his followers did not, however, join the pro-French secessionist rebellion in 1980.)

There remain two stark interpretations of condocolonialism: one that views the French with fondness and casts the British as oppressors; the other that reverses these roles. Whereas islanders in the remote bush had the relative luxury of ignoring the Condominium, dual imperialism forced many other condocolonized New Hebrideans to choose between rulers. In "normal" — that is, territorial — partition, identification with the colonizer is imposed or engineered from above. The colonized endures, adapts to, suffers from, or collaborates with the colonial regime; she/he is not, however, otherwise obliged to choose it. However ambivalent or distasteful the relationship, the association between colonized and colonizer is a given. For the nationalist, the enemy is clearly known.

In New Hebridean condocolonialism, in contrast, even the pro-independence militant had to discriminate between the British and the French and, by so doing, identify with one colonizer against the other. Such voluntary identification may have been more tactical than affective, but it nevertheless heightened and complexified the anticolonial response. Once independence came, it was more difficult to disassociate from the favored colonial power than it was in places, as in Africa, where the adversary had been unequivocal and one. Even though there is general consensus over the desirability of independence in Vanuatu, beyond a vague acknowledgment of the disunity and inefficacy of *tufala gavman*, ni-Vanuatu have no common interpretation of condocolonialism and their preindependence. Indeed, in public discourse the very existence of a latent, internalized Anglophone-Francophone schism has taken on the character of — to borrow from a core concept in many an indigenous culture in Melanesia — political taboo. The inability to transcend this taboo and to forge a unifying interpretation of condocolonialism constitutes an ongoing challenge to the construction of a unifying myth of Vanuatu national liberation.[9]

KASTOM AND NATIONALISM

Creating national unity out of social diversity in contemporary Vanuatu is advanced through a paradoxical combination of Bislama and *kastom;* for Bislama, which proliferated on Australian plantations and is larded with an English lexicon, is an undeniably quintessential outcome of colonialism. *Kastom,* though ideologically understood by anthropologists also to be a Westernized construction, is supposed to incarnate indigenous cultural authenticity in opposition to colonialism. (Indeed, *kastom* existed as long as Melanesian culture did but only achieved explicit definition when pitted against missionization.) As Chapter 6 examines Bislama specifically, here I will concentrate on the nationalist implications of *kastom.* (The relationship between *kastom* and religion is discussed in Chapter 3.) But even before *kastom* emerged as a discrete concept, protonationalist movements had prepared the ground.

Protonationalism in the New Hebrides

Although the emergence of nationalism in the New Hebrides is usually treated as a 1960s phenomenon, localized resistance movements bear witness to anticolonial politics of an earlier era. It was their inability to unite or otherwise perceive a general interest in opposition that doomed these movements to be only easily repressed, short-lived rebellions.

Most of these actions had some land dispute at their source and often resulted in the killing of a covetous European. Often there was some cargo-cult connection, which is why subsequent cargo cults of a peaceable nature (such as John Frum, discussed at greater length in Chapter 3) were severely repressed. Even before the Condominium had been officially established, in 1890 a planter under British protection, George Latour, was killed. Latour was a blatant racist who posted a signboard prohibiting "Dogs and Niggers" from entering his property—under penalty of death—and perhaps poisoned wells to eliminate inconvenient islanders. In 1891 one Peter Sawyer was also killed as a result of a land dispute. British planter P. C. Greig and his two teenage daughters were hacked to death in 1908 in a labor dispute.

In the 1920s a reputedly immortal would-be king of Santo, Ronovuro, inveighed against the white men of his island and collected money for their deportation from Santo. During an epidemic, Ronovuro specifically targeted a plantation owner, and R. Clapcott was murdered. Though Ronovuro and two other *man Santo* were subsequently executed for the Clapcott killing, Ronovuro followers emerged in the 1930s (Avu Avu) and 1940s (Atori). Another cult founder of Santo, Tieka, advocated a communal reconstruction of society, including wife sharing, to follow the elimination of private homes and agricultural plots.[10] Jean Guiart recounts how, during his trek through south Santo in the 1950s, the memory of Greig and Clapcott still soured relations between islanders and government representatives, particularly because innocent women, including a girl, had been killed during an expedition to capture Greig's murderers.[11] Jimmy Stephens' family also had ties to persons implicated in the Clapcott-Ronovuro affair, a fact that presumably reinforced his anti-Condominium sentiments and following.[12]

Protonationalist movements were not confined to Santo. On the island of Tongoa, in the Shepherds group, Chief Samuel Kora is credited with having been, as early as the 1930s, the "first chief to move against colonialism."[13] In the 1940s, a renegade group of Anglicans, the Danielites, both tried to purify Christian practice and "usher . . . in an age in which Melanesians would rule themselves and the island of Pentecost would achieve a pre-eminence."[14] On West Ambae, resistance both to the Condominium and to European institutions, including the church, stemmed from the imprisonment of a "Christian Chief" (Sale Bani) by the French Residency in 1914, presumably for inciting a boycott against local French traders. A half-century later, the legacy of Sale Bani was an Ambae welcome for Jimmy Stephens. On Malakula in the 1940s, Ragrag Charley, inspired by John Frum promises of salvation from America, decided to carve out an airstrip to receive cargo-bearing planes from the United States, while on Pentecost Bule John started to build a cargo road. Condominium authorities, perceiving these initiatives as threats to their authority, jailed or deported these cargo-cult leaders.

None of these activities was generally recognized to be political. In popular parlance, politics only "came out" (i.e., emerged) when nationalist and opposition parties surfaced in the 1960s. For many ni-Vanuatu, "politics" is narrowly associated with Western forms of mobilization and organization; it is not viewed as either a universal or an indigenous contest over power. (Jimmy Stephens' genius lay in rejecting this common understanding.) Democratic politics in particular is often rejected as negating the "natural" order of governance through chiefs or bigmen. *Politik* is foreign, several informants said, "something of the Whiteman."

"Those who have gone abroad may know how to use it but not ordinary folk." "It creates division and jealousy." Such attitudes represent a challenge to democratic entrenchment in many developing societies.[15]

It would be interesting to compare Melanesian cargo-cult movements to early colonial resistance initiatives in Africa.[16] Both represent anticolonial reactions before modern nationalist ideology crystallized in the colonies. For our purposes here, it is sufficient to realize that nationalist ferment in the New Hebrides in the 1960s did not spring forth all of a piece but rather had its roots in sporadic, disparate, and often millenarian outbursts.

Nagriamel and Kastom

Nagriamel is a neologism formed from the name of two leaves, *nagria* (nan[n]garie) and *namele*. According to Stephens' Santo interlocutors in 1960, *nagria* represented the people, particularly the females, who previously, in time of war, had been exchanged as peace offerings. The *namele* leaf symbolized traditional law. When, upon Jimmy Stephens' advice, frustrated land-dispossessed islanders on Santo began to weave *nagria* and *namele* leaves together, literally (as baskets) as well as symbolically, the Nagriamel movement was conceived.[17] Five years later, in 1965, at a meeting with Chief Buluk, others from Santo, and Simon Garae from Ambae, the movement was officially born. Removal of plantation boundary markers and squatter occupation of alienated land netted Condominial jail terms for both Stephens and Buluk. It also galvanized the movement.

Nagriamel represents the most cohesive attempt to create a society based on the ideal of *kastom*. Under Jimmy Stephens, Nagriamel functioned as a cross between an opposition political movement and a self-help association. As Vanuatu's wider independence loomed, political circumstances and external forces ultimately obliged Stephens to conjure an independent state of Vemarana in an ill-fated attempt at secession. This was Nagriamel's undoing, for its real strength was in creating an autonomous society based on a reconstructed notion of *kastom,* not in constructing another nation-state. Neither in ideology nor infrastructure was Nagriamel equipped to handle the demands of modern nationalism. In current social scientific terminology, one could describe it as an early instance of civil society's disengagement from an alternately ineffectual and repressive state, one here spanning both colonial and postcolonial regimes. It is therefore more accurate to view Nagriamel as a localized and protonationalist movement, with strong civil societal tendencies,

The making of a *tam-tam*.

rather than as a full-blown nationalist one. Stephens and Nagriamel did not strive for independence for all of the New Hebrides—indeed, they rejected the very notion of a New Hebridean political entity—but rather preferred to carve out an autonomous space for themselves in their twenty districts of Ambae, Maewo, Malakula, Ambrym, Paama, and, especially, Santo, with Fanafo, a scant fourteen miles from Luganville, as their headquarters. Still, through its powerful and effective invocation of *kastom* for mass mobilization, Nagriamel showed how revitalized and hitherto denigrated notions of custom could be tapped for political, including nationalistic, purposes.

Nagriamel under Stephens was a familiar nationalist blend of customary belief with modernist techniques and ideological suppleness. Although he himself was not technically a *manples* (local person or native),
Stephens followed customary pig-killing rites so as to achieve the traditional chiefly title of *moli*. Pig exchange and wife offerings solidified
relationships with communities on other islands. Indeed, upon his release from prison in 1991, Stephens' major preoccupation was to orga-
nize the collection and distribution of pigs on different islands to official-
ize reconciliation in customary terms. Yet Stephens also followed the
European plantation model to develop an agricultural community and
put into place an elaborate committee system to administer Nagriamel.
He collaborated with American land speculator Eugene Peacock and his
libertarian colleague (and founder of the Phoenix Foundation) Michael
Oliver, as well as with French millionaire businessman André Leconte
and, eventually, the French Residency itself.

It is difficult to pigeonhole Nagriamel. Although adopting "some of
the trappings of a cult hero," Howard van Trease explicitly states that
Jimmy Stephens "was not . . . the classical cargo cult leader. . . .
Nagriamel was . . . not a form of government, but a system for ordering
Melanesian society based on custom, which the government of Vanuatu—
both the Condominium and a future independent government—had to
recognize."[18] John Beasant characterizes Nagriamel as a "creed that was a
curious amalgam of Christianity, custom and cargo cult."[19] Though wary
of conventional politics—Stephens believed that political parties, unlike
Nagriamel, were sullied by their intimacy with money[20]—Nagriamel not
only participated in the preindependence elections of 1979 but, under the
stewardship of Jimmy's son Franky, joined the UMP coalition in elections
following Jimmy's release from prison.

Although formally uneducated and liable to manipulation by
profit-seeking outsiders, Jimmy Stephens was also rather "savvy" (a
well-worked loan-word in Bislama) in understanding the psyche of his
people. He predicted that independence would perpetuate the dispdsses-
sion of ordinary islanders, with educated New Hebrideans merely taking
the place of Condominium officials but not effecting structural change.[21]
More than a decade in prison mellowed his secessionist proclivities, and
he reconciled himself both to Vanuatu independence and Father Walter
Lini's leadership.[22] But in an interview one year after his release (and two
years before his death), Stephens lamented the obsession with money
and materialism that was taking hold throughout Vanuatu society and,
by implication, revealed doubts about the future of his own movement

and ideals.[23] That Nagriamel survived at all with its leader in prison[24] is testamony to Jimmy Stephens' inimitable charisma; whether it outlasts his death will depend on his followers' accommodation, not only with the regime in Vila, but with their memory of and fidelity to *kastom* as preached by the late Moli Jimmy Moses Stephens.

Vanua'aku Pati and Kastom

Even as Jimmy Stephens was invoking customary symbols to reclaim colonized land on Santo, other New Hebrideans, coming from a more classically nationalist mind-set, were construing *kastom* in familiar ideological terms and with broader political aims in mind. In 1971 two Anglophone teachers from the Shepherd islands, Donald Kalpokas and Peter Taurakoto, joined with Walter Lini, the Anglican priest from Pentecost, and Father John Bani, to form an organization to "promote, to preserve, to revive and to encourage New Hebridean culture. To seek the advancement of the New Hebrideans socially, educationally and politically in relation with New Hebridean culture and Western civilization." Thus was born the New Hebrides Cultural Association, which shortly thereafter declared itself the first modern political party in Condominial history: the New Hebrides National Party (NHNP). Like Nagriamel, the NHNP was largely motivated by land grievances and renamed itself in 1977 the Vanua'aku Pati (Our Land Party); unlike Nagriamel, its leadership consisted of educated and urban Anglophones acquainted with the decolonization process elsewhere in the Pacific and Third World liberation movements more broadly.

But party leaders, "cultural half-castes in a land of tradition,"[25] were not as familiar with the customs and traditions of their less cosmopolitan rural compatriots. Nor were they sufficiently assimilated to sit at the table of the European colonials. The political disenfranchisement of the New Hebridean elites was therefore not only a problem of nationalism, but it also constituted a crisis of identity. A rehabilitated *kastom* could restore social dignity and impart national identity if only its long-entrenched denigration by Christianity and colonialism could be overcome. This was a difficult goal to accomplish, for whereas the Condominium was a legitimate target of nationalist denunciation, Christianity was not. By reinvesting *kastom* ceremonies and practices with historical and cultural meaning, and conveniently ignoring their animistic and magical origins, National Party leaders succeeded, on the whole, in elevating *kastom* without contradicting Christianity.

For the National Party no less than for Nagriamel, invoking

kastom was equated with reclaiming the land. It was the land which provided spiritual meaning and physical sustenance to the people. Land imparted social identity by making one a *manples*. But the National Party politicized the land in a way that Nagriamel did not know how to do, by linking its redemption to more familiar, global referents of national sovereignty and political independence. Indeed, independence was "customized" by associating it with the freedom that islanders had possessed prior to colonial rule. Rehabilitating customary chiefs *(kastom jif)*, who had lost much of their authority to the Condominium-appointed assessors was another explicit goal of the National Party.

National Party leaders spatially expanded the *kastom* idea to encompass a "Melanesian Way," uniting not only all New Hebrideans but New Guineans, Fijians, and Solomon Islanders alike. "Melanesian Socialism," "Melanesian Democracy," and "Melanesian Brotherhood" all cropped up in National Party and Vanua'aku discourse as elevated, Anglicized versions of *kastom*. Such innovation eventually revolutionized the lexicon of Bislama, now promoted from mere pidgin to a language of nationalism (or, as Joan Larcom has noted in Malakula, *langwis blong politik*).[26] Common language and compatible objectives created a political affinity between the British Residency and New Hebridean National Party leaders. Though the British could not unilaterally dismantle the Condominium and withdraw, Britain's overall postwar Pacific policy was predicated on decolonization. The British would not leave the New Hebrides to the French alone, but they could indirectly, if tacitly, support the aims of the Anglophone independentists.[27] Such implicit collusion spurred rapprochement between Nagriamel and the French.

On one level, the resulting competition between Nagriamel and NHNP/Vanua'aku Pati was a surrogate for the rivalry between France and Great Britain. Yet, on another level, it spoke more intimately to two distinct paths of political evolution in the New Hebrides. One path, represented by Jimmy Stephens and Nagriamel, looked inward to the ground and common people in a fundamentalist revolt against local land alienation. The other, represented by Walter Lini and the National Party, looked outward, tapping popular symbols of cultural identity to build a conventional political party that would succeed the Condominium government. Both created, interpreted, and constructed *kastom* selectively; only Lini's version, however, was self-consciously nationalist in its appropriation and use of *kastom*.

In the decade following independence the government of Walter Lini continued to cultivate *kastom* as the foundation of ni-Vanuatu national unity. When either the prime minister or the president of the republic went on national tour, it was common for local communities to accord them local chieftaincy titles within the framework of ritual grade-taking ceremonies. Pig killing by the chief of government and head of state became a common *affaire d'état*. Annual independence celebrations were a time to publicly perform *kastom* dances and songs. The National Arts Festival held on Santo in 1991, the first since independence (the previous one was organized in the waning days of the Condominium) overcame major logistical impediments at great expense to bring *kastom* celebrants from throughout the archipelago. Opening and closing speeches were laced with expressions of nationalism, the oft-repeated motto being Unity Within Diversity. President Timakata, mounted on a leaf-and-branch Aneityumese throne chair and bedecked in custom dress, was carried to the stage-ground by dancers in warrior costume and inaugurated the proceeding by ritually killing a pig by clubbing it on the head. In the days that followed displays of traditional cooking, artisanship, fire making, and magic were interspersed with dances and songs from throughout the nation. Exposing ni-Vanuatu to the different varieties of *kastom* practiced on other islands was a major accomplishment of the National Arts Festival.[28]

By the time it splintered and lost its vitality as a political party, the Vanua'aku Pati had nevertheless succeeded in normalizing and nationalizing *kastom*. This will perhaps prove to have been its single greatest postindependence accomplishment. By 1991, eleven years after independence, the compatibility between *kastom* and nationalism was no longer in question. To the contrary, particularly on those islands where traditional songs and rituals had been fading in memory and practice, the necessity and intensity of pre-Festival preparations demonstrated that *kastom* now needed Vanuatu nationalism as much as Vanuatu nationalism required *kastom*. Whereas Anglophone nationalists in the 1960s and 1970s may have politicized indigenous customs for tactical purposes, by the 1990s the survival of *kastom* in several locations (particularly the longest Christianized ones) depended on governmental encouragement and support. *Kastom* had also become a unifying element of national consciousness. This is all the more remarkable given the wedge that, for those who called it *la Coutume*, it had once constituted between Francophones and their adversaries.

Francophone Opponents and *Kastom*

Even as Francophones opposed the mounting of a nationalist movement of Anglophone ascendency, they too were obliged to embrace *kastom* as part of their own platform; for one could not possibly be against *kastom* and expect any following among rank-and-file islanders. Certainly, the educated, Francophile, "moderate" leaders of the UMP were skeptical that progress could be achieved by harking back to old-fashioned practices that smacked of precivilization. But *kastom* had such a strong resonance among so many islanders that Francophones could ill afford to stress such skepticism on their part. Rather, they challenged the Anglophones' monopolistic pretense of interpreting *kastom* for selfish partisan purposes. *Kastom* existed, for sure, but it was not what the National Party and later the Vanua'aku Pati made it out to be. In their view, *kastom* was inherently conservative and stabilizing and could not properly be corrupted into a force for revolutionary independence. Francophone politicians attempted to recuperate *kastom* and use it to resist their adversaries' vision of a National Party/Vanua'aku Pati–dominated state. In indigenous strongholds such as Tanna and, reinforced by Nagriamel, Santo, the combination of Catholic missions, Francophone schools, and *kastom* survivalism catalyzed into an anti-Anglophone opposition that challenged the nationalist interpretation of *kastom*. Ironically, then, although the Vanua'aku Pati based its legitimacy in large measure on its appeal to *kastom,* it was also on the basis of *kastom* that the Francophone opposition and its allies resisted it.

A good example of Francophone-inspired *kastom* is Jean-Marie Léyé, "the parable man." A solid French-speaker and founding member of the UMP, imprisoned in the wake of the Santo rebellion, opposition politician throughout the 1980s, and president of the republic since 1995, Léyé is renowned for his mastery of Bislama folk wisdom and metaphorical oratory. Throughout his career Léyé has used popular language and imagery to enhance his credentials as a man of the people and, by extension, an advocate of *kastom*. (That this prominent Francophone has achieved popular legitimacy through Bislama is but one of Vanuatu's political paradoxes.) As opposed to the Lini-inspired version, which syncretized *kastom* with Christianity, the Léyé brand relied on rural references to island cultural life. Francophone expressions of *kastom,* as embodied by President Léyé, thus take on a different tenor than do Anglophone and Protestant ones. While the ultimate objectives may be no less political, *kastom* sounds less ideological and change-oriented when it comes from Francophone, in contrast to Anglophone, lips.

KASTOM AS DIVIDER AND INTEGRATOR

> Many ways of the past are with us,
> Ways of today [too],
> But we are all one,
> This is our way
> —National Anthem of Vanuatu, second verse

The use of *kastom* to create national identity is not unique to Vanuatu. Indeed, the "invention of tradition" paradigm was first advanced in the context of Great Britain and was immediately applied to South Asia and Africa.[29] Perhaps in no region but the Pacific, however—and here, in no country more than Vanuatu—has it been so quickly compressed and utilized by political movements for the purposes of national unity and independence. But critical observers of *kastom* fault its vagueness and shallowness. Though they do not employ the term, it is criticized in the same way that some in the West find fault with civil religion for becoming a hollow, watered-down version of religion for the sake of political, nationalistic unity.

Island-specific studies have shown how differing interpretations of *kastom* have given rise to very different outcomes. Competing political groups on Tanna (Anglophone Vanua'aku Pati followers, Francophones of the Federal Party, John Frumites) deliberately understood *kastom* in ways that legitimated them vis-à-vis rivals.[30] In South Pentecost, the land dive *(gol)* has become both a symbol of traditional ritual and a casualty of commoditizing tourism.[31] Whether to call one island Aoba or Ambae became a test of will between chiefs and youth, the former basing their claim on customary, and the latter on democratic, legitimacy.[32] Among the Mewun of Southwest Bay, Malakula, *kastom* has been reinterpreted from knowledge subject to dynamic market transactions to a more rigid body of ritual conduct.[33] In South-East Ambrym complementarity evolved between believers in *kastom* and in Christ,[34] just as symbiosis developed on Maewo.[35] And on Santo Jimmy Stephens mounted an organized movement that, based on Nagriamel's particular interpretations of authenticity, went so far as to attempt secession.

These and other, more general treatments of *kastom* in Vanuatu highlight the ambiguous nature of the term: the more open-ended the meaning, the more instrumental the usage. Likewise, as *kastom* is understood in specific terms, it becomes more divisive. In as culturally diverse a society as Vanuatu's, it is chimerical to suppose that there is a common catechism of customary belief or ritual. Robert Tonkinson identifies "a major problem with *kastom* as a dominant unifying symbol: it is inherently divisive if treated at any level more analytical or literal than an undifferentiated and vague symbolic one."[36]

National-scale studies (comparative studies have also been elaborated with respect to Fiji,[37] the Maori,[38] and Hausaland[39]) all agree with the island-specific ones in this respect: *Kastom* is not what national leaders in Vanuatu pretend it to be. *Kastom* for ni-Vanuatu nationalists is an easily identifiable, indigenously recognizable, unifying set of customs and practices steeped in the history and tradition of the archipelago. Social scientists rarely examine the effectiveness of *kastom* in constructing the Vanuatu nation-state. Rather, they problematize it by pointing out its inconsistencies and contradictions. "Because of the inherent ambiguity and potential for divisiveness contained in *kastom,* its heuristic use in the development of laws, structures, and policies is dangerous."[40] A "generic 'no-name brand' culture is being codified to serve as the basis of nationalistic sentiments as well as a rallying point for a civil polity. . . . [T]he irony of the situation in Vanuatu [is that] a Westernized elite which knows least about *kastom* is busy inventing" it.[41] "[S]tate *kastom* . . . appear[s] . . . as a sort of gigantic neocustomary or neotraditional 'bricolage,' a medley of disparate cultural traits from different cultures, broken up, extracted from their context, and juxtaposed with elements directly inspired from Western or Westernized practices. . . ."[42]

Still, for the purposes of public display, four rituals have come to constitute a common core of *kastom:* pig killing, kava drinking, mat trading, and chieftaincy conferring. Presidential and prime ministerial visits to outer islands invariably include all four of these. Yet it is the consumption of kava that perhaps best represents the reinterpretation of traditional ritual for nationalistic purposes.

Kava: Narcotic of Nationalism

Kava (Latin: *Piper methysticum*) is a tuber in the pepper family that has long been appreciated by Melanesians for its seminarcotic properties. When the roots are pulverized (traditionally, either by chewing or mortaring) and liquified, their consumption induces a state of heightened sensory perception combined, above all, with deep mental relaxation and a sense of well-being. Elaborate rituals and strict taboos associated with the preparation and consumption of kava developed, groups on certain islands (such as Tanna) going so far as to prescribe death for any female witnessing portions of the sacred ceremony. In many locations the taking of kava was relatively rare and reserved for chiefs whose grades so permitted them.

For the masses, particularly those able to participate in the Westernized economy, alcohol (particularly beer and wine) replaced kava as the mind-altering drink of choice. Devoid of ritualistic connotations, alcohol was so easily abused that the Condominium long prohibited its sale to New Hebrideans. When the ban was lifted, in the 1970s alcohol abuse became a preoccupation of Condominium authorities and nationalist leaders alike. For, unlike kava, whose most serious mental side effect is torpor, alcohol among young New Hebrideans more often led to aggression. Group fights between outer-island youths would break out, with island of origin constituting a ganglike basis of identification.

Commercialization of kava by a local Chinese entrepreneur coincided in the late 1970s with its rehabilitation by New Hebridean nationalists as part of their *kastom* campaign. Kava not only was indigenous, it was solidaristic: Where alcohol divided, kava united. Unlike beer or wine, kava did not require cash to acquire, but merely the determination to cultivate it in one's garden.

Popularized as never before, kava, once restricted by island and status, has become a common beverage throughout all Vanuatu. Kava bars have become a popular nightlife scene in the capital and, at least in the towns, even women can imbibe carefreely, not to mention with impunity. State ceremonies include a ritual coconut shell's draught. Alcohol has not disappeared—indeed, Vanuatu now produces its own beer, Tusker—and the vulgarization of kava has led to urban problems of overconsumption, dependence, and abuse.

Even in the outer islands, the regular after-work evening custom of communal kava making in the village *nakamal* (clubhouse)—as seemingly authentic a ritual as one might imagine—masks inroads into true *kastom*.[43] Before, *nakamal* gatherings were occasions to swap custom stories and to sing and dance on the nearby *nasara* (dancing ground, village square). Kava was infrequently taken, and then only by the chiefs and their selected retainers. Now, however, kava has become the focus of the *nakamal* assemblage. Primary *kastom* activities *(singsing, danis, storian)* have consequently been neglected.

Such problems, however serious, are by-products of a triumphant nationalism, for they reflect the success of the nation's leaders in rehabilitating and popularizing the once exotic brew. Though infused with different meaning and consumption patterns than before, kava is as much a consumable national symbol for Vanuatu as apple pie is for

America. Despite continuing opposition by some churches (e.g., Apostolic, Church of Christ, Seventh-Day Adventist), kava is a solid, if liquid, symbol of the Vanuatu nation.

The widespread drinking of kava by ordinary ni-Vanuatu, in the towns as well as the outer islands, by plebes as well as chiefs, reflects not only democratization but also development. Inasmuch as the regular preparation of kava requires a ready supply of water, consumption used to be ecologically limited in those many areas where rivers were relatively distant. Only with the installation of artesian wells and the widespread distribution of water taps could kava be prepared so regularly. Once again, the recuperation of a supposedly traditional custom, the drinking of kava, was not only promoted for a modern ideological end (nationalism) but was facilitated by modern technology. The conversion of kava into a cash crop, the commercialization of the drinking ritual, its industrial processing, and its export to the overseas pharmacological market all reveal how a consumable icon of custom can be transformed by politics. "As Port Vila's busy nakamals grind kava rootstock into 50- and 100-vatu shells of 'redimed' [ready-made] drink, they are further processing sacred kava into a cash crop and into a rooted but inventive emblem of cultural identity."[44]

Penis Wrappers and Grass Skirts

One of the least discussed aspects of *kastom* and Melanesian identity concerns dress.[45] While state leaders uphold pig killing, kava drinking, and mat trading as activities worthy of preservation, there has been a circumspect silence in official circles and among *kastom* ideologues about how ni-Vanuatu ought to dress in their daily lives. On high ceremonial occasions even state leaders don the leaves of customary dress, as do most participants in arts festivals and other elevating *kastom* events. But in ordinary life ni-Vanuatu women are still expected to wear the modest Mother Hubbard, a relic of nineteenth-century missionary fashion, while standard male attire consists of short-sleeved shirts, shorts (on the islands), or long pants (in town), and thongs. On Sundays and other non-*kastom* holidays men will, wardrobe permitting, wear long-sleeved shirts, long pants, and closed shoes.

Mountain dwellers in the outer islands, a relatively small and diminishing proportion of the ni-Vanuatu population, preserve an indigenous style of dress, which covers little more than the genitalia.[46] This is done not for conscious, ideological reasons but rather reflects a continuity in dress style and limited disposable income. Mountain dress constitutes a source of embarrassment for coastal and town dwellers, who regard this, like most manners of the "bush," as primitive.

A few communities have nevertheless decided to return to the *nambas,* the penis wrapper, as a mark of *kastom.* For them, there is nothing more customary than the way their ancestors dressed, and there should be no shame associated with it. On the island of Tanna, a *kastom* school in the village of Iohanen is distinguished more by the customary dress of its pupils than by its curriculum.[47] In and around Fanafo, the center of Nagriamel on Santo, a faction of followers of Jimmy Stephens (himself a conservative dresser by contemporary Vanuatu norms) have adopted the *nambas* (not a traditionally Santo garb) and leaf dress for women. And on Pentecost, cradle of the globally commercialized bungee jumping, men perform the land-dive ceremony wearing *nambas* and cheered on by similarly clad men and leaf-wearing women.

Yet even in this return to *nambas,* which otherwise divides believers in *kastom* between those who mouth it and those who dress it, there is an ambiguity. For the impact of Western customs of dress has affected even the wearers of leaves, bark, pandanus, and string. It was not a *man Tanna* who convinced the men to cast off their shorts and return to the *nambas,* but a *National Geographic* stringer, one Kal Muller, whose legacy of his early 1970s visit includes the *kastom* school itself.[48] Some young Tannese walk to school in shorts and change into their *nambas* (to the delight of picture-taking tourists) only for class. Even the thrill of the *gol* is tempered when, after the spectacle is concluded, one realizes that the *nambas*-clad land diver changes back into shorts and white sneakers, like any professional athlete emerging from his locker at the end of the game.[49] Kastom clothing, too, while ostensibly imparting identity, is no less subject to the overlapping boundaries of Western and Melanesian prudery, fashion, and practicality.

String Band Music

Although the role of martial bands and music in the development of nineteenth century nationalism is well known, studies of Third World nationalism often overlook the integrative potential of music. The ni-Vanuatu gift for music making, long expressed in indigenous singing and, since evangelization, in hymnal prayer sessions, now popularly takes the form of the string band. Vaguely reminiscent of the Hawaiian ukelele beat, ni-Vanuatu string bands rely on the acoustic guitar to achieve their distinctive melodic style.

Although some string bands do perform in island languages, success and national acclaim is reserved most for those whose lyrics are in Bislama. Thanks to Radio Vanuatu, string bands from even small islands are known throughout the archipelago. Island-wide and national string-band competitions are held regularly, and national anniversary celebrations invariably feature string bands.

Love of country competes with love of woman as a favorite theme in string-band music. String bands are also popular because they deal with social issues and problems (e.g., kava drinking, money culture, and materialism) that touch upon contemporary life. In terms of nationalism, though, perhaps less crucial than the themes and lyrics themselves is the sheer emergence of the string-band sound as a familiar expression of national culture. While foreign music, particularly West Indian (both French and Reggae) has also become popular, the popularity of the native string band, combined with its inherent localism (the foreign market for Vanuatu music is very limited), is a melodious by-product of Vanuatu nationalism.

REGIONAL AND ISLAND IDENTITIES AND LIMITS TO STATE KASTOM

Concomitant with the emergence of a Vanuatu national identity has been a growing salience of home island identity. This has been made possible through inter-island migration and the emergence of a national political life. Prior to condocolonialism there was relatively little consciousness, particularly on the larger islands, of belonging to an island-based community. Indigenous language boundaries, geographic barriers, political rivalries, and outright warfare precluded any sense of solidarity arising on the basis of shared islandhood. As mentioned earlier, often there was not even any common name for the island—*man Santo*, for example, is a postcontact designation.

Congregation in Port Vila or Luganville, however, has fostered a new sense of shared islandhood. This situation is similar to that experienced by rural African communities with only the dimmest sense of common ethnicity when they were thrust into urban centers in the first half of the twentieth century. Shared place of origin and common language (here, Bislama) transcend previous barriers to identity. For some mobile islanders, such as those from Ambae and Pentecost, the sense of solidarity is stronger than for others. Shared islandhood is also beginning to transcend, to a certain degree, older divisions based on language and religion. (The ambivalent relationship between the Anglophone Lini and Francophone Boulekone families, both from Pentecost and representing distinct political tendencies, is significant in this regard.)

There is a negative side to this emerging sense of shared islandhood: among young, semi-educated, displaced males, it is becoming a basis for aggressive affirmation of collective identity. Fights break out in the bars of Luganville whose only basis seems to be the rivalry, imagined or real, between young men of different islands. The same processes that give rise to an appreciation of national unity—mobility, common language, *kastom*—also enhance the subnational, island-based focus of identity.

With or without the sanction of *kastom*, the first decade of independence spawned a certain degree of disillusionment, if not cynicism. Particularly in the outer islands, in both Anglophone and Francophone villages informants expressed dissatisfaction with certain postindependence trends. Economic difficulties—lower prices for copra, the levying of taxes, a rise in school fees, and inflation—were major complaints. Respect for school, church, and *kastom* is also said to be less today than before independence. "Life was good but hard," stated a prominent Malakulan. "There was obedience, respect and honesty. Today, people have money but they are never satisfied with the amount they have." An elder on Malakula said that, before independence, "men would work together, as one. Now the young men are divided amongst themselves." Another informant claimed that on his island, Pentecost, *kastom* indeed remains strong but that on other islands it has been losing ground. "Politics," he claimed, "leads to fighting."

One chief on Tanna criticized the police: "During the Condominium, they would go out on tour, and spend two or three days in each village, speaking with the people. Now they put on their shoes and high stockings, stay in the station and fill their pockets with *vatu*." On Santo another chief concurred: "Before, if you did something wrong in the day, the police would come that night. Now the police is for play." Similar sentiments were voiced in the Banks: "Today, we call out, call out but the police don't come."

"For the moment we can pay the school fees for our children," an Ambae bigman said, "but in ten years only MPs, civil servants, and office workers will be able to. The people will be divided again. During the Condominium, the difference was between black and white. But now the big difference is between [poor and rich] Blackmen." "Our ministers are the new Whitemen." Since independence, "life has been good only for government ministers," declared a diehard critic from Fanafo

(Santo). "'We are glad, we are free,'" he mocked. "What freedom are they talking about?"

"People think independence means they don't have to listen to anyone anymore, that *they* are independent," complained another Ambae notable. A purported rise in illegitimacy ("children of the road") is also linked to the advent of popular sovereignty. "When the British were here," claimed an Anglophone on Pentecost, "things were good, clean, straight. But now there are quarrels all the time." A Maewo man admitted improvement in the numbers of high school graduates and work. "But in the rural areas," he went on, "it's just as in our grandfathers' time, when people cut coconuts to sell copra. Progress is on paper." "Vila and Santo are pulling ahead," one Ambae septuagenarian stated, "but there isn't so much development in the islands."

Obviously, not all the changes noted above are in fact due to political sovereignty. Societal evolution would invariably have occurred even in a nonindependent New Hebrides, and few ni-Vanuatu would want to turn the clock back to before 1980.[50] However one wishes to measure change, perhaps the most poignant observation in this regard was made by a Torres islander: "We didn't think much about independence. Things are the same as before. I can't say they're better and I can't say they're worse. We were poor then. We're still poor."

Construction of a Melanesian regional identity has gone hand in hand with Vanuatu nationalism. Uniting Vanuatu with the Solomons Islanders, Papua New Guineans, and Kanaks of New Caledonia within the Melanesian Spearhead Group was the crux of foreign policy under the Lini prime ministry and has continued since. Yet regionalism is still one of the most nascent elements of identity, for Vanuatu as well as Oceania at large: "Pacific identity is largely something for the elite."[51]

Ron Crocombe classifies Vanuatu, as part of inner or central Melanesia, as one of those Pacific nations experiencing the lowest degree of access to external sources of identity change. But basic identity is evolving there, too, even if the stimulus for change is more domestic than international or regional in origin. This provides the young nation with privileged opportunities to shape its own destiny and identity. *Kastom*, however problematic outside observers make it out to be, is the instrument for doing so. What is essential is that the mallet of *kastom* be pointed rather than blunt, that it tap lightly rather than smash flatly.

Melanesian identity is only vaguely emerging within Vanuatu consciousness. Eventually, *man Melanesia* may enter the commonly used lexicon beside *manples, man Tanna* (*man Santo,* or *man Aneityum,* etc.), and ni-Vanuatu. The closest local term yet approximating this notion of Melanesian social unity is *Wontok* ("One Talk"), which encompasses speakers of Pacific Pidgin (Bislama in Vanuatu, Tok Pisin in New Guinea, and Solomons Pidgin).[52]

KASTOM AS BOUNDARY MARKER

Identity in precontact Oceania was remarkably nonethnic in basis.[53] Distinctions were based on locality and genealogy, and sometimes on bush-coastal differences, but only with colonialism were "we–they" dualisms thrust to the forefront of consciousness. Previously, personhood was a matter of interlinking relationships and "shared biographies." The individualization of identity, followed by the objectification of cultural groups (now perceived as ethnic categories) is a by-product of Westernization. "[B]oundaries come to be emphasized over interpenetrating networks of relations."[54]

Still, there were—and remain—within *kastom* methods of physically demarcating in-group from out-group spaces. Boundaries are marked by the placement of certain leaves, which is understood to be *tabu*. Trespassing beyond these boundaries is to invite punishment. In the lead-up to the struggle over Santo, members of the pro-French Tabwemassana movement placed such *kastom* leaves on the outskirts of Luganville, inflaming tensions between local partisans and between the local British and French district agents.[55]

For all its ambiguity and contradictions, *kastom* in Vanuatu has come to signify the proper, or indigenously authentic, way of living, acting, and behaving in society. Such a general understanding of *kastom* is analogous to the way morality is used in the West. Everyone claims to be moral, even if reaching a consensus on what constitutes moral behavior is well-nigh impossible. *Kastom* marks itself off from colonialism (though not Christianity), from Westernization, from unwelcome modernity.

To the extent that *kastom* succeeds in resisting modernity, it reinforces the colonial-imposed boundaries between Western and Melanesian worldviews. Only, now, the balance of power is reversed in that it is the indigenous and traditional which is considered superior to the alien and imported. It is no less dualistic, however. Whereas the bridging of boundaries between Francophone and Anglophone is a matter of mental decolonization, transcending those between *kastom* and modernity is a question of socioeconomic development. In theory, state-sponsored

Table 2 Textbook Contrast of Values

Traditional	Western
Dependence on extended family, with family obligations	Personal independence
Communal ownership of property	Individual ownership of property
Time is not so important.	Punctuality is important.
Wealth consists of traditional items. Money is not so important.	Money economy is of great importance.
Respect and success are based on human relationships.	Success is based on material gains, e.g. education, wealth.

Source: *Our Changing Society. Social Science Unit*, 1985, p. 50

kastom is perfectly compatible with national development, and so these boundaries would seem to be artificial. In practice, however, "development" has introduced capitalistic, consumer-oriented, materialistic, individualistic, and competitive values into collectivistic societies—albeit ones whose competitive streak previously took the form of intervillage warfare and revenge or "payback" killings.

There is, of course, nothing unusual or inconsistent about aspects of traditional culture being recuperated for nationalist and transnationalist purposes and by modernist means. The very validity of the "traditional versus modern" distinction has long been explicitly disputed by scholars, and implicitly by politicians. It is for this very reason that the dichotomy between the official ideology of *kastom* and education policy in Vanuatu is so striking. Whereas the former stresses the importance of integrating *kastom* into national development and the compatibility between Melanesian and Occidental notions of progress, the latter imparts a dualistic understanding of traditional Pacific vis-à-vis Western values. A tenth-grade social studies text illustrates the value difference in tabular form.

Although classes in woodworking and artisanship do impart time-honored skills to young ni-Vanuatu (a miniature *nalnal*—a combination warrior club and chiefly scepter—carved by primary school children on the island of Hiu, adorns my office as testimony), by and large the Vanuatu educational curricula, despite their emphasis on the interrelationship between indigenous *kastom* and Vanuatu nationalism, are of Western foundation and exclude indigenous languages, culture, and knowledge. As with the rehabilitation and transformation of kava, the reality is one of blurred boundary lines between the paradigms of the "modern" with the so-called traditional.

Kastom symbols: Statue of boar's tusk at Bauerfield Airport, Santo.

TREES, CANOES, AND NATIONAL IDENTITY

In his metaphorical analysis of Melanesian identity, at least as lived by the ni-Vanuatu of Tanna, Bonnemaison employs an indigenous tree-canoe analogy to explain the relationship between individual and group. Man (no gender distinction here) is likened unto the tree, which implants itself downward into the earth and draws its sustenance and strength from the depth and vibrancy of its roots. Personal identity is tied to a specific place, location, ground, soil, land: To be a *manples* is the highest mark of belonging. Ground roots also preserve the memory, and therefore the existence, of the *bubu,* the ancestors. There is a timelessness in Melanesian identity; one is by virtue of what was.

Yet while enrootedness remains the highest of values for the Tannese/ni-Vanuatu/Melanesians, their origins as "people of voyage" are not forgotten. It is the canoe (itself a product of the tree) that represents social identity, for it is this vehicle which reunites the spaces and people divided by oceanic expanse. "Man-tree only lives through the group-canoe, which gives him the alliances necessary to his survival and his reproduction."[56] The physical world may be broken up, but collectively traveling the route restores both geographical and social wholeness.

Bonnemaison's insights into the Melanesian mind are brilliant but problematic, particularly regarding that aspect of identity we must qualify as "national." Personally and intellectually enrooted in the archipelago, he tends to dismiss, as do many outer-island sojourners, the linguistically linked identities superimposed during the Condominium. These identities are viewed as superficial in hold and alien in origin, and therefore unworthy of integration within a grand conceptualization of Melanesian authenticity.

Vanuatu, as a distinct Melanesian society, is nothing if not the product of a dichotomous imperialism and a nationalist project aiming to overcome its condocolonial heritage. There is no indigenous, anthropologically conceived identity in Vanuatu that subsists apart from French and British, Catholic and Protestant influences and affinities. There is no intrinsic Melanesian identity separate from its Papuan, Fijian, or ni-Vanuatu variants. Fourth-world theorists who elaborate a stark dichotomy between the oppressive state and the embattled nation[57] miss the mark by ignoring the extent to which indigenous peoples also yearn for the dignity that shared membership in an internationally recognized state, even a multinational one, confers.

Nationalism in Vanuatu functions both by elevating that which is indigenous *(kastom),* so as to create a sense of cultural unity, and by promoting the virtues of bilingualism, so as to turn a condocolonial handicap into strategic advantage. Only by first recognizing the reality of inherited mental boundaries, and their place in ni-Vanuatu identity, can the nationalist project succeed. Even *kastom (especially kastom),* as a consciously articulated ideology, is a by-product of, even in being a reaction to, Western condocolonialism.

By expanding the spatial referents in the original model, Joël Bonnemaison's tree–canoe analogy can, in fact, be usefully applied to the question of ni-Vanuatu national identity. The verticality implied in the metaphor of the tree remains intact: Identity among ni-Vanuatu is indeed rooted in past and place (though this may now be expanded to the entire island) whence the individual emerges. The nationalistic "trick" is to enlarge and privilege the horizontal relationships represented by the canoe. Indigenous Tannese paddlers must be reimagined as new-style ni-Vanuatu relayers who extend their network society from local group to national society. Spanning not only reticulated space as cosmologically comprehended but condocolonial boundaries more recently encoded, outriggers of nationalism add Vila and Luganville to their more parochial cognitive maps. They think more and more horizontally and look increasingly outward, to their nation and to the future. Vertical vision, downward, groundward, loses its primacy. Young Melanesian mariners navigate new linguistic channels, English or French, off the straits of Bislama. National routes ply over ancestral roots. The wooden canoe is upgraded to ship of state.

KASTOM AND GLOBALISM

Commenting on the dialectic that gives rise to both national uniqueness and global uniformity, Immanuel Wallerstein has written, "At the very moment that we have been creating national cultures each distinct from the other . . . flows of commodities . . . of capital . . . of labor . . . have been breaking down . . . national distinctions." I was staying overnight in Renuvwe village in Malakula in 1991 when the full reach of globalization hit home. Renuvwe is a rather unremarkable and out-of-the-way village; "village" is actually an aggrandized term for what is really a cluster of scattered homesteads. Development is minimal: There is no electricity, no running water. Villagers possess few material goods, no furniture, not even beds; they sleep on enormous banana leaves which they stretch out on the hard, dank earthern floors of their huts. Clothing is rudimentary.

But it was to such an economically unassuming settlement in the remote reaches of the South Pacific that a letter had been sent, in the name of the village's bigman, from Hamburg, Germany. Receiving mail at all in Renuvwe is unusual. A letter from overseas was extraordinary and exciting. This piece of correspondence was, to me, a sign of globalization at its darkest: a slick, ingenuously personalized, pay-in sweepstakes offering. My host, of course, was excited at the prospect of becoming a multimillionaire, as the finely nuanced printout indicated he might (should he purchase a ticket and win). I failed to dampen his enthusiasm for his computer-generated cargo-cash chance, the junk mail in the antipodes.

Outer-island ni-Vanuatu cannot, nor should they, be shielded from processes of globalization transforming the world at the dawn of the twenty-first century. (Denizens of Vila and Luganville, of course, have long been affected by international, interregional, and intercontinental flows of people, goods, and information.) In fact, as Anthony King has pointed out, it is in the periphery of the Third World, not the core of the First, that the "first globally multi-racial, multi-cultural, multi-continental societies on any substantial scale" emerged.[58] In terms of identity, the psychological ramifications of globalization are more significant than the economic ones. Replacing exclusionary myths of origin with a psychic sense of world community bridges a critical boundary in a social group's understanding of itself. Nationalism plays an essential, intermediary role in this process, but *national* identity is not an end point. Through participation in the community of nations—and it is here that the sheer existence of Vanuatu's Permanent Mission to the United Nations in New York plays an important role—the boundary between geographically isolated outer-island community and greater humanity is transcended.

Perhaps the ultimate dissolution of boundary, the obliteration of physical space between people is, to the Western mind, the most abhorrent one: the literal consumption of one human being by another. Far from denoting disdain for the cannibalized, ritual anthropophagy, as practiced throughout the South Pacific, betokened acknowledgment of *mana,* the essential, transcendent spirit or humanity which inheres in all people, including one's enemy, and which can best be neutralized through corporal ingestion. Eating one's enemy, for the pre-modern Melanesian, was more a mark of respect than an expression of inhumanity.

"Increasingly, one goes through life . . . picking up identities . . . [I]dentity construction is never finished."[59] In an age of globalization, the ultimate boundary for ni-Vanuatu to bridge is no longer that between rival villages, between *kastom* and Christianity, between Anglophones and Francophones, or between competing islands. It is that between being *manples,* a person rooted in and defined by the soil of his or her birthplace, and *man blong ol wol,* a citizen of the world. Deepening Vanuatu nationalism is an essential step along this path, just as developing Melanesian identity is.

Kastom in Vanuatu no longer sanctions the consumption of man by man, the ultimate boundary expunger. *Pawa* (power) can no longer accrue from ritualistically cannibalizing, but it can from successfully globalizing. During the Condominium, the inhabitants of the New Hebrides ceased to partake of man.[60] Under independence, the citizens of Vanuatu cannot help but partake of mankind.

CHAPTER 3

Religious Boundaries Constructed and Bridged

We the people of the New Hebrides . . . hereby proclaim the establishment
of the united and free Republic of the New Hebrides founded on
traditional Melanesian values, faith in God, and Christian principles.
> —Preamble to the Constitution of the Repub-
> lic of the New Hebrides

The Republic of the New Hebrides recognises that . . . all persons are
entitled to . . . fundamental rights and freedoms of the individual without
discrimination on the grounds of . . . religious . . . belief. . . .
> —Chapter 2, Part 1—Fundamental Rights,
> Constitution of the Republic of the New
> Hebrides

Even before the new nation had settled on its name, ambivalence about
the religious character of Vanuatu had been constitutionally enshrined.
On the one hand, crafters of the constitution wanted to ensure a democratic and secular polity, at least in the sense that there would be no
officially sanctioned state church and that religious freedom would be
guaranteed. On the other hand, as the preamble clearly shows, most
ni-Vanuatu also wished to be defined as a Christian people. Such a
dichotomy reflects both the deep penetration of European-exported
Christianity into Melanesian society and a sensitivity to parallel divisions, animosity, and intolerance fostered by denominational cleavages
throughout Vanuatu's religious and condocolonial history.

RELIGION IN THE NEW HEBRIDES

Throughout the nineteenth century various Christian denominations
viewed the South Pacific, as they did Africa, as fertile ground for spiritual and institutional expansion. Earlier reports of explorers, traders,
and travelers spoke of half-naked savages practicing such inhumane cus-

toms as cannibalism, infanticide, and skull worship. Missionaries strongly believed that it was wrong to leave the natives to their ignorance and superstition. The metaphor used then, and still in vogue today, was that of bringing the unsaved "from darkness into light."

Islanders were not initially well disposed to being saved, however, and many of the early European missionaries paid dearly for their zeal. John Williams is considered the first of the "martyrs" in the missionary cause. The day after dropping off three Polynesian catechists on Tanna in 1839, he was killed while coming ashore on the island of Erromango. While the Nisbet and Turner couples from Scotland survived their seven-month ordeal on Tanna, their trauma of besiegement—they were caught between two warring tribes—reinforced the sense of sacrifice that white missionaries to Melanesia were making. Several Polynesian Christians, primarily Samoans, were recruited as intermediaries in accordance with missionary strategy and also lost their lives.

Williams and his Scottish counterparts had been sent by the London Missionary Society, a non-denominational organization close to Congregationalism. Prominent Anglicans who followed later in the century included Bishop George Selwyn, his assistant Codrington, and John Patteson (killed in the Solomons in 1871). In the meantime, however, Presbyterian missionaries had implanted themselves throughout much of the archipelago. These included the Canadian John Geddie and New Zealander John Inglis, who established themselves on Aneityum, and the Scotsman John Paton, who settled on Tanna. Inherent denominational differences between the Anglican and Presbyterian traditions were deepened by the particularly fundamentalist stamp of the Scottish Reformed Presbyterian church.

The Reformed Church of Scotland, distancing itself not only from the Church of England but from all official state churches, aimed to create a Christian nation, a biblical nation, in all its purity. To this end Presbyterian missionaries in the New Hebrides felt compelled to Christianize by stamping out those indigenous customs, practices, and rituals deemed incompatible with a chaste and holy life. Dancing, singing, drumming, divination, exorcism, immodest dress, and elaborate hairdos were outlawed, in addition to warfare, polygamy, widow strangulation, and ritual sex initiation. Local police forces and courts, composed of the converted, were set up to enforce the new code, the most rigid and totalitarian version taking its name from its island of implementation: Tanna Law.

The heyday of Tanna Law occurred between 1905 and 1925 under the missionary reign of Dr. Nicholson. Nicholson, assisted by his "Very Christian [but Melanesian] Kings"[1] sanctioned fines, imprisonment, forced-labor punishment, public whippings and, it was alleged, garrotings to coerce abandonment of traditional customs, enforce participation at prayer services, and isolate prospective volunteers from French labor recruiters. Despite opposition from the resident British administrator, Wilkes, and from the French Resident Commissioner, Nicholson and his "Christian Kings" ruled Tanna as their personal theocratic fief, waging a religiocultural war on the "pagans" of the interior. When the culturally sympathetic Wilkes was replaced in 1915 by the Scottish Presbyterian partisan James Nicol, the forces besieging indigenous Tannese life were double: religious (qua Presbyterian) and political (qua Condominial). Nicol, officially representing the Crown but acting more as a scriptural steward, saw to it that Tannese adulterers were harshly punished, that polygamy was legally suppressed, and that the last of the women to ritually initiate pubescent boys were married off.[2]

The naming by Anglophone missionaries of Tannese Christian "chiefs"—antithetical to the system of fragmented polities on the island—recalls the appointment of warrant chiefs by the British administration among the acephalous Igbo of southeastern Nigeria. Here, however, parallel authority was instituted not by colonial authorities but by religious outsiders. Intervention by French authorities to protect indigenes from involuntary "civilizing" by Anglophones is also an interesting departure from the colonial model then operating in Africa. Studies of African colonialism contrast the cultural policy of indirect rule by Britain, according to which indigenous customs and governance would be only gradually modified, with the French regime of direct rule, which aimed to transform African society more radically. In the New Hebrides, where British officials were in tacit agreement with Protestant missionaries, French authorities found themselves, first in Tanna and later in Santo, in the unusual position of defending native rights and cultural autonomy against Western intrusion and ecclesiastical despotism. Certainly, France embraced this early endorsement of enlightened cultural pluralism out of competition with Britain and British-protected evangelists, not out of any intrinsic sympathy with Melanesian culture per se. Nevertheless, French and British cultural policy in the New Hebrides, especially in the nineteenth and early twentieth centuries, relativizes the otherwise stark contrasts in colonial policy that emerge from studies of the colonial experience elsewhere, particularly in Africa and the Caribbean. Such a perspective denationalizes colonial policy formulation a step by focusing on factors of political contingency rather than metropolitan national character.

The new Presbyterian polity had as its focus the "teacher": a catechist trained to impart Bible, prayer, and morality. To this end—but only to this end—literacy was valued and taught. School and church, from a linguistic as well as functional standpoint, were the same: In Bislama one word, *skul,* still denotes both institutions.

Anglican evangelization in the New Hebrides employed a some-what softer, less puritanical, more intellectual and indirect approach than did Presbyterian proselytization. More progressive than the Presbyterians, Anglican ecclesiastics believed that indigenous society could be Christianized without being deracinated. To the extent that traditional customs were not outrightly incompatible with Christian principles and morals, they would be tolerated. Moreover, Melanesians themselves—not the foreign white men—would, after an appropriate period of study in New Zealand or Australia, spread the gospel. Overseas training also spoke to the higher Anglican commitment to education as an intrinsic moral good, consistent with the Anglicans' own social and intellectual background vis-à-vis that of the more plebeian Presbyterians. Less confrontational and competitive than the Presbyterian Protestants, the Anglican church in the New Hebrides—whose Melanesian diocese became independent of New Zealand in 1861—was willing to concede those islands (particularly those in the north) which had already been staked out by other denominations. There was even a democratic impulse to Anglican Christianizing, in that traditional chieftaincies were replaced by elected local councils that gradually assumed progressively greater decision-making powers.

One must not exaggerate the differences in conversional outcome between Anglicans and Presbyterians. Although the philosophy and style were indeed distinctive, Anglicans no less than Presbyterians concluded that indigenous Melanesian religion and tradition were antithetical to Christianity.[3] The abolition of secret societies and the disappearance of political hierarchies based on grade-climbing were applauded on both sides of the denominational fence. Both discovered the danger that wholescale conversion could entail for the indigenous work ethic: Complacency and mysticism, not Protestant industriousness, often followed; the arrival of missionaries could just as easily be associated with the coming of material goods and an easier way of life as with finding spiritual salvation.

But the more important reason for downplaying the differences between Anglicans and Presbyterians is that such distinctions paled next to the larger theological divide in the Christian partition of the New Hebrides: that between Protestants and Catholics.

CATHOLIC VERSUS PROTESTANT

> Observing the coastline with spyglasses, we saw long shadows
> dressed in black robes marching up and down in front of the
> shacks. At that moment we recognized the sign of the beast. . . .
> A new enemy was there [and had] preceded us on the ground. The
> battle would take place not only against Paganism, but against
> Paganism and Popery together.
>
> —John Geddie, 1848

Although Father Rougeyron had established himself on Aneityum two months before John Geddie arrived there, the relative poverty of Catholic missionaries impeded long-term settlement and early expansion in the New Hebrides. Unlike the Presbyterians and Anglicans hailing from Great Britain, New Zealand, and Australia, Catholics could count on little support from their own host government: France's post-Revolution, anticlerical strain remained strong. (The 1887 French naval expedition, which at the behest of John Higginson transported missionaries from New Caledonia under military protection, was a much regretted exception.) Vowers of poverty were difficult role models for Melanesians more readily impressed with white man goods and trinkets; celibacy was downright incomprehensible. As the wife of the rival pastor in Banam Bay reported, gloatingly, at the reception of Father François-Xavier Gaudet in 1887: "The Malekulas do not like the French Missionary. 'He got no boat, no wife, no children. He no got nuthin'."[4] Still, as the above quote from John Geddie suggests, Protestant missionaries (particularly Presbyterians) viewed Catholics as a real threat to their own soul-saving endeavors. Though Catholics were to remain forever outnumbered by Protestants in the New Hebrides, their later success in building a highly developed infrastructure of mission stations and high-quality schools has bestowed on the Catholic church great organizational strength and all the political advantages ensuing from tightly linked networks that foster morale and group solidarity.

Rivalries between neighboring Catholic and Protestant missionaries festered in much of the archipelago throughout the colonial era. Geddie, based on Aneityum, entertained one rather cool meeting in a two-year period with missionaries based in New Caledonia. On tiny Wala, off the coast of Malakula, Father Casimir Salomon and Reverend Crombie—having been set against each other by rival islet factions—bickered constantly at the turn of the century, usually in notes dispatched through Melanesian intermediaries. On nearby Rano, a pastor (and former Queen's Dragoon) reportedly attempted to trip a Catholic priest into a well![5] Different denominations, different origins, and different languages meant that Catholics and Protestants had little in common besides their foreignness and skin color.

Despite its material poverty (at least until the 1930s), the attraction of the Roman Catholic brand of Christianity lay in its optimistic spirit and cultural suppleness. Rather than "saving souls"—an obligation that Protestants believed could only be accomplished by combating the devil who dwelt in retrograde society—Catholic missionaries sought the divine spark intrinsic in all manner of men and customs. Marist missionaries were particularly imbued with this tolerant spirit. Catholicism in Melanesia was not as austere as Calvinism (as embodied by Pacific Presbyterians) and accommodated those indigenous groups who, in response to the Protestant crusade, had remained most defensive of their cultural specificity.

As a result of these religious rivalries, theogeographical boundaries emerged in the New Hebrides. These boundaries were in no way official but rather reflected a precarious, denominational balance of power of the Anglican-Presbyterian-Catholic trinity. An 1881 territorial entente delimited zones of influence between the Presbyterian and Anglican churches but excluded the Catholics. Though it was never formally validated by the Condominium government that followed, the informal partition stuck. Presbyterian churches were strongest in the southern islands (Aneityum, Erromango, Efate, Tanna, the Shepherds); Anglicans dominated in the northern ones (the Banks and Torres groups, Maewo, Ambae, Pentecost); and Catholics concentrated in the middle space between the two (Santo, Malakula, Ambrym). (See Map 3.) The political influence of the British and French residencies followed accordingly, no matter how hard the Catholic mission attempted to maintain its distance from French colonial strategy.

Spatial divisions were often fluid, however; rarely did a single church establish a monopoly on a given island. Certain islands—Efate, Tanna, Pentecost, Ambae, plus the islets off of Malakula (Wala, Rano, Atchin, Vao)—were the sites of particularly strong religious rivalry and divisions between Catholics and Presbyterian Protestants. Not surprisingly, political rivalries between Francophones and Anglophones eventually erupted most strongly in such locations.

As conversions proceeded, so did New Hebridean internalization of denominational boundaries. Melanesian catechists and "teachers" displayed religiously based suspicions and intolerance worthy of their

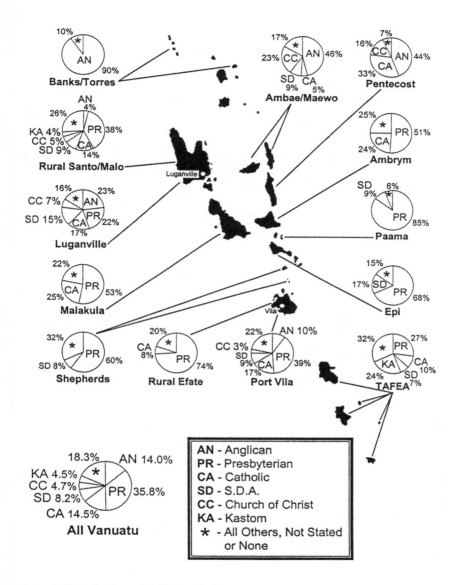

Banks/Torres
10%
*
AN
90%

Ambae/Maewo
17%
*
23% CC AN 46%
SD 9%
CA 5%

Pentecost
7%
*
16% CC AN 44%
CA
33%

Rural Santo/Malo
AN 4%
26%
*
KA 4%
CC 5%
SD 9%
PR 38%
CA 14%

Ambrym
25%
*
PR 51%
CA 24%

Luganville
16% 23%
CC 7% * AN
SD 15% PR 22%
CA 17%

Paama
SD 6%
9% *
PR 85%

Malakula
22%
*
CA PR 53%
25%

Epi
15%
*
17% SD PR 68%

Shepherds
32%
*
PR 60%
SD 8%

Rural Efate
20%
CA 8% *
PR 74%

Port Vila
22% AN 10%
CC 3% *
SD 9% PR 39%
CA 17%

TAFEA
32% 27%
* PR
KA CA 10%
24% SD 7%

All Vanuatu
18.3% AN 14.0%
KA 4.5% *
CC 4.7%
SD 8.2% PR 35.8%
CA 14.5%

Luganville
Vila

AN - Anglican
PR - Presbyterian
CA - Catholic
SD - S.D.A.
CC - Church of Christ
KA - Kastom
* - All Others, Not Stated or None

Map 3. Distribution of Religions in Vanuatu

respective priest and pastor patrons. Conflict and competition were often quite localized, setting village against village. Even after independence, the continuing presence of foreign missionaries, and in particular Catholic priests, animated nationalistic (if not xenophobic) responses in some non-Catholic and non-Francophone circles. A letter written in Bislama by the executive committee of the Vanua'aku Pati of North Pentecost and sent in April of 1985[6] to the Catholic bishop of Vanuatu (himself American-born)[7] expresses this sentiment in no uncertain terms:

> The Executive Committee of the Vanuaku Party notes that there is no cooperation between the Roman Catholic Church and any other organization here, only division. [It also] observes that the Roman Catholic Church is overly politicized, violating the law of the Republic prohibiting involvement by the Church, Government, and Chiefs in politics. . . . We don't want any white man or priest. . . .[8]

Despite concerted attempts since independence to indigenize the Catholic church—as of 1991, all five diocesan clergy were local and a dozen or so ni-Vanuatu seminarians were in training—the image still remained of a foreign-dominated denomination. Of the seventeen Marist missionaries then serving throughout the archipelago, only three were Melanesians, and one of these was from Fiji. One of the reasons for the slow extension to Melanesians of leadership positions within the Vanuatu Catholic church were the high standards set by the French priests both for baptism and ordination. Only in 1955 did Cyriaque Adeng become the first local priest, and in the 1960s only two more ni-Vanuatu, Gérard Leymang and Noël Vutiala, were so ordained. All three were trained in New Caledonia.

Yet the popular assumption that the foreign priest hailed from France no longer withstood scrutiny: Fewer than half of Vanuatu's fourteen white priests were French by the early 1990s, the others hailing from Great Britain, Ireland, Italy, New Zealand, and the United States. Though historical forces militate against it, there has been a tendency on the part of the church hierarchy to unlink Catholicism from Francophonie. After all, the linkage in Vanuatu between the religion of Rome and the language of France was coincidental, not theological. Logistics as well as politics are influencing this change. While the three first ni-Vanuatu priests were trained in New Caledonia, and hence in French, the four succeeding ones (Jules Bir, Blaise Buleban, Noël Molvis, and Michel Visi) studied either in Anglophone Fiji or Papua New

Guinea. All succeeding seminarians have gone to divinity school in Fiji, Papua New Guinea, or the Solomon Islands. Closing of the seminary in New Caledonia has obliged ni-Vanuatu priests-in-training, all Francophone in origin, to master English in order to study theology.

Under the initiative of Bishop Lambert, Vanuatu's first Anglophone Catholic parochial school was established in the early 1990s. Although the French–Catholic separation is important for national political reasons (i.e., to reinforce the image of the Catholic church as a religious, not a linguistically partisan, institution), ni-Vanuatu Catholics tend to resist defrenchification on the local level. Marist missions have been too long associated with French language and education, elements of social success and upward mobility, for ni-Vanuatu Catholics to "convert" easily to another language. Anglicizing the Catholic Mission is perceived as a double linguistic abandonment, not only by France, but also by the church.[9] In Vanuatu, where linguistic and religious boundaries have so closely overlapped, disassociating the French language from the Catholic religion will be one of the more difficult barriers to bridge.

For sure, Christian activity did not create conflict out of a peaceful anteregnum: Melanesia was no Eden. Superimposed Catholic–Protestant divisions did, however, contribute to elevating a multiplicity of local conflicts into wider, bipolar patterns of competition. It is important to note that the "Protestant versus Catholic" dichotomy is a Western one and not so common among ni-Vanuatu themselves. "Catholic" is a familiar referent, but there is little understanding that Anglicans and Adventists and Apostolics and Presbyterians and so on all fall under the general rubric of "Protestant." Theologically derived divisions, we have seen, did become linked to boundaries of language (English versus French) and loyalty (Great Britain versus France). But the boundaries were far from watertight, and were often crisscrossed by religious and linguistic countermovements.

BREAKING THE RELIGIOLINGUISTIC CONNECTION: FRANCOPHONE PROTESTANTS

Perhaps no example belies the simplistic Catholic = Francophone, Protestant = Anglophone correlation more than the movement of Francophone Protestants concentrated on the islands of Santo and Malakula. They are a spinoff of the Free Evangelical church established in New Caledonia by Raymond Charlemagne, a French evangelist born in Nancy. Charlemagne's campaign to convert New Caledonian Kanaks to evangelical Protestantism represented a kind of Melanesian Reformation. Most notable has been the movement's work in the realm of education.

In the 1970s Kanak missionaries came to the New Hebrides to establish a branch of the Federation of Protestant Free Teaching (FELP). The activities of the FELP reinforced the familiar linkage between religion and language in Vanuatu, but in an unexpected way—by imparting Francophone education within a uniquely Protestant framework. Linguistic particularism has nevertheless maintained the distance between French-New Caledonian and British-Australian-New Zealand strains of Protestantism.

Compared with the resources available to Catholic parochial schools, those of the FELP are rather meager. Even its headquarters, situated in the village of Orap on Malakula, pale next to even the more modest mission stations of the DEC, its Catholic equivalent. In 1991, the FELP's eleven schools taught 626 pupils, representing a little under 7 percent of all Francophone primary school enrollments.

In addition to the Francophone evangelical Protestants of the Charlemagne movement, there are uncounted, less organized non-Catholic Francophones in Vanuatu. The presumed association between Catholicism and Francophonie or, inversely, between speaking English and being Protestant, is challenged when one looks at the religious profile of the foremost leader of French-speaking ni-Vanuatu. Maxime Carlot Korman, Vanuatu's first Francophone prime minister, is a Presbyterian.

MELANESIAN LIBERATION THEOLOGY

From the independence struggle until today there has been a direct relationship between Vanuatu nationalism and liberation theology. Liberation theology, perhaps best known as a radical movement within Latin American Catholicism legitimating class conflict on theological grounds, has also stimulated antiauthoritarian and anticolonial politics throughout Christendom. Given the religious background of Vanuatu's pre-independence leaders, it is not surprising—indeed, it was inevitable—that nationalism be justified on theological grounds.

Christian-inspired nationalism in the New Hebrides actually predated liberation theology as it is known today. Independence for the New Hebridean missionary church, granted by the Presbyterian churches of Australia and New Zealand in 1947, was regarded as a first step toward devolving policy-making, initially within church affairs, among New

Hebrideans. Such responsibility was extended in 1965 to encompass all administrative and financial duties. Pro-independence sympathies were overtly expressed in 1973 (by which time liberation theology was an acknowledged belief system) when the General Assembly of the Presbyterian church declared itself to anticipate favorably "the goal of responsible self-government of the New Hebridean people as a nation . . . without violence and with the due preparation . . . for the duties, functions, rights and responsibilities of independent government." Two years later the Anglican Diocese of Melanesia was officially indigenized, sectioned off from the New Zealand church, and became a province of its own. Ecclesiastical responsibility among Melanesians within the Presbyterian and Anglican churches of the New Hebrides, augmented by overseas training in progressive theological seminaries throughout Australasia, naturally translated into political leadership for ni-Vanuatu pastors and preachers with a theologically buttressed belief in national independence.

According to liberation theology, colonialism is incompatible with Christianity; oppression must give way to liberation, for all people are equal in God's eyes. Political freedom for a nation is no less important than spiritual freedom for the individual. The maintenance of alien rule over indigenous peoples, with its attendant discrimination and exploitation, is contrary to divine law, be it in Asia, Africa, or Oceania.

"Colonial" status offended the dignity of religious leaders conscious of decolonization elsewhere. Clergy throughout the Pacific encouraged independence sentiment. Prominent in this regard was Bishop Derek Rawcliffe, an early and staunch advocate and adviser for Vanuatu independence. It was Bishop Rawcliffe who oversaw the ecclesiastical change granting independence to the Anglican Diocese of Melanesia (encompassing Vanuatu and the Solomon Islands) in 1975. There may be dispute over whether foreign clergy actually organized the Vanuatu nationalist movement, but there is no doubt that its encouragement in the face of French opposition and original British reticence was crucial.

Although there has been some ideological mellowing in the years since he cofounded the Vanua'aku Party, even after his losing the prime ministership Walter Lini retained his belief in the inseparability of church and state, religion and politics. In an interview in 1992, Father Lini maintained:

> We in Vanuatu cannot separate religion from politics because in our own society any leader is also a religious and political leader. . . . I believe firmly that as a priest . . . in Vanuatu I have a duty to continue to

be a religious leader . . . and as a political leader I also have a duty to
make sure that I represent what I believe to be Christian. . . . [M]ost of
our human rights today derive from Christian principles . . . Jesus
Christ is a political leader and I cannot see Christians saying, "We want
to follow in the footsteps of Jesus [but if] you are a political leader you
should not be a religious leader." I cannot put those two together.[10]

Although he did not come from a formal theological background
like Father Walter (as he is familiarly called throughout the archipelago),
Lini's successor as prime minister, Maxime Carlot Korman, also sponta-
neously reaffirmed the religious character of Vanuatu in a 1992 interview. Asked to justify his decision to introduce television to the nation,
a move that Father Walter had long opposed on moral grounds, Prime
Minister Carlot Korman gave as one of his reasons "to show that
Vanuatu is a constitutionally Christian country. [There is a role for]
churches in television. It is very important."[11]

Less prominent leaders also reinforce the link. Pastor John Peter,
who built a Seventh-Day Adventist church on Malakula, put it thus:

People will only be satisfied if they are honest, have respect [and show]
obedience and love for God and fellowmen. It is the same with governments. . . . When I took over the job of local government, the people
did not trust it. I was not educated in universities but I ran three coalition forms of government. The people were surprised. I worked with
love for all mankind.

Into the 1990s Sunday sermons, broadcast nationally by Radio
Vanuatu, commonly invoked the analogy between obtaining personal
freedom through Christ and enjoying group freedom in independence.
Salvation of the soul was incontrovertibly tied to sovereignty for the
nation. Political independence remained a religious imperative; a good
Christian was a Vanuatu patriot. Governmental sponsorship of religion
did not limit itself to general references to the deity, as the national
motto, Long God Yumi Stanap (We Stand With God), would have it;
parliamentary sessions were inaugurated with prayers invoking Jesus
Christ per se. Independence anniversary celebrations invariably com-
mence with opening prayers by the Vanuatu Christian Council (VCC)
and include a short church service; at the twelfth independence celebra-
tion in July 1992, between the advancing of the Vanuatu Military Forces
(VMF) Honor Guard and their hoisting of it, the Vanuatu flag, lying on

the same *tam-tam* (slit drum) used in the original independence ceremony in 1980, was blessed by a VCC churchman.

The intertwining of Christian religion and patriotism is no less
prominent at the level of island governance. On the eighth anniversary
of the establishment of local government on the island of Epi in April
1991, prayers and a sermon were a major part of the ceremony. The
pastor read from Mathew 22 to highlight the responsibility that citizens
have toward government—specifically, to pay taxes ("Render unto Caesar what belongs to Caesar.") Each person possesses two citizenships,
the pastor went on, one to God and the other to country. "Every country
has its own system for collecting taxes. It is the duty of everyone to pay
those taxes." The pastor then enumerated the purposes for which public
service taxes were collected: water, health, education. "A Christian is a
man of honor and respect. Every Christian should help the local government." A parable of two sons was then recounted: "One of the sons
agrees to work in the garden, and the other does not. [By implication,
it is a community farm.] But then they change their minds. The one who
says he will work but does not is committing a sin. Not fulfilling one's
promise is sinful." The moral: "One should not depend too much on
outside help. People have a responsibility to strengthen their [local gov-
ernment] council, their commmunity, and their island. Amen."

It would be premature to claim that a distinctive ni-Vanuatu civil
religion has developed out of Melanesian liberation theology.[12] Denominational identities are still quite strong and religious institutions still
overshadow governmental ones on most of the islands. Still, a unique
blend of nationalism, *kastom,* and Christianity is emerging in Vanuatu.
National identity is no less dependent on religion, particularly Pacific
Protestantism, than it is on reconstructed indigenous culture and international principles of self-determination. The missionary heritage remains a major component in the identity of the Vanuatu people.

Although Catholics were reluctant partisan players and, as Francophones, initially skeptical of independence—at least under Anglophone terms—the archdiocese of Vanuatu has subsequently embraced
the spirit of a politically engaged church. The tenth independence anniversary issue of the church's news bulletin, in a response to certain
parliamentary discussions, carried these lines, in an article entitled "Re-
vising the Vanuatuan Constitution is to Celebrate Love":

Changing, amending or improving a constitution is not only a matter
for custom chiefs, politicians or jurists, specialists of custom law or In-

ternational Law. . . . Whether it be Melanesian, American, European or
Asian . . . every Tradition and Culture derives its source and finality at
the very heart of the Trinity: Father, Son and Holy Spirit. Any Constitution must be clear, obvious, and reflecting of the Love of God for the
Man created in his likeness. . . .

   In spite of a preface with a Christian view, the Constitution of
Vanuatu sins greatly through exclusivism, compounded by xenophobia.
[It] is stuffed with political compromises which forced a hasty signing:
In other words, a Death attitude.[13]

Momentum for the women's movement in Vanuatu has also come
from within the framework of Melanesian liberation theology. European
missionaries had already fought against the most egregiously chauvinist
customs,[14] though different denominations approached the question of
sexual equality to markedly different degrees. Because Catholic and Anglican missions were more tolerant of *kastom* and traditional gender relations than, for example, Church of Christ ones were, separate meeting
spaces, male-only kava-drinking rituals, and sister exchange and bride-
price persisted in the former, but not in the latter, communities of even
the same island.[15] In the late twentieth century, and particularly since
independence, protection and extension of rights for ni-Vanuatu women
has been embraced by indigenous church leaders. These believe that
equality for women must occur within the church for it to be achieved
throughout society. In this vein, Sethy Regenanu—at the time both government and Presbyterian minister—urged ordination for women in the
nation's churches. Melanesian liberation theology in Vanuatu is evolving
from a religiously guided movement toward achieving political sovereignty and decolonization to being a force for patriotism, moral renewal,
gender equality, and domestic change.

A RELIGIOUS PROFILE OF THE VANUATU FOUNDING FATHERS

An insightful biographical portrait of the leading figures of Vanuatu at
independence, published by the Institute of Pacific Studies at the University of the South Pacific and copyrighted by the Pacific Churches Research Centre, well illustrates the prominent role played by clergymen
and lay preachers in the nation's first independence government. Succes-
sive governments throughout the first decade continued to reflect this
religious character.

   Of the sixteen national leaders and "politicians" depicted in *Yumi*

Stanap,[16] three (Willie Korisa and Sethy Regenvanu, cabinet ministers, and Fred Timakata, deputy prime minister) were Presbyterian pastors. ("Pastor Fred" later went on to become president of the republic, serving from 1989 to 1994.) Two others (George Kalsakau, first preindependence chief minister and postindependence mayor of Port Vila, and Thomas Reuben, cabinet member) were elders in the Presbyterian church. Two cabinet ministers (Presbyterian Donald Kalpokas, who briefly served as prime minister in 1991, and George Worek, Anglican) were lay preachers. Gérard Leymang, successor to George Kalsakau as chief minister in 1978 and appointed in 1992 as first secretary to prime minister Maxime Carlot Korman, was an ordained priest (Catholic) as, of course, was Prime Minister Walter Lini (Anglican). Even anti-establishment Jimmy Stephens headed a "church"—albeit a non-Christian one—the Royal Church of Nagriamel. Four of the remaining six leaders who did not hold official church positions were identified as having been educated in schools either of the Catholic Mission (Vincent Boulekone, leader of the opposition, and Jean-Marie Léyé, chairman of the Federal Party and president of the republic from 1994), the Presbyterian church (John Naupa, cabinet minister) or the Methodist movement (Ati George Sokomanu, first president of the republic). The fifth—Maxime Carlot, then speaker of the parliament—had attended both Catholic and Presbyterian schools!

Another category of ni-Vanuatu leaders described in *Yumi Stanap* included seven churchmen: Father Blaise Buleban, Roman Catholic priest; Pastor Reuben Makikon, chairman of the Vanuatu Christian Council; Pastor Ephraim Moli, Apostolic church; Dr. Titus Path, principal of Tangoa Bible College; Pastor Dick Joel Peter, Assemblies of God; Harry Sivehi, bishop of Vanuatu; and George Kuse, director of the Catholic Mission Schools (later, under Prime Minister Carlot Korman, director-general of the ministry of education). It is particularly significant that all three "custom chiefs"—Chief Willie Bongmatur, head of the National Council of Chiefs; Chief Graham Kalsakau, chairman of the Efate Council of Chiefs; and Chief Tom Tipoloamata, chief of Itakoma—are self-consciously and actively Christian. Chief Tipoloamta is described as a Presbyterian Church elder, Chief Kalsakau trained as a Presbyterian catechist and preacher, and Chief Bongmatur, "[d]uring the service of worship which preceded the raising of the flag at the main independence ceremony . . . was the one who received the Bible presented to the National Council of Chiefs by the Vanuatu Christian Council and the Bible Society in the South Pacific."[17] Chief Bongmatur then pledged to uphold Christian principles along with Melanesian values. Eleven years later, when the president, prime minister, and finance minister were all priests or pastors, Chief Willie Bongmatur, still head of the National Council of Chiefs, formally opened the sixth assembly of the Pacific Conference of Churches held in Mele on Efate island. Though at one level it may appear contradictory, the melding of *kastom* with Christianity pervades the religious as well as political scene in contemporary Vanuatu society.

KASTOM AND CHRISTIANITY

Understanding the relationship between *kastom* and Christianity is the key to unraveling the complexity of identity in Vanuatu today. This is no easy task, for among ni-Vanuatu themselves, particularly when the issue is posed in religious terms, there is no consensus over the meaning of *kastom*. Does *kastom* connote a general nostalgia for traditional life that nevertheless remains compatible with Christianity? Or is it a fundamentalist movement against both Westernization and Christianity, the only genuine movement that preserves the authentic traditions and religions of the indigenous peoples of Vanuatu? Subscribers to each of these positions claim *kastom* as their own.

If we opt for the first meaning, the one that legitimates the authority of the founding fathers mentioned in the previous section, then most ni-Vanuatu—over three-quarters of whom identify themselves as Christian—clearly subscribe to *kastom*. But if we adhere to its stricter meaning, the one that appears to be incompatible with Christianity, then fewer than 5 percent of ni-Vanuatu (80 percent of whom are Tannese) are followers of customary, non-Western religions. This represents a 3 percent drop from ten years previously and confirms Tanna, over a quarter of whose inhabitants name *kastom* as their religion, as the largest outpost for an otherwise dwindling number of followers of non-Christian beliefs. (Santo Bush, the Malakula hills, and South Pentecost constitute secondary redoubts.) The problem with this interpretation, we shall see, is that even on Tanna, *kastom* has evolved more as an idiosyncratic reaction to Westernization than as an orthodox preserver of indigenous belief.

Missionaries as well as their critics acknowledge that one of the unfortunate consequences of Christianization has been the devitalization of indigenous society. After noting the success in implanting new forms of worship (i.e., formal services, English hymns) among the Melanesians, an Anglican missionary admitted in 1917, "there is no doubt that social life as a whole is a more drab affair now than it used to be."[18] The upshot of the totalitarian "Christian Nation" constructed on Vanuatu's most southern island was that "The population of Aneityum, deprived of any response pattern, decimated by a kind of slow death which continued well after . . . 1860, fell into a profound lethargy noted by all visitors."[19] Even the Catholic Mission of Vanuatu, in its centenary retrospective, acknowledged that "the boundaries of the mission often became a trap where the new Christians became lazy and lost their initial vigour."[20] Missionization heralded the death knell of much of traditional Melanesian culture as practiced in the contact years. In this light, the reconciliation of *kastom* with Christianity is all the more remarkable.

Indigenous Theological Views

> I find it really difficult to understand some of the practices that were taking place when the missionaries came, up to the time when we began to struggle for independence. Even up to this time, I cannot reconcile some of the things that they believed was [*sic*] right. . . . For example, cannibalism. It was done as revenge, not just killing and eating people . . .
> for meat [but] religiously eating, to show that they have completely overpowered the enemy.[21]

The above represents a mainstream view among ni-Vanuatu Christians. There is frank admission that some of the customary and religious practices of their not-too-distant ancestors were evil and were rightly suppressed by missionaries and colonial governors.[22] Even Vanuatu nationalists such as former Prime Minister Father Walter Lini, quoted above, express gratitude that missionaries brought the gospel to the New Hebrides and eliminated some indigenous depravities. Yet there is also a need for theological fine tuning, for some legitimate—indeed, divinely inspired—elements of Melanesian culture were needlessly attacked in the process: "Some people believed that the customary dances were wrong, and some people still believe that today. I don't believe that it is wrong. I think it is [something] that God has given our forefathers and fathers to express themselves."[23]

Catholic leaders, too, steer a course to avoid excluding either Christianity or Melanesian authenticity. Taking aim at *kastom*-based land disputes, Father Leymang declaimed: "Before being a 'Melanesian custom property' the Earth is Common Property. It belongs to every human being living on planet Earth. Any land policy must . . . reflect . . . Love of God. . . . Ignoring the source and finality in God of

Melanesian Tradition and Culture will continuously create multiple problems, such as the one with the Lands Office. . . ."[24]

Some ni-Vanuatu religious leaders, in their opposition to indigenous rites, perpetuate the more puritanical side of nineteenth-century Protestantism. Differing attitudes toward such practices, particularly ritual dancing and kava drinking, have long constituted a significant ritual boundary among Christians in Vanuatu. Presbyterian missionaries condemned kava, Anglican ones tolerated it, and Catholics freely indulged in it.

The public and ceremonial consumption of kava, especially on state occasions, is a powerful symbol of the rehabilitation of a formerly damned practice. No less than the spirted *kastom* dancing, the drinking of kava at the National Arts Festival on Santo in 1991, where even a visiting dignitary from France publicly downed a shell,[25] was an important theopolitical ritual.

Religious leaders in Vanuatu have selectively reexamined indigenous belief and practice in light of contemporary universal norms of human rights and Third World ideologies of national liberation. Some aspects of Melanesian life that Christian missionaries condemned—those which violate modern moral sensibilities—remain banished to the era of "Darkness." Those which express cultural diversity and national identity are now regarded as God-given. Cognizant of the multiple faces of Christianity introduced by the white man, many ni-Vanuatu now transcend the spiritual boundaries not only between old-time Catholicism and Protestantism, but between liberal Christianity and sanitized *kastom*. A passage from a primary school textbook illustrates the reconciliation between an indigenous activity once condemned as idolatrous but now praised as cultural:

> A long time ago, people in Vanuatu carved figures out of wood or made them with clay. . . . [T]he figures represented the spirits that people believed in at that time [and] were carved to help people in their worship. When missionaries brought the Christian Gospel, the objects were no longer considered to be important since people on many islands no longer believed in spirits. Today such carvings as the face on a tamtam are reminders of the past, but are no longer believed to have power. They are a part of the history of our civilisation.[26]

As the survival of John Frum attests, however, the state can go only so far in harnessing religion.

John Frum as Anti-Prophet

As with cargo cults in general, the John Frum phenomenon can be mapped on either side of the hermeneutic divide between inspired religion and mass psychosis. Emerging as a millenarian response to harsh years of Tanna Law, and stimulated by the prospect of American liberators at the outset of World War II, John Frum has developed into a pseudosovereign community and a permanent embarrassment to both local governmental authorities on Tanna and national leaders in Vila.

It was during the tenure of John Nicol as British District Agent on Tanna that rumors of a supernatural or divine being, promising a utopian era, began to surface. In 1940 Nicol reported that a certain John Frum, bedecked in red suit and shiny buttons, had been preaching, for three years already, that the rejection of Christianity and other European customs (such as money) would help ring in the new age.[27] Once money had disappeared, went the new gospel, the Whitemen traders would also leave, their raison d'être for being in the South Seas having gone. Drinking kava again, said John, would also presage redemption.

Masses of Tannese, including church leaders, became John Frumists. Kava was drunk en masse and money was either profligately disposed of in binge-buying sprees or literally thrown into the sea. In hindsight, the John Frum movement has been characterized as a would-be "neo-pagan national theocracy,"[28] as a "forerunner of Melanesian nationalism,"[29] and as a "dreamtime" effort toward social reconstruction.[30] At the time, however, Condominium officials viewed it as an immoral and dangerous delusion that warranted repression. John Frum leaders were jailed or sent into exile. One man, Nelawiyang, who claimed to be John Frum, eventually died in a mental asylum in New Caledonia. But suppression never killed belief.

Described by his original "ropes," or messengers, as light of skin (even if "dusky"), John Frum was believed to have originated from America.[31] (The embarking of GIs in the New Hebrides when the Pacific theater was opened was viewed as confirmation; in 1943 an airstrip was begun to receive John Frum's soldiers.) Alternatively, he was seen as an incarnation of Karaperamum, the god of Tanna's greatest mountain. No contradiction or invalidation (such as American soldiers disavowing knowledge of John Frum) damaged the myth. Though John Frumists ostensibly opposed Christianity as introduced by the missionaries, they in fact incorporated several elements of Old and New Testament belief and claimed theological primacy. "The entire mythology of John Frum rests on attempts to reconcile opposites: it consists, on one hand, of wanting to 'paganize' Christianity, by localizing it within the pagan pantheon of the island, and on the other hand of christianizing Custom by giving it a messianic and universal meaning."[32]

During the Condominium, the political rationale of the John Frum movement was clear: "first to get rid of the totalitarian grip of Presbyterian Christianity, then to eliminate the European merchants . . . thought to be responsible for variations in the price of copra."[33] Today, Presbyterianism has lost its totalitarianism and Europeans no longer manage the copra trade. Yet John Frum remains strong, as evidenced by a following on islands other than Tanna and its paramilitary drills and Friday all-night dancing sessions at Sulphur Bay.

The accession to independence of Vanuatu has changed little in the political perspective of John Frum leaders. In a 1991 interview with Peter Poita, Tom Meles, and Isaac Wan, I was told that the change which came about in 1980 is not the one John Frum had envisioned: it was a British- and French-imposed sham independence, a mirage of politics, not a true, American-granted liberation. The Condominium had merely set up a government and political parties to govern in its stead. Such a government suppressed belief in John Frum and stifled the true desires of the people. It was opposed to *kastom,* antagonistic to chiefs, and hindered contact with the American government. If the northern islands wanted to be part of Vanuatu, fine; but freedom for Tanna meant joining with the United States.

A tug-of-war had been going on between the followers of John Frum and the government of Vanuatu over possession of the American flag, the symbol of the movement. Twice the government of Vanuatu had confiscated their Stars and Stripes; now the men in Vila were frightened to take the one the Frumists managed to obtain in 1987. Perhaps, they went on, the Vanuatu government now realized that the United States would replace any stolen flag. Frustration and yearning frequently surfaced in the course of our talk. "This 'independence' is wrong," went the refrain. "The time for America is long overdue."

John Frum blurs several boundaries. As a "new *kastom*" movement, with heavily borrowed biblical imagery (John is reminiscent of the Baptist, Noah is a prominent figure), it combines the Christian with the pagan, the innovative with the indigenous. It reposes on a kind of *kastom* ideology, but not one compatible with Vanuatu nationalism. Indeed, in its remarkably continuous urging for unity with America, it audaciously spans geographical and political boundaries. Regarded by local government leaders as retrograde, and by national leaders as unpatriotic, the John Frum community is denied the meager elements of governmental assistance available. Sulphur Bay's lack of development elicits ambivalence: It is a reason to lambast the government but also a manifestation of the community's independence. Along with other sects which believe that Prince Philip is actually a Tannese doppelganger, the followers of John Frum test the credulity of all would-be students of the Condominium's legacies.

Nagriamel

Although Nagriamel is best known for its impact on Vanuatu politics—reclaiming indigenous land in the 1960s, claiming national sovereignty in the 1970s, proclaiming secessionist independence in 1980—its cultural and religious dimensions are also important. These in turn revolve around Jimmy Stephens' own complex syncretism of *kastom* and Christianity.

It is unclear what kind of religious education Jimmy Stephens received as a youngster; it was only in his middle age that he was baptized into the Church of Christ (presumably for tactical reasons) and assumed the name of Moses, mark of his intention figuratively to lead the people of Santo out of the slavery of colonialism and into an era of freedom. Other marginalized believers, such as Seventh-Day Adventists and Presbyterians from south and west Santo, joined the antiestablishment movement early on. Stephens went on to found the Nagriamel Federation Independent Royal Church, whose clergy, former pastors from the Church of Christ, sermonized in ways akin to liberation theologians, but with a specifically land rights focus. "Remove not the ancient landmarks which your fathers have set" was a favorite verse.[34]

Stephens' (and hence Nagriamel's) ultimate relationship to Christianity was ambiguous. While he rejected the established churches, particularly those which he identified as colonially collaborationist, he did not reject outright the fundaments of New Testament theology. Yet he also expressed, in an interview with the author two years before his death, a skepticism, if not cynicism, relating to basic missionary preaching.

One of the controversial aspects of Steven's *kastom*-cum-religious movement, and the one that put him most at loggerheads with the Christian establishment even after his release from prison, concerned polygamy. At least partly in the name of Nagriamel-interpreted *kastom*, Jimmy Stephens had over the years taken dozens of wives. In honor of his seventy-seventh birthday, in 1992, he took a few more, prompting criticism by the Vanuatu Christian Council, the minister in charge of religion and culture, and the director of the Vanuatu Family Health Association. The criticism was directed as much at the institution of polygamy as at Stephens' liberal practice of it. The acting chief justice, however, reaffirmed that polygamy, as an exercise of indigenous custom, was constitutionally protected. By the time Jimmy Stephens passed away in 1994, he reportedly had married thirty-one women.

Nagriamel's vision of *kastom,* and particularly its endorsement of polygamy, remains a challenge to the conventional (and ideologically comforting) rhetoric that softpedals basic incompatibilities between *kastom* and Christianity. With Stephens' demise it is unclear what future Nagriamel will enjoy as an "independent *kastom* movement." If it fades away with its leader, then *kastom* will come one step closer to being fully Christianized.

The National Arts Festival Controversy

Although *kastom* may be largely reconciled with Christianity in Vanuatu, Christianity is not always reconciled with *kastom.* This is particularly the case in the more fundamentalist and millenarian denominations, which do not accept the accommodation that mainstream churches have made with indigenous cultural practices. Thus, while the official Presbyterian church no longer bans kava drinking or condemns pig-killing ceremonies, smaller offshoot sects are as uncompromising with these and other customs as the most restrictive of nineteenth-century missionaries.

In the lead-up to the National Arts Festival on Santo in 1991, the first such event since the one that rang in independence, such churches opposed the festival on religious grounds. Radio reports carried government refutation of the charge that "black magic" and other un-Christian activities would be performed at the festival. Some churchmen also took exception to the festival beginning on a Sunday. There were also related reports that some so-called religious leaders instructed people not to vote in upcoming elections, though the source of these reports is unclear.

The challenge to the legitimacy of the National Arts Festival from religious quarters was troubling. The underlying aim of the festival was ideological. One decade after Vanuatu's accession to independence, it was felt important to reinforce the message of "unity in diversity" — diversity being represented by the multifaceted *kastom* as practiced throughout the archipelago. Unity was enthroned in Vanuatu nationhood, which all of Vanuatu's peoples shared. But they all were also supposed to share a religious commonality, Christianity. That certain denominational leaders would balk at the festival on purely religious grounds was galling to festival organizers.

In his response to the Arts Festival boycott, secretary of the Santo/

Malo local government council, Joe Joseph, after defending *kastom,* charged that some ni-Vanuatu had gone too far in adopting European ways and thinking. His example of the wearing of white dresses and high heels at weddings may not have scored many points among the radio audience, but it did underscore the lengths to which the rhetoric over authenticity in Vanuatu's cultural and religious traditions could go.

Opening and closing prayers and speeches at the festival, by religious as well as political leaders, took pains to invoke religion to legitimize the festival. The inaugural sermon was based on the Creation story from Genesis and was developed along these lines: God, in creating the world, endowed it with many different kinds of flora, fauna, and colors. He also provided for a multiplicity and diversity of human customs, arts, and traditions. *Kastom* and Creation are thus equivalent. National identity is also God-given.

It is also true, the sermon went on, that Creation gave way to the Fall, to the curse, and to shame. While some customs and traditions are in line with Christian principles, others are "not straight." People should examine and choose between those practices which are legitimate and those which should be discontinued. But it is the people themselves who must choose: This is not a matter, it was implied, for self-appointed judges to dictate.

In addition to Genesis, there was a reading from Corinthians. The message contained a warning: Who is to judge which is a proper Christian life compared with a traditional one? Some things are for God alone to judge—individuals should not condemn the practices of other groups. Tradition and custom are ways of praising God, by practicing people's God-given talents: "Glory, glory, glory to God. . . . Art, culture, custom, tradition: all go together, all glorify the Lord. Because, in the Beginning, God; in the End, God."

Chief Willie Bongmatur, president of the National Council of Chiefs (Malvatumauri), was even more direct in his speech intended to counter Arts Festival critics: "God has made all peoples, all beliefs. It is not true, as some have been claiming, that some customs are satanic. . . . Long Live Vanuatu *Kastom!* Long Live God's Blessing!"

ESTABLISHMENT VERSUS MINORITY CHRISTIANITIES

The plethora of Christian churches practicing in the New Hebrides gave rise in the late Condominium era to recognition of the need for some ecumenical body to manage interdenominational relations. Thus was born, in 1963, the Vanuatu Christian Council (VCC). Five churches are permanent members of the VCC: the Anglican, the Apostolic, Churches of Christ, the Presbyterian, and the Roman Catholic. In addition to its evangelical, social welfare, Bible translation activities, and overseeing those of independent religious organizations, the VCC enjoys a formal channel of communication with the Vanuatu government through the Prime Minister's Office. Yet this does not mean that the VCC exercises unbridled influence, as this October 1985 complaint to the Ministry of Home Affairs (708/5) attests. (The major issue was the delay in issuing a visa for an Australian one-year lecturer for its Bible College. Grammatical and typographical errors of this and ensuing archival documents appear as they do in the originals.)

> As we sit and watch we can see that certain people have freedom to do things as stated in our constitution, but we cannot do it. . . . If people have a right to sell liquor, sell kava, perform pig ceremony which is really against God, Why not our church build Bible College or teach Christian things to help both the spiritual man and the physical? . . . Why not stop sectarian movements such as Jehovah Witness, Bahai, Mormon, etc. . . . which really hinders God's Holy Spirit from working in His Church?

Other religious denominations and movements have indeed proliferated and expanded the traditional tripartite Presbyterian–Anglican–Catholic division of spirituality in Vanuatu. Though quite different in theology and expression from one another, their common successes may be linked to material dissatisfaction with the religious status quo. Not coincidentally, there has been an American connection with virtually all of them.

Seventh-Day Adventism (SDA) emerged out of an American Baptist tradition that adapted and extended Old Testament proscriptions to the realm of personal consumption. In return for renouncing alcohol, tobacco, meat, and caffeine products, Adventists in the New Hebrides, to which the movement came in 1917, were entitled to the benefits of a tightly organized and relatively prosperous community network. Voluntary, communal acceptance of such prohibitions, according to Joël Bonnemaison, was facilitated by viewing it as replacement of one set of taboos, the indigenous ones, by another, albeit modern, set.[35] Ni-Vanuatu Adventists came to enjoy comfortable homes, well-endowed health and educational systems, and a headstart on salvation when the impending end-of-the-world arrives. The Adventist movement has made impressive gains as a denominational share of Vanuatu Christianity, going from 8 percent in 1979 to nearly 11 percent in 1989.[36]

The Assemblies of God, of more recent (circa 1970) vintage, also emanated from the United States. Sharing with the SDA a millenarian streak, the Assemblies of God employ an aggressive proselytizing technique characterized by fiery and charismatic preachers, rhythmic musical attractions, and electrified (and electrifying) public-air jamborees. It is a youth-oriented denomination with an American pop-culture appeal.[37] Unfortunately, Assemblies of God were not included as a category in the 1989 census. Yet both the Assemblies of God and Seventh-Day Adventists enjoy observer status in the Vanuatu Christian Council.

During the 1980s other denominations—for instance, Jehovah's Witnesses, Holiness Fellowship, the Revival Movement—sprang up, causing grave consternation within the ranks of the Christian establishment. They have also raised concern within the government because of their theologically antipolitical and electorally abstentionist stances, and the former two have been accused of hindering electoral registration. The universalist but non-Christian Bahai faith also gained a foothold in the 1970s and 1980s. Not only have these novel sects made inroads into traditional church membership—proportionally, Presbyterian, Anglican, and Roman Catholic affiliations all declined slightly between 1979 and 1989, whereas "other religions" climbed from 5 percent to 12.5 percent (see Table 3)—but a few are perceived as downright cultist. Such fears explain the 1993 decision by the (Presbyterian) Onesua and (Anglican) Vureas High Schools to reject children who had passed the Primary School Leaving Examination but belonged to revival group churches. As explained by the head of the Christian Education Department of the Presbyterian church, such churches are "anti-Presbyterian breakaway sects," whose children, even, had previously caused disturbances.

Denominations that emphasize ecstatic revelation, laying on of hands, speaking in tongues, and trances may strike a precontact cultural chord, one of which born-again ni-Vanuatu may not even be aware.[38] But such movements also have political implications: They are devoutly abstentionist and are alleged to hinder electoral registration, preferring to count on the "cargo" of God.

From some of the more idiosyncratic, charismatic churches, reports of all-night sexual tests of temptation (repeated failure of which has resulted in a rise in illegitimate births) have been particularly alarming to mainstream religious leaders. Extracts from the following letter from

Table 3 Religious Groups in Vanuatu, 1979–1989

Religion	1979	%	1989	%	Rank Change
Presbyterian	40,843	36.7	50,951	35.8	nil
Anglican	16,778	15.1	19,949	14.0	-1
Roman Catholic	16,502	14.8	20,613	14.5	+1
Not Stated	10,828	9.7	5,755	4.0	-4
Kastom	8,460	7.6	6,484	4.5	-1
S. Day Adventist	6,817	6.1	11,737	8.2	+1
Other Religions	5,532	5.0	17,748	12.5	+4
Church of Christ	4,241	3.8	6,745	4.7	+3
No Religion	1,250	1.1	2,437	1.7	nil
Total	111,251	100.0	142,419	100.0	

Source: Derived from data in *Vanuatu National Population Census 1989*, Table 13.3, p. 38.

a representative of the Vanuatu Red Cross Society and local chapter of the National Council of Chiefs in the Shepherd groups to the Department of Investigation of the Vanuatu Police, received at the Ministry of Home Affairs on September 20, 1983, and catalogued at the National Archives (708/6/6) reflect such concern.

Dear Sir,
    Re-Revival movement in the Shepherd Groups
. . . The so call revied Presbyterian Church in the Shepherd Groups is creating lots of unrest, desunity, physcial damages and desordered. These are some of the evidence of the pratical actions of the above movement especially course by the ring leaders of the groups

1. They have encourage their membership to leave their wives, children and gone after other men's wives. . . . This create lots of problem to the kids and relatives and course lots of violence to couples. EG. Mrs [W. D.] completely lost her eye. . . .
2. W.F. will never course any women to be pregnent because, back in 1960 Mr, M. wrote a letter to apply for his operation to tye off his spermatic cord or prostatectmy. . . . Because of this he feels, he can have sexual intercourse with any women and not worry about pergnecy. But this is very miss leading for those men who have not have the operation. This was done only for the sake of his family control and not to be used for his selfish desire. [He] must be taken to court immediately. . . .

The letter catalogs various other infractions of W.F. that are not related to church activities (impounding a community center motor wood-saw machine against uncompensated use of a speedboat, theft of corrugated iron sheets, embezzled bank funds, etc.). Letters of denunciation, signed and not, are not uncommon outcomes of village disputes and should be treated with great caution, both in terms of motivation as well as accuracy. This and the next letter (708/5), however, do demonstrate how religious conflict still gives rise to intracommunity, interpersonal, and transdenominational divisions:

22-7-1985

Labour Department
Vila

SUBJECT: NEO PENTICOSTAL MOVEMENT PANGO VILLAGE

Dear Sir,

We would like to bring your attention concerning the new Penticostal Movement which is been set by . . . Ex-Holiness Fellowship President. . . . [He] does not respect the chiefs authority in some of the pass matters concerning this movement. . . . New Penticostal church teaching is oppose to the fundamental truths of the scripture. We have seen too much division in our community, especially in having too many religion in the village. . . . We the chief, council, Pango church session, with its congreation disagree totally to this idea of building a Neo Pentecostal Church at Pango Village. . . .

Thanking you in advance,
Pango chief
Council Secretary
Pango Moderator
Session Clerk

Conflict between the principles of religious freedom and national sovereignty surfaced shortly after independence. In October of 1980, then minister of home affairs, Fred Timakata (himself a Presbyterian minister), issued an opinion to the deputy principal immigration officer refusing work permits to an applicant (apparently a Jehovah's Witness) and three other Jehovah's Witness couples, "as I believe that there are too many religious sects in this country" (MHA 012/1). The following letter reveals the conflict that arises on the local level when community control vies against freedom of religion:

5th July, 1982

President
S. D. A. Mission
Santo

Dear Sir,

Thank you very much for your childish letter dated 29th June, 1982. You seemed clearly to be totally ignorant of our way of life. Such phrases as "freedom of worship" in the national constitution does not mean that you be free setting up your Mission wherever one or two agrees upon. We do not live on individualistic society like you do back home. . . . Rather [you are] bringing disunity and unsettlement of hearts which makes me cry over my people as Christ did over Jerusalem. . . .

Yours,
[Signed]
For Erromago People

A "Policy Proposal on the Religion [*sic*] Freedom" on file at the National Archives (708/5 PA) offers an interesting perspective on this ongoing dilemma.

During the colonial times, missionaries from overseas used to come to the colonies and preach the Gospel. . . . The local people, however, were never asked if they wanted Christianity, or what type of Christianity they preferred. . . .

Today the former colonies have reached independence and are able to make their own decisions. . . . Religious freedom should not be understood as a freedom for outsiders to come in the country and hunt down again those who do not want a certain religion, but rather as a freedom of the citizens to decide themselves what religion they want. . . .

It is recommended that the Vanuatu Government keep the notion of religious freedom in its constitution with the understanding that is a *freedom of choice* for the citizens of Vanuatu and not a *freedom of conquest* for any new foreign religions or sect. . . . Authority should be given to the local council chiefs to bar any religious minister from spreading a new religion in their territory, if they feel that the religious peace will be disrupted.

Despite its concern for religious fractionalization, the Government of Vanuatu has not succeeded in limiting Christianity to the establishment churches. In July of 1993, at a speech delivered on the occasion of the ordination of an Anglican priest, Sethy Regenvanu, then minister responsible for religious affairs, put at twenty-one the number of religious groups that were not part of the Vanuatu Christian Council. In a society where so many services provided by government in other nations—notably education and health—are the province of religious institutions and personnel, coordination and harmony among the various churches is essential.

Denominational schism is thus viewed not as a doctrinal problem alone but as a risk to national unity. In a private conversation with Samuel Turgett, the president of the Santo/Malo government council likened the mushrooming of sects to the proliferation of political parties. Just as more parties do not necessarily make for better democracy, so more denominations do not bring more religiosity. Both politics and religion need to be limited, Turgett claimed, for the society to prosper.

The Vanuatu Christian Council is less inhibited about taking positions on foreign affairs. Over the years the VCC has expressed sympathy with the secessionist movement in Bougainville vis-à-vis the government of Papua New Guinea. In 1994 the VCC went a step further in criticizing its own government for agreeing to participate in a South Pacific Peacekeeping Force in Bougainville.

Members of the Vanuatu Christian Council are usually circumspect about assuming the role of mediator and critic when a crisis erupts within and among the nation's political parties. A noteworthy departure occurred during the schism of the ruling party in 1991. The prime minister's draconian measures to retain control of the Vanua'aku Party elicited this statement to "the Honorable Prime Minister Father Walter Lini" by the executive assembly of the Presbyterian Church of Vanuatu and was broadcast on Radio Vanuatu:

> We as the Church are concerned about the life and good of the people you dismissed without warning. . . . The increase in nepotism in your government is alarming and the church considers this undemocratic and unchristian. . . . The Presbyterian Church in Vanuatu cannot keep quiet [and] humbly requests you and your government to keep peace and harmony and stability in the country. . . . We remain united in God's mission.

RELIGION IN EDUCATIONAL CURRICULUM

Perhaps on account of the resilience, success, and autonomy of Catholic Missions schools, religious education in Vanuatu's public schools has not generated the kind of opposition that it has in other predominantly Protestant nations.[39] Perhaps in no other domain does Vanuatu so belie the separation of church and state that is supposed to prevail in democratic societies as in the prominent role accorded religion in the classroom.

Religious education in Vanuatu's public schools is not a generic, spiritual program of moral sensitization for young children. Though no state church is established, and no denomination is officially favored, religious education is unambiguously Christian. Even the social studies curriculum reinforces this aspect of ni-Vanuatu identity. The very first chapter of part 2 of the revised (1983) edition textbook for upper primary school students, *The Story of Our Islands—The People and Government,* emphasizes as one of the "three rocks which are the foundation of the constitution" (after traditional Melanesian values and faith in God) "Christian Principles which means that the teaching and work of Jesus Christ is the guide to all the affairs of the Nation."

Even through high school, Christianity (with a vaguely liberal Protestant bent) is an integral part of the curriculum, taught and tested like any other subject (though with fewer hours per week). In seventh grade, the emphasis is on divine revelation. Thus, in the first term, "God reveals himself in the Old Testament." The second term is devoted to Jesus Christ ("What is a gospel?" and "The Life of Jesus from birth to Peter's confession"). Term three covers how "God reveals Himself to Vanuatu" (missionary activity) as well as how to pray ("adoration, thanksgiving, confession, intercession, supplication"). In eighth grade the religious education begins with Jesus's life (part 2) and then moves on to God's communication with mankind (including "false prophets" and "other religions").

In ninth grade, the Old Testament and teachings of Jesus are revisited in Term One. Term Two stresses responsibility to self (hygiene, smoking, alcohol), to family ("the ideal Christian home"), and to others (relationships, marriage, unmarried parents, illegitimate children, and "reasons for and against dancing").[40] In the third term, church history and contemporary church relations are covered. Reflecting the politically liberal theology of mainstream Vanuatu Christianity, the modern-day "persecution" of Christians is exemplified in difficulties faced by clerical activists in promoting racial equality (e.g., Martin Luther King, Desmond Tutu) and socioeconomic reform (e.g., Korean pastors imprisoned for advocating just wages and land rights for workers).

Tenth-grade religious education begins again with the teachings of Jesus. In the second term, such topics as choosing a job, prejudice, and world poverty and hunger are covered. The curriculum concludes with "finding out about other denominations." Given the sensitivities arising from competition between the somewhat aggressive millenarian and the more established denominations in Vanuatu, this final year tackles "The Final Coming of the Kingdom" section gingerly but inferentially. "If it's not in the Bible," teachers are urged to tell the children, "don't believe it."

Religious observance is also advocated for teachers in training. The *Handbook* for the Vanuatu Teacher's College/Ecole Normale de Vanuatu states (p. 8): "All students are expected to attend morning assembly every weekday, and to take their turn at leading it. . . . Students are encouraged to attend services at their own churches in the town and to make a personal contribution, for example as Sunday School teachers."

VANUATU RELIGION IN A COMPARATIVE LIGHT

Anthropologists and historians of religion use the term "syncretism" to describe the remarkable blending of indigenous animist religions with monotheistic ones. Catholicism in vodun-practicing Haiti and elsewhere in Latin America, Protestantism and Catholicism in East and Central Africa, and Islam throughout West Africa provide comparative examples of the accommodation between native and imported religion. The melding of *kastom* and Christianity in Vanuatu has imparted a theoretical richness to these other cases by adding to the phenomenon of religious syncretism the political perspective of nation building. Nonconformist religious movements, such as Nagriamel and the John Frum cargo cult, simultaneously erected new political boundaries while blurring theological ones.

It is ironic that while the mental political boundaries introduced during condocolonialism are diminishing, new religious boundaries are arising in their wake. Although the traditional Protestant–Catholic divide is far from bridged, the mainstream churches, as represented by the VCC, are closing ranks against the burgeoning of minoritarian, evangelical, and "upstart" sects. It is in this sense that the situation in Vanuatu

resembles that of the Middle East, where leaders of previously antagonistic religious traditions are forging common ground in a parallel response to fundamentalism.[41] Vanuatu demonstrates how some of the
most rigid of mental boundaries—in this case, religious ones—can be
transcended not only in the name of spirituality but also for the sake of
nationality, for *raison d'état* as well as *gloria Dei*.

Language, Education, and National Identity

The classroom looked as if a tornado had recently paid a call. Large holes yawned from the ceiling. Windows were broken. A puddle of rainwater occupied part of the floor. Several desks were broken and makeshift benches only barely elevated the occupant above the ground.

Textbooks were streaked with watermarks. They carried a faint whiff of mold. One storeroom had been converted into a bachelor teacher's living quarters. His married colleagues lived in cramped, thatched huts on the school grounds.

In a group interview the three teachers for this Francophone primary school on an outer island revealed that the devastation I was witnessing had actually occurred years before, with Cyclone Uma. Yet the government, they went on, cared little for French education in the country and therefore rehabilitated English medium schools instead. Such neglect was reflected not only in disaster relief, they claimed, but was a standing policy of English-speaking government ministers.

"How do you go on?" I asked, referring to the deplorable working, living, and political conditions under which these colleagues labored. "How can Francophonie be maintained under such circumstances?"

Confronted by this implausible question, the schoolteachers shrugged and laughed in recognizable, Melanesian fashion. "We just do our best to muddle through," the most junior of the three finally responded. "We still feel that, despite the difficulties and hardships involved, we need to keep Francophonie alive. *Il faut se débrouiller.*"

This vignette, reconstructed from an actual school visit on Tanna island in 1991, illustrates how closely language can be linked to politics. Although by constitution French is an official language on the same par as English, Francophone ni-Vanuatu had reason to believe that in the decade following the nation's independence in 1980 the government in fact pursued a discriminatory policy to reduce, if not eradicate, French influence (political, cultural, linguistic) in the nation. Throughout the educational system, from local community to school district, classical fault lines resurfaced along rival, if not antagonistic, linguistic lines. Unification did not eliminate competition between French- and English-medium schools; it merely transformed it from an intersystemic rivalry to an intrasystemic one. In Vanuatu, schools were the battlefield and primary schools the front lines.

The allure of nationalism is inextricably bound up with the politics of language. Long before the political scientist Karl Deutsch claimed in the 1950s that communication networks are at the heart of nationalist bonding[1]—that nation building consists of deepening and intensifying the communicative interaction of people within a given set of political boundaries beyond those prevailing internationally—nineteenth-century philosopher Johann Herder identified language as the driving emotional and intellectual force behind nationalism. Linguist Joshua Fishman also locates the power of language in its capacity to provide links both with a people's "glorious past" and with its authenticity, and points to the need for language planning to rationalize the process,[2] particularly in bilingual societies.[3] Brian Weinstein investigates the consequences of actual language planning (which he defines as "a government authorized, long term sustained and conscious effort to alter a language itself or to change a language's functions in a society for the purpose of solving communication problems"),[4] in a worldwide survey that highlights the politics of language.[5] James Jacob and William Beer advance a theory of linguistic mobilization that explains language conflict in terms of perceived or relative inequality among linguistic minorities in their social status, economic rewards, and political power.[6] Concentrating on Africa (though using India as a model), David Laitin presents the paradigm of "language repertoire": "the set of languages that a citizen must know in order to take advantage of . . . occupational mobility and middle-class urban opportunities . . . in his or her own country."[7] All of these studies are pertinent to disaggregating the complex interplay between language and politics in Vanuatu.

Studies of ethnicity acknowledge the degree to which language is critical in imparting identity. Yet it is not necessarily the use of a distinctive language which creates a collective sense of self; mere identification with a tongue different from that used by the majority may provide the requisite sense of group difference. "The language which gives a person his or her social identity . . . may be just a label the person uses to form an association with a felt ethnicity."[8] Thus, Italian-Americans do not generally speak Italian, nor is Navaho any longer spoken by most persons who identify themselves as Navaho.

In Vanuatu a similar process is at work, minus the ethnic factor. Most so-called Anglophones speak no English, just as Francophones do not necessarily speak French. It is their identification to a group linked, however tenuously, to those two languages which long provided a sense of collective belonging. That neither English nor French is indigenous to any ni-Vanuatu culture has enormous theoretical implications. Here, language identification constitutes a nonethnic identity marker. The experience of Vanuatu highlights the transformational power of language, *independent of ethnicity*, to crystallize group identity.

GENERAL TRENDS IN VANUATU EDUCATION AND LITERACY

According to data derived from the 1989 census, 76.8 percent of ni-Vanuatu aged six years and older had received some formal education. Of these, approximately two-thirds (67 percent) were educated in English and somewhat less than one-third (29 percent) were educated in French. Taken at face value, this would mean that a little more than half of ni-Vanuatu could qualify, linguistically, as Anglophones and between one-quarter and one-fifth as Francophones. But asked whether they could actually speak either of these languages, only 39.1 percent of ni-Vanuatu claimed to speak English and 19.4 percent French (see Table 4). This gap between those *schooled* in a language and those *actually speaking* should be noted: a 15 percent spread for putative Anglophones but only 4 percent for Francophones. Given that a higher proportion of English-schooled ni-Vanuatu were awarded primary school certificates or higher than were French-schooled ones (38 percent compared to 34 percent), and that 48 percent of the former who achieved only primary certificates did so within six years, as opposed to 33 percent for the latter, it would appear that Francophone schooling has indeed been more rigorous and its standards higher, at least as measured by oral mastery of the target language.[9]

But even the lower figures indicating that well over half (58 percent) of ni-Vanuatu can speak either English or French should be suspect for anyone who has traveled throughout the archipelago. Currently enrolled primary and secondary school pupils alone constitute nearly one-quarter of all ni-Vanuatu above the age of five (1989 census figures). Yet the ability of schoolchildren to converse with any proficiency in English or French is highly variable and, especially among primary schoolchildren (70 percent of the student total), often close to nil. Even more problematic is the case of primary school graduates and leavers in

Table 4 Percentage of Ni-Vanuatu by Schooling and Language

	English Educated	English Speaking	French Educated	French Speaking
Rural	50.3%	34.9%	20.4%	15.9%
Urban	57.3%	57.5%	31.6%	34.9%
Total	51.7%	39.1%	22.3%	19.4%

Source: Compiled from data in tables B4, B59 and B61 of the *Vanuatu National Population Census 1989*. Percentages of English- and French-speakers include non-ni-Vanuatu residents who also speak Bislama and exclude bilingual English-French speakers (4.8%). Table covers population six years and over.

the outer islands who, lacking occasion to practice their school-learned language, may be unaware or reluctant to admit that they have lost their ability to speak it. My own estimate of true speakers of either French or English is somewhere between 10 and 20 percent, with the higher end inversely correlated with level of fluency.

A geographical analysis shows some linguistic concentration within an overall mixed distribution of language. Ni-Vanuatu Francophones are everywhere a minority, though their percentage (when calculated in terms of formal education in French) ranges from a high of 36.5 percent on Pentecost to a low of 11.2 percent on Epi (see Table 5). Education within both Francophone and Anglophone systems has been higher in the towns. Sixty-four percent of ni-Vanuatu in both Port Vila and Luganville (Santo town) have been schooled in English. Forty percent of ni-Vanuatu in the capital were educated as Francophones, and in Luganville 36 percent.

There do not appear to be any language-linked correlations by gender. While male ni-Vanuatu are slightly more likely than females to have had some formal schooling (83 percent versus 78 percent), there is no significant difference in the proportion of females educated within Anglophone as opposed to Francophone systems: 46.5 percent of the Anglophone-schooled are female, 47.4 percent of the Francophone-schooled are. In either language, rural females are the least educated category: 74.6 percent as opposed to 93.2 percent for urban females and 94.3 percent for urban males.

FOCUS ON FRANCOPHONIE

Francophonie is a cause: the desire to partake of and promote French language and culture for its intrinsic value. If one could speak of "An-

Table 5 Distribution of Francophones and Anglophones by Island/LGR

| | Formally Educated Ni-Vanuatu 6 Yrs+ 1989 | | Claim to Speak All Residents 1989 | |
	F	A	F	A
Pentecost	36.5%	57.4%	16.7%	28.6%
Malakula	35.5%	61.5%	23.2%	34.2%
TAFEA (Tanna, Aneityum, Futuna, Erromango, Aniwa)	32.1%	63.7%	10.3%	22.3%
Ambrym	30.0%	64.1%	22.2%	41.3%
Santo/Malo	28.7%	69.4%	12.9%	27.3%
Efate	26.8%	68.1%	25.6%	56.2%
Tongoa/Shepherds	19.9%	69.8%	17.0%	45.3%
Paama	17.9%	66.4%	15.3%	40.8%
Ambae/Maewo	14.4%	83.8%	9.5%	44.0%
Banks/Torres	14.0%	82.3%	8.9%	39.6%
Epi	11.2%	86.6%	9.3%	44.3%

Source: Compiled from data in tables B4, B59 and B61 of the *Vanuatu National Population Census 1989*.

glophonie," it would merely be a choice of or facility for the English language, driven more by expedience and convenience than by a sense of mission. Given the minority status of Francophonie in Vanuatu, it is worthwhile to focus on its status within the educational system.

Except for a sporadic rise in 1983, the proportion of Francophone pupils in primary schools steadily declined in the first decade after independence. The 1990 share, 38 percent, was precisely what it had been twenty years prior (see Table 6 and Figure 1).

Officials in the Ministry of Education denied that such drop-offs were a result of linguistic favoritism.[10] In the pre-1992 period, however, the popular perception that the government favored Anglophones was a drag on Francophone enrollments, and this in turn justified governmental disinvestment in Francophone schools. The end result was creeping Anglicization.

In as small an island-nation as Vanuatu, the impact is most dramatically seen at the level of local village schools. Records from the Francophone primary school of Wonesky on Mota Lava in the Banks group, for instance, reflect a 1975–1978 average range of enrollment of 150 to 160 pupils. Between 1981 and 1985, enrollment plummeted from 100 to 35 pupils. In 1986, Wonesky was forced to close its boarding facilities. The neighboring Anglophone school of Telhei was the chief

Table 6 Primary School Enrollments in the New Hebrides-Vanuatu

Year	Francophone #	%	Anglophone #	%	Total #
1971*	7,037	37.0	11,972	63.0	19,009
1972	7,190	39.1	11,211	60.9	18,401
1973	7,472	40.3	11,050	59.7	18,522
1974	8,234	42.6	11,081	57.4	19,315
1975	9,196	44.8	11,315	55.2	20,511
1976	9,104	45.3	10,987	54.7	20,091
1977	10,171	46.6	11,634	53.4	21,805
1978	10,147	48.3	10,870	51.7	21,017
1979	10,655	48.9	11,149	51.1	21,804
1980**	10,802	48.9	11,303	51.1	22,105
1981	9,931	44.8	12,224	55.2	22,155
1982	9,722	42.8	12,990	57.2	22,712
1983	9,603	45.0	11,748	55.0	21,351
1984	9,816	43.6	12,691	56.4	22,507
1985	9,294	41.4	13,136	58.6	22,430
1986	9,831	41.2	14,025	58.8	23,856
1987	9,173	38.1	14,887	61.9	24,060
1988	9,448	38.4	15,186	61.6	24,634
1989	9,374	37.5	15,626	62.5	25,000
1990	9,407	38.4	15,064	61.6	24,471
1991	9,400	37.7	15,552	62.3	24,952

Source: Compiled from data provided by the Ministry of Education, Port Vila.
* Data for 1971 from April 1976 Monthly Report of *Résidence de France*.
** Independence on July 30.

beneficiary: Its enrollment rose from 140–150 in 1980 to nearly 200 in 1991. In 1991, Wonesky's two remaining teachers taught 32 youngsters in three classes and saw protecting their school's supplies from being "pinched" by Telhei as a major challenge. On the nearby island of Vanua Lava, the statistics at the Arep Francophone school were also stark: In 1977 enrollments stood at 206; in 1991 they were down to 50. With Francophone enrollments in certain locations dropping off so precipitously, many French-medium classes were closed outright.

It is at the secondary school level that the politics of education is at its touchiest. Unlike primary school, for which entry is very much a matter of free choice, competition for entry to secondary school is keen. In the postindependence decade, thanks to British, Australian, and New Zealand aid, English-medium secondary schools mushroomed. In 1986 alone the total number of secondary schools doubled from ten (four Francophone, six Anglophone) to twenty. Seven of the ten new schools were purely Anglophone; two of the remaining three (Isangel on Tanna

Table 7 Secondary Schools in Vanuatu, 1991, by Level, Language, and Sponsorship

| | Francophone | | Anglophone | | | |
	Junior	Senior	Junior	Senior	Mixed	Subtotal
Government		2	5	2	3	12
Catholic	1	1				2
Anglican			2			2
Presbyterian			1			1
Seventh Day Adventist			1			1
Church of Christ			1			1
Protestant		1				1
Subtotal	1	4	10	2	3	20
Total		5		12	3	20

and Rensarie on Malakula) were mixed Anglophone-Francophone. Overall, the breakdown was twelve Anglophone secondary schools to five Francophone ones, with three secondary schools maintaining dual-track systems (see Table 7).

Given the paucity of comparable statistical data, it is difficult to compare the Francophone and Anglophone systems in a quantitative way. About the only such published data is an analysis of the 1985 results of the primary-leaving exam performance by the School Location Planning Team.[11] Even such results must be used carefully. Score results broken down by medium of instruction and region were provided for math and language (French for Francophones, English for Anglophones). Francophones had a higher pass rate than Anglophones in nine of the eleven administrative regions into which the country was then divided. The average difference for the regions as a whole (not weighted by actual numbers of students) for these nine regions was 14 percent; factoring in the two regions in which Anglophones outscored Francophones, the Francophone advantage was 10 percent.

As measured, in eight of the eleven regions Francophones performed higher in French than Anglophones did in English. The average difference was 22 percent and, weighted with all eleven regions, 14 percent. In light of the consensus on both sides of the language fence that French is harder to master than English, these results are all the more striking. Although Francophone primary students outperform their Anglophone counterparts in final examinations, on account of the limited places for Francophone students relatively fewer of them have gone on to secondary school. In the same year for which examination results were analyzed (1985), in eight of the regions the percentage of Anglophones going on to secondary school exceeded that of Francophones. As a result, one informant on the island of Tongoa told me, Francophones who fail entry into secondary school are coopted into Anglophone schools. Another informant from the same island claimed that parents, aware of the greater competition for Francophone secondary schooling, began to prefer the Anglophone track.

Independence brought the diverse schools under the wing of the Vanuatu Ministry of Education, but to different degrees. In 1980 identical agreements were signed between the new republic and both the Roman Catholic and Anglican churches of Vanuatu. According to the agreement, the government of Vanuatu, "[b]earing in mind the nature of religious education provided in [them] . . . acknowledges the need to maintain and develop Roman Catholic (and Anglican) Schools at all levels" (chap. I, art. 1). Though granted autonomy in terms of religious education, these religious systems would be subject to ministerial regulations, supervision, and confirmation of personnel postings.

After 1990 the role of the Catholic Education Service (DEC) in maintaining Francophonie in Vanuatu became all the more crucial. From the mid-1970s until independence, French government (secular) schools accounted for over half of the Francophone primary school enrollments.[12] A decade after independence, 54 percent of young Vanuatu became Francophone through Catholic schools. (Another 6 percent studied in Protestant parochial schools.) This does not mean that only Catholics were trained to become Francophone: Several factors could induce non-Catholic parents to send their children to DEC schools. The Lolopuépué school on North Ambae, for instance, has Anglican, Church of Christ, and Seventh-Day Adventist children along with Catholic ones. But it is safe to say that the majority of pupils in DEC schools are Catholic. As a religiolinguistic minority, alumni of the Catholic Mission system have come to constitute an informal fraternity. Likewise, the ties between Anglican and Presbyterian education and the government intensified. Before independence, British government services schooled only about 4 percent of young New Hebrideans who were studying in English: The bulk were educated in missionary schools.[13] Today, virtually all ni-Vanuatu studying as Anglophones do so through government schools as a result of the smooth and uncontested transfer to the Ministry of Education (see Table 8).

Table 8 Primary School Systems, 1991

	No. Schools	No. and Percent of Pupils	
Government Anglophone	166	15,552	(62%)
Government Francophone	49	3,835	(15%)
Catholic Mission	39	4,993	(20%)
Francophone Protestant	13	572	(4%)
Total	267	24,952	(100%)

Source: Planning and Implementation Unit, Ministry of Education, Port Vila, Vanuatu.

RATIONAL LANGUAGE CHOICE

Rational choice and moral economy literature for developing societies has focused on the agricultural and food production dimension to the peasant's apparent conservatism. James Scott explains risk-averse behavior among Indochinese farmers in terms of the safety-first principle: "subsistence-oriented peasants typically prefer to avoid economic disaster rather than take risks to maximize their average income."[14] Samuel Popkin applies investment logic and individual decision-making theory, also in Indochina (Vietnam), to elaborate "an expanded conception of the role of the village in peasant economic life."[15] However much these studies explain in terms of economic thinking on the subsistence producer level, the moral-economy and rational-peasant literature underestimates certain kinds of political calculations that peasants may also make. Politics is presented as a transcendent realm or structural framework within which peasants make microeconomic decisions; but the peasants are not seen to make explicitly political calculations in their investment choices. The case of Vanuatu illustrates how adept self-subsistence cultivators can be at making, and acting on, their own political risk analyses for the purposes of maximizing economic gain *and* security.

Rather than categorically rejecting one linguistic camp for the other, many ni-Vanuatu parents made the much shrewder decision of spreading their risks. As education is the single most important economic investment families in developing countries can make, one might characterize this strategy of ni-Vanuatu parents as "educational portfolio diversification": Some children would be sent to French-medium schools while their brothers or sisters would be enrolled in English-medium ones. This did not only occur in the case of "mixed" Anglo-Franco marriages, as when Wuro-Fali couples married.[16] Confounding crude analyses of religiolinguistic determinism, ni-Vanuatu parents in both the outer islands and the towns reasoned that such a strategy guaranteed that some members of the family would be well positioned whatever direction electoral politics might take. This politically savvy but linguistically chancy calculation proved to be most successful twelve years after independence, when the helm of state did revert to a Francophone-led government. Although no statistics exist to document the frequency of this strategy of linguistic sibling-splitting, it was reported to me repeatedly throughout the archipelago and is common knowledge to long-term observers of the Vanuatu scene.

One of the most consistent and unexpected findings in my first set of interviews before the changeover to a Francophone-led government was the overwhelming support for the retention of French as an official language and language of instruction. Regardless of language affiliation, island of origin, partisan allegiance, religious faith, and socioeconomic class, ni-Vanuatu supported the continuation of a dual linguistic track in Vanuatu education. Given the postindependence dominance of Anglophone parties still prevailing, such sentiment represented an indirect endorsement of Francophonie (as narrowly conceived) even among the Anglophone population. This was not merely a question of enjoying a familial edge based on domestic electoral calculations: Informants invoked national interests, such as expanded employment possibilities for ni-Vanuatu both abroad (i.e., in other Francophone countries) and at home (i.e., with French companies inside Vanuatu); a more diverse tourism industry (more visitors from France and other French-speaking nations); and the exploitation of (bilingual) Vanuatu as an international conference or diplomatic center. (Anglophone) Vanua'aku Pati members cited such reasons as readily as (Francophone) UMP partisans did. Those of the UMP also defended Francophonie in terms of the cultural horizons opened to ni-Vanuatu by virtue of their exposure to French language, culture, literature, and civilization. Such grass-roots support for bilingualism should be encouraging to the Vanuatu government (particularly a Francophone-led one), for it is the underpinning of much of its platform. Indeed, so popular is this idea that in government circles, the very expression "Francophonie" is considered uncouth and is on the road to becoming taboo. The politically correct term to acknowledge the presence of French-speakers in Vanuatu is "bilingualism."

Although there is popular sentiment for retaining some form of French-language instruction in Vanuatu (to be sure, divested of its politically charged aspects), it overlooks two counter realities: creeping Anglicization (regional and international) and the real meaning of "bilingualism."

UNIFICATION AND BILINGUALISM

As used in the Vanuatu context, the term "bilingualism" is misleading, for the retention of French does not in and of itself make for a bilingual people there. This assertion is irrespective of the critical role that Bislama plays in Vanuatu society and the importance of indigenous Melanesian languages. To the extent that there are both French- and English-speakers, on an aggregate, national level one may arguably regard Vanuatu as bilingual. But *as individuals* few ni-Vanuatu are: only 5 percent of the population (according to the 1989 census) claim to speak both English and French, and one can assume wide discrepancies in degree of language mastery among those who do. Vanuatu is not bilingual in the sense of promoting dual competency among its citizens, as is the case, for example, in Canada or on the Indian Ocean island of Mauritius, where all pupils are exposed to English as the main medium of instruction but also learn French from early primary school. As with ni-Vanuatu, few Mauritians speak either language studied in school as a maternal tongue, and virtually all speak a slave-based lingua franca (Kreol) that is not taught in the schools.[17] Despite the persistence of a Franco-Mauritian elite, the highly pluralistic population, which includes many Asian immigrant groups, is not divided along Anglophone-Francophone lines.

Those few ni-Vanuatu who are truly bilingual are usually Francophones who have gone to Australia, New Zealand, the Solomons, Fiji, or New Guinea for higher education. Not even the offspring of "mixed" Melanesian Francophone-Anglophone marriages necessarily become bilingual. In terms of official-language use, it is more accurate to view Vanuatu as linguistically dualistic than as truly bilingual.

Since independence the educational policy in Vanuatu has been one of unification: to create out of two systems of education, British and French, a single curriculum with common methods of evaluation but taught in separate language tracks. For Francophones this has meant shifting from a twelve-year program (beginning with *Cours Préparatoire* and culminating in *Terminale,* counting "down" through *sixième, cinquième, quatrième,* etc.) to a thirteen-year program, from grade 1 to grade 13. Kindergarten, which prior to independence was available to Francophone children, is not provided by the Vanuatu Ministry of Edu-

Language amalgamation headquarters.

cation at all. Primary school in Vanuatu is a six-year sequence (not five, as in France), followed by four years of lower secondary school (grades 7–10) and then three years of upper secondary (11–13). At the end of primary, lower secondary, and upper secondary school, examinations are taken to determine eligibility for continuing education. University coursework is offered at the Vila branch of the University of the South Pacific (USP). Ni-Vanuatu university students (usually Anglophone) may easily transfer to USP campuses in Fiji and Papua New Guinea.

A vocational track following primary school is also available. Two years of vocational training qualify students for entrance into the Vanuatu National Institute of Technology (INTV), of three years' duration. INTV, founded as a French vocational school *(collège d'enseignement technique)* in 1970, fell under the Vanuatu Ministry of Education in 1980 and continued to cater mainly to Francophone students, who constituted 70–85 percent of the student body. In 1991, though 17 out of 22 teachers (and 233 out of 284 students) were Francophone, a parallel English-French system of teaching was introduced. Expectations were of achieving Francophone-Anglophone intake parity within a few years. For Francophone students, the DEC also maintains a vocational school at St. Michel on Santo.

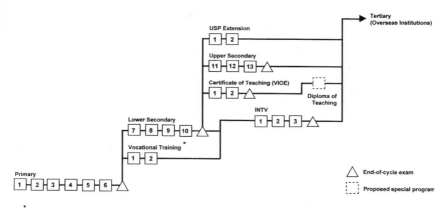

Figure 3. Vanuatu Educational System
Source: World Bank, Primary and Secondary Education Project (Vanuatu),
c. 1991

Students who prefer a teaching career on the primary level may
enter the Vanuatu Institute of Education (VIOE, the early Kawenu College) after lower secondary school, to which French teacher-training
classes were moved in 1981. This teacher-training is a two-year program
culminating in a Certificate of Teaching.

One decade after independence, unification of the primary school
curricula had still not been completed, despite progress made by the Curriculum Development Centre (CDC) at Malapoa College. Only three subjects out of twelve (health, nutrition, agriculture) had identical curricula.

Curricular unification at the secondary school level has proceeded
more smoothly. Thanks largely to the support of New Zealand, the Curriculum Development Center has designed textbooks and teacher guides
for a unified dual language ("double stream") program. Francophone and
Anglophone students study the same subjects at the same time and, in
principle, in the same way (though of course Francophones study English
as a foreign language and vice versa). End-of-cycle examinations are also,
despite the language difference, identical. One consequence of unification
at the secondary level is that students in the French-language track no
longer take the French national baccalaureate exam. Though few Francophones ever successfully pursued this option—in 1986 only two of
Vanuatu's 161 postsecondary students did so as Francophones[18]—the
suppression of the "bac" option in Vanuatu secondary schools closed this
major avenue to higher education in the Francophone world. In response,

a preparatory program for Francophone secondary graduates was set up at the University of the South Pacific branch in Port Vila. Those who successfully complete the program then transfer to the Université Française du Pacifique (UFP), established in New Caledonia in the 1980s. UFP degrees are recognized by the Vanuatu government.

Unification of curriculum has alienated many of the Francophone secondary school teachers. They maintain that the effort to accommodate weaker Anglophone educational standards has lowered quality: the Francophone system has been held back so that the Anglophone one can catch up, goes one refrain. Francophone teachers also contend that "unified" pedagogy and testing (which now include, for instance, multiple-choice exams) promote the "Anglo-Saxon" model at the expense of the Francophone system. They also bristle at the elimination of *redoublage,* whereby weaker students repeat classes, in favor of a budget-motivated automatic promotion to the next class. Teachers in French-medium high schools resent having to adopt what is, in their view, an inferior methodology. "Unification" represents much less of a change for Anglophone teachers and, consequently, they voice no opposition to it.[19]

The *administrative* union or amalgamation of primary schools had been effectuated, though, with contradictory results.

Amalgamation includes programs to increase interaction and understanding between the two linguistic camps. English and French instructors may be exchanged one hour a week to teach their respective languages. Pupils of each language learn to sing songs from the other, and they may play sports together once a week. But the degree of enthusiasm for and cooperation in such activities varies considerably from faculty to faculty and community to community. When aggravated by the intrusion of factional cleavages already dividing the local community, such school mergers become positively debilitating. Francophones dramatically experienced creeping Anglicization at the local level with the literal takeover and occupation of formerly French school buildings in the community for Anglophone pupils and classes.

Conflict between Fali and Wuro villages in West Ambrym provides an example. Fali, with its Francophone Catholic primary school, had been under government pressure to merge with Wuro, a neighboring Anglophone school. As of 1991 the Fali headmaster had successfully resisted the proposed merger, partially for fear that the better-quality French-built facilities would be taken over by the Anglophone section. Combining Anglophone and Francophone schools would also encourage the use of Bislama, according to the Fali school committee, a process that would undermine the facility to manipulate French. On Tongoa, where the Kutundaula French-medium school had been merged with the Naworaone English-medium one, the weekly joint sports and agriculture programs have indeed increased Bislama usage among children.

Another scenario developed at Itakoma, also on the island of Tongoa. There, in the Shepherd group a year after independence, the parents requested an Anglophone school to supplement the French-built one. When the Anglophone educational adviser could not comply, the villagers built their own hut to serve as a kindergarten. The number of children sent for Anglophone schooling rapidly increased and the number of Francophone pupils declined. In 1983, the Ministry of Education handed the French-built school building over to the Anglophone school.

Vilakalaka represents a variation on this theme. In the 1960s the French built a primary school in this small village on the western side of Ambae. When Nagriamel was at its peak the Francophone school was very popular. But following independence, and particularly with Nagriamel's decline, some Vilakalaka parents strongly believed that the prospects for jobs and continuing education scholarships had become greater for those villagers schooled in English. The introduction of school fees also removed an incentive for some families to educate their children locally. Consequently, a number of parents began to send some of their children to Anglophone schools elsewhere on the island. But the village as a whole remained loyal to the Francophone camp.

In 1986 the Vanuatu government decided to establish an Anglophone high school, Nivutiriki Junior Secondary, in the village. So as to reduce personnel redundancy, the headmaster of the new secondary school was supposed to administer the preexisting primary school as well. And as a cost-containment measure, the secondary school was to use the primary school classrooms that declining Francophone enrollments had emptied. Vilakalaka's ardent Francophones were outraged and resisted, as they saw it, this Anglophone occupation. The headmaster of Nivutiriki Junior Secondary School never managed to wrest control of the primary school. Nor did the local populace allow the secondary school to use the empty classrooms. The new secondary school was forced to acquire its own building, and a prefabricated structure was erected.

With the spatial separation of the Anglophone and Francophone schools established (though theoretically Vilakalaka-Nivutiriki remained a single educational institution), enmity between the two camps in the small village was contained. A compromise was reached that provided for joint use of the dining room and dormitory facilities. But as of 1991

one small classroom remained empty, rustic testament to the internalized, conflictual, condocolonial legacy that had yet to be fully resolved.

Merging of neighboring French- and British-built schools (a typical
Condominium legacy) under the single leadership of an Anglophone headmaster was a common scenario. Depending on the personalities involved,
the tension between headmaster and Francophone staff could be high.
("Amalgamation is very fragile," reported one schoolteacher in the Banks.
"The French won't let the English dominate them.") Teachers at Unmet,
Malakula, convey similar sentiments: "In meetings with Anglophone colleagues in training sessions, Francophones grasp what is being said more
quickly. The Anglophones have to keep on asking questions before they
catch on. It's boring for us." Such sentiments were not confined to school
administration. Francophones who managed to remain in other branches
of government service often viewed themselves as serving under hierarchi-
cally superior but intellectually inferior Anglophone administrators. Anglophone bosses accordingly felt inadequate and hostile toward Francophone colleagues. It was not much easier for the rare Francophone in a
supervisory capacity over Anglophones: "After independence there was a
need to unify the administrative systems. It was rather difficult [for the
Anglophones] to accept a Francophone director. They tried everything to
take my place but their level of education was too low. Really, to compose
an administrative letter, they would take hours, three hours!"

At least initially, the two-track language system merely reinforced
the linguistically dualistic nature of society rather than creating a truly
bilingual people. Low government revenues have also aggravated the
linguistic situation, because each linguistic camp perceives that the other
is receiving an unfair share of scarce educational resources. This was
particularly the case in the period 1980–1992, when Francophone educators were convinced that Anglophone education was being favored in
budgetary allocations. For example, recalling the vignette with which I
began this chapter, Francophone educators were convinced that cyclone
relief went first to Anglophone schools, and only then (if at all) to Francophone ones. Anglophones, for their part, justified any favoritism for
English-medium schools on the grounds that this only balanced the pro-
Francophone bias of the preindependence decade. Efforts to promote
Francophone education in the years following the UMP victory were
similarly defended as balancing the pro-Anglophone tilt of the Lini era.
Such pendulum swinging in the name of righting historical wrong serves
to perpetuate this major legacy of Condominium rivalry.

Based on appointments at the level of local school districts, the system did appear to be politicized along linguistic lines. Right up to the rout of the VP in 1991, virtually all of the Regional Education Officers (REOs) who headed the education districts were Anglophones: Not all of them had been professional educators. Their second-in-command Francophone deputies were not alone in viewing this as a deliberate policy to buttress Anglophone hegemony and favor English language within the educational system. At least in one region, it was said that the REO and his deputy would have come to blows had they not been restrained by the janitors. Under such circumstances, interlinguistic collegiality within a unified education district administration had difficulty materializing.

School amalgamation was intended to help create an English-French bilingual school environment. In practice, however, it tends to diminish the role of each of these international languages in favor of a monolingual usage of Bislama. When ni-Vanuatu teachers from both language sections assemble for school meetings, they invariably communicate in Bislama; yet most schools generally prohibit students from using Bislama on school grounds during school hours. (In some schools, such as Arep in the Banks, students heard speaking it are placed in detention.) Minutes from the executive committee meeting of the Rensarie Junior Secondary School on Malakula illustrate some of the contradictions (translations are in brackets).

> Sipos yu raetem eni jenj long [lanwis Environment] wanem nao wan wea yu sapotem bigwan? [What major method do you suggest for improving the language environment in the school?]
>
> "Mi think se i moa gud blong aplyem wan strong rules long ol pikinini we oli stap tock strong long language mo bislama."
>
> [I think it preferable to apply strong rules against pupils who frequently speak indigenous language or Bislama.]
>
> "Mi happy long luk se English mo French language tufalla i kam antap big wan. French speaking pupils are beginning to speak English. English speaking pupils i sud mekem sem mak. Hem nao samting mi wantem luk mo supotem bigwan blong yumi every wan i promotem"
>
> [I am happy to observe that both English and French languages are being used more and more. English-speaking pupils should do the same as the French-speaking ones. This is something I wanted to see and support for all of us.]

"Yes mi wantem spos yumi gat wan "LANGUAGE EXCHANGE" between anglophone students mo francophone students. Aim blong hem hemi blong promotem "BILINGUALISM" insaed long RJSS."

[Yes, I am in favor of a language exchange between Anglophone and Francophone students for the purposes of promoting bilingualism inside the high school.]

"Mi think se igud blong stopem lanwis mo bislama long skul wantaem."

[I think we ought right away to forbid the use of indigenous languages and Bislama at the school.]

Unification at the Vanuatu Teacher's College in Vila, the premier institution for the training of both primary school and junior secondary level teachers, has also had a similar result: Anglophone and Francophone teachers-in-training communicate with each other in Bislama. This also tends to increase the use of Bislama *within* language camps. Francophone teachers, much more than Anglophone ones, express unhappiness with having to conduct official business in what they still consider an inferior, pidgin version of English. Differences in approach toward the use of Bislama are apparent in the policies of Malapoa College and the Lycée Bougainville: Whereas the latter prohibits Bislama, the former "encourages" the use of English.

To create a unified wage scale, salaries of Anglophone teachers were significantly raised after independence. Francophone teachers' earnings, which initially took a large cut, have increased much more slowly. Scholarship opportunities for postgraduate training in nearby Anglophone countries (Australia, New Zealand, Fiji, Papua New Guinea) are also much greater than they are in Francophone ones (restricted, essentially, to New Caledonia). It is not difficult to see why the morale of Francophone ni-Vanuatu teachers and high-performing students plummeted in the first decade of independence.

BIFURCATION IN PRINT

Vanuatu has only one regular news publication, the government-produced weekly *Vanuatu Weekly-Hebdomadaire*. Although the newspaper is trilingual, in that articles appear in Bislama as well as English and French, I shall concentrate on the English and French sections of the paper to demonstrate the pitfalls and misleading nature of official bilingualism.

One might reasonably assume that a national newspaper in a bilingual country would carry identical articles in both languages; in other words, the same stories in translation. In fact, English and French articles regularly offer different versions of the same events. Often, some stories are reported in one language and not the other.

For example, issue number 400 of August 1, 1992, headlined, in English, the independence anniversary address of the newly appointed prime minister, Maxime Carlot Korman ("Gov't Brings Back Economic Situation in 7 Months"). There was no English-language account of the prime minister's speech, however, only articles in French and in Bislama. By the same token, the lead story on July 18, 1992 (no. 399), carried as its headline and major story, in English, the imminent introduction of television to the country, despite pending parliamentary legislation on the same. There was no account in French of this item. (In contrast, there was no English-language mention of a major French-language story in that same issue—Bastille Day celebrations hosted by the French chargé d'affaires).

Compare two versions of the same lead story that did appear a year later, on July 24, 1993 (no. 451). The two appeared side by side; the French version is translated into English.

English Version	French Version
KORMAN SECURES ANOTHER VT 740 M	A VISIT THAT BRINGS MUCH TO VANUATU
The government head Prime Minister Maxime Carlot Korman has signed an agreement with the European Economic Community allowing Vanuatu to obtain VT 740,000,000 from the Community.	*After having been in Paris, Prime Minister Carlot was in Brussels this week where he signed an important agreement with the authorities of the European Economic Community.*
According to a press statement, STABEX Funds to Vanuatu ceased in 1989.	The prime minister, Maxime Carlot Korman, returned to the country on Friday, 23 July, after two weeks of official visits overseas. Mr. Korman traveled to Paris at the invitation of the mayor of the French capital where he participated in celebrations for the fourteenth of July. Last week he signed a financial accord with French authorities
But after hard negotiations between the government and EC leaders Prime Mnsiter [sic] finally succeeded in persuading EC officials to release STABEX funds for 1988, 1989, 1990 and 1991.	
The funds secured will go	

towards these projects: Copra/Cacao prices; Animal Health Survey (to facilitate export); Agriculture research at Saraoutou; Constitution [*sic*] of new Sarakata bridge and Road construction on Ambae, South Pentecost, South Tanna and Lulep on Paamaa.

To mark the important event a party was hosted by Prime Minister Korman which saw prominent members of EC, ACP Secretariat and every ambassadors [*sic*] of Pacific countries and their staff.

During the function Mr Korman announced that Vanuatu will soon appoint an ambassador to Brussels.

Prime Minister who described the agreement as "a big success" appeals to the government and the people of Vanuatu to continue to work with EC to implement the projects and to finalise the Lome IV programme for an amount of VT 850 million to be issued begging [*sic*] 1994. The Union of Moderate Parties has expressed satisfaction over the mission headed by Prime Minister Korman.

estimated at 450 million vatus, which France will sign over to Vanuatu within the rubric of cooperation between the two countries. Moreover, a "Puma"-type helicopter of the French army will soon be placed at the disposition of the government of Vanuatu.

The head of the government of Vanuatu then went on to Brussels where he met with officials of the European Economic Commission (EEC), the secretary-general of the APC group, and ambassadors from nations of the Pacific, such as Papua New Guinea, Fiji, Western Samoa, and the Solomon Islands. Negotiations were begun among these officials to establish economic development projects in Vanuatu. With the EEC, Mr. Korman signed an agreement to release 740 million vatu for export stabilization funds (STABEX), which were again made available. During a reception he hosted and to which he invited the personalities he met, Mr. Korman announced that Vanuatu is on verge of naming an ambassador to Brussels. Regarding the agreement signed in Brussels, the prime minister asked the people of Vanuatu to work in close collaboration with the EEC so that the proposed projects can be realized as soon as possible and to take into consideration the program of the Lome IV convention, representing a sum of 850 million vatu already signed for and that will start at the beginning of next year.

Radio news accounts follow a similar pattern: Stories that are likely to interest Francophones in particular may not receive any coverage in English. Even when events are reported in both languages, significantly different versions commonly appear. As in the example above, a particular political slant, one emphasizing French relations and aid, may be present in the French-language article and absent from the English-language one. Disjunctures also appear in stories with no political content. Details may conflict or be simply absent from one language version compared to the other. With different sets of editors and journalists operating in English and French, there is no structural norm of uniformity of communication. The hypothesis that different languages condition different perceptions of the same reality requires no psychological basis for verification in Vanuatu: Journalistic "bilingualism" often results in factual contradiction.

One price of maintaining a dual official-language policy is the cost of official document translation. No attempts have been made to estimate the aggregate expenses associated with having French and English as the two languages of official business in Vanuatu. There is a budget for the Language Services Department, however, whose main task is to translate government documents (parliamentary minutes and legislative enactments). All translation is done in both French and English; usually, the direction of translation is from English into French. In 1991 the budget for the Language Services was 10.2 million vatu, or approximately U.S. $100,000; expatriate experts financed by their host governments dampened the true costs of the department, as reflected in the budget. Although Francophobes might criticize the need to translate documents into a language read by so few as a waste of sparse resources, defenders relativize the cost by pointing out that this represents little more than 2 percent of the overall central government recurrent expenditure. Manpower gaps are a major problem for the Language Services Unit, and the backlog in document translation is considerable.

Fortunately, most ni-Vanuatu get their information from the same Bislama language sources, reducing the contradictions in facts from which Vanuatu residents who rely only on official language sources often suffer. Indeed, the Bislama rumor mill is believed by many to be more reliable than official reportage in either the newspaper or on the radio. But for the ni-Vanuatu elite who do read and listen to English- or French-language news sources, linguistic dualism within the area of journalism, by presenting different versions of the same national reality to Anglophones and Francophones, unwittingly fosters mental boundaries.

CREEPING ANGLICIZATION

During the Condominium era, Francophonie's promoters had to defend themselves mainly from their Anglophone New Hebridean adversaries. Linguistic battles were in this sense domestic. The withdrawal of the two condominial powers and the conferral of independence have greatly increased Vanuatu's exposure to its broader regional environment. And this Pacific zone—dominated by Australia and New Zealand and reinforced by the Solomons, Fiji, and Papua New Guinea—is even more heavily tilted toward English-speakers than the New Hebrides alone were. A much more sophisticated transportation and telecommunication infrastructure has opened Vanuatu up to its Oceanic neighbors. Economic and diplomatic interventions have magnified the Anglophone influence in Vanuatu. To take an example from tourism, which has been a cornerstone of economic planning since independence, in 1986, 72 percent of holiday visitors hailed from English-speaking nations (particularly Australia); only 17 percent were from Francophone ones (mostly New Caledonia). Vanuatu's offshore banking center is also dominated by English-speaking firms.

Anglicization in Vanuatu is not only due to regional forces but to global ones as well. It is not in the Pacific alone that Francophonie is on the defensive; indeed, France has raised the menace to Francophonie on a worldwide level as an issue of highest priority.[20] Non-French Francophone individuals and organizations have also taken up the banner.[21] The saturation of the international video market with American products has been particularly high in developing nations that lack an indigenous commercial entertainment industry. In Vanuatu, to which television came only in the 1990s, video entertainment has had a particularly Anglicizing impact. Video boundaries—Anglophone cassettes are only viewable in black-and-white for French cassette players, and Francophone tapes cannot be played at all on Anglophone VCRs—are reminiscent of condocolonial technological divisions, such as differently pronged electrical outlets. In 1992 there were three Anglophone and two Francophone videotape rental shops.

Precisely to anticipate and counteract the disproportionate Anglophone influence of television, it was France which, as part of its foreign assistance package, set up TV Blong Vanuatu in 1992. Though the initial decision to permit (and to pay for) television was controversial—it did, after all, reverse a long-standing cultural policy—it has been instituted in such a way as to guarantee approximate parity between English- and French-language programming.[22]

The overall impact of international penetration, an inevitable consequence of decolonization, has been a progressive Anglicization among an already dominantly English-speaking population within an overwhelmingly Anglophone regional environment. Global trends toward cultural Americanization also extend into the hinterlands of Vanuatu.[23] Regardless of political will and popular sentiment in favor of Francophonie's retention, creeping regional and global Anglicization will always keep it on the defensive.

One of the ironic legacies of condominial rivalry is that, from a comparative financial perspective, Vanuatu is "overeducated" (see Table 9). The Anglo-Franco school race of the 1960s and 1970s bequeathed an overabundance of facilities and personnel that the present government is struggling to finance and to streamline, particularly at the primary level. (Geographical dispersal and small catchment areas also raise education costs.) This perspective has been vigorously advanced by the World Bank, whose soft-window loans to the Vanuatu government, cofinanced with Australian development assistance, have raised concerns among Francophones about an Anglophone recolonization in the guise of international donor assistance.

BISLAMA

Although condocolonial rivalries in education policy have continued since independence, Vanuatu has made great strides toward national unity through the promotion of Bislama, its national language. Bislama, long referred to as Pidgin English (or just plain pidgin), was born as a lingua franca among Melanesian indentured laborers in the plantations of Queensland, Australia in the mid-nineteenth century.[24] Though its vocabular foundation is a simplified English, its grammatical structure owes much to Melanesian syntax. Loanwords from French also pepper Bislama (or Bichelamar, as Francophones render it.)[25]

Preindependence Development

Denigrated as "a rough and inadequate plantation language, unworthy to communicate the word of God" acquisition of Bislama was nevertheless useful for both Melanesians and Europeans residing in the New Hebrides.[26] Probably on account of the politicolinguistic competition between French and British, however, pidgin was not used during the Condominium as a language of colonial administration to the extent that it was by the Australians in Papua New Guinea,[27] thereby never

Table 9 Comparative Education Costs in the Pacific

Country	Central Govt. Expenditure on Education as % of Total Govt. Expenditures	GNP per capita	Costs per Pupil in $ U.S.	
			Primary	Secondary
Vanuatu	24.0	880	232	950
Papua New Guinea	16.0	680	223	612
Solomon Islands	17.0	510	67	361
Indonesia	9.3	530	40	90
Philippines	16.0	580	50	280

Source: Compiled from data in Republic of Vanuat, *Second National Development Plan 1987-1991;* World Bank, *World Development Report 1987.*

achieving the level of prestige that it did in preindependence PNG. Though New Hebridean chiefs and other local leaders originally suspected that Bislama was a language of rebellion—for those who ran away to the plantations returned with both this new language and often a contumacious streak—utility overcame misgiving.

Publication of the New Testament in Bislama (1971–1980), a formal sign of its acceptance by the churches, did enhance both its scope and status.[28] By bringing together schoolchildren from various districts and islands in the 1960s and 1970s, the boarding schools set up by European authorities (particularly the French) also unwittingly promoted its expansion. Bislama became the single vehicle for nationwide communication among Melanesians, bridging both French–English and inter-Melanesian linguistic divides. It is not surprising that nationalist leaders, particularly those of the future (Anglophone) Vanua'aku Pati, should have made the promotion of a single national language, Bislama, a linchpin of their nationalist platform. Their use of Bislama for political purposes, in fact, greatly expanded its diffusion throughout the archipelago.

By using New Hebridean pidgin to promote Vanuatu independence, nationalist leaders subtly began to transform the basis of popular attachment to Bislama from mere instrumentality (qua communication) to sentimentality (qua nationalism).[29] "Moderate" (Francophone) opponents, in return, viewed Bislama politics as a strategy for eventual Anglicization and the complete eradication of Francophonie. However exaggerated their specific fears, Francophones correctly intuited some of the revolutionary implications of status language displacement: that it changes political identities, alters access patterns to resources, and replaces ensconced elites with new ones.[30]

Radio Vila, founded in 1966 by both the French and British residencies (not the Condominium per se), gave an unintended fillip to both Bislama and Vanuatu nationalism. Although Bislama was used no more than English or French, broadcasts in it were by far the most widely listened to. British and French alike used Bislama radio broadcasts to appeal to the opposing camp among the population—the overall winner being the language itself. In the aftermath to the election of 1975—the first ever electoral campaign in the New Hebrides—political parties crossed a politicotechnological threshold by appealing to the electorate directly over the airwaves.[31]

The distinction between Anglophone and Francophone versions of Bislama (dialectical differences in accent and vocabulary) has faded since the 1960s and 1970s. Familiarity with the Bislama of Radio Vanuatu has given rise to a certain uniformity in pronunciation and terminology. The Bislama of radio does not necessarily translate into a language of common understanding, however. We shall see how the earlier condocolonial division between Anglophone and Francophone Bislama has given way to another linguistic bifurcation based on Anglicization, education, and urbanization.

Bislama Today

Today both Francophone and Anglophone camps acknowledge the usefulness of Bislama as a vehicle for national unity. Its enshrinement in the Constitution, in fact, means that Vanuatu is one of only two countries in the world—the other is the Seychelles—to have elevated a pidgin language to the status of national language.

Between two-thirds and four-fifths of all ni-Vanuatu can now speak Bislama.[32] Elderly rural females report the lowest frequency of knowing Bislama; still, 60 percent of these women can speak it. Urban males between fifteen and fifty-nine years of age are the most Bislamaphone (94 percent). Although it is still rare to find individuals who are monolingual in Bislama (0.4 percent, according to the 1989 census), the rise in interisland marriages resulting in urban households will certainly create a new kind of ni-Vanuatu Melanesian, one whose mother tongue is Bislama and who knows no indigenous language. Already nearly 10 percent of ni-Vanuatu living in urban areas speak no Melanesian language,[33] and the percentage of monolingual Bislama speakers in Luganville is three times the national rate.

From a pedagogical perspective, the popularization and permeation of Bislama has blurred the distinction among Anglophones between "pidgin" and "proper" English. As Bislama becomes the language of choice, schoolchildren in English-medium schools suffer from a linguistic interference that impairs their ability to master standard English. Because French is several degrees removed from Bislama, Francophone pupils are not as vulnerable to this threat as their Anglophone counterparts. There is a real risk of widening gaps in educational performance, with Francophone pupils learning French much better than Anglophone ones do English.

Still, the spread of Bislama can also be inimical to the French language. One secondary school principal claims that French has deteriorated because the young now think in Bislama and translate into English. Thus, instead of the more grammatically correct "D'où viens-tu?" ("Where do you come from?") young Francophones, translating directly from the Bislama *Yu kam we*, will say "Tu viens d'où?" A number of educated Francophones remain skeptical about the intrinsic value of *bichelamar* as a civilized language. In interviews one Francophone schoolteacher called it *un charabia anglais*—an English gobbledygook— and another *l'anglais batârd*—bastard English.

For its part, Bislama is undermined by a lack of standardization and increasing Anglicization. Examples are legion of rural ni-Vanuatu shaking their heads over incomprehensible Vila Bislish—a kind of highbrow Bislama—as broadcast by Radio Vanuatu or printed in *Vanuatu Weekly-Hebdomadaire.* Without using these terms, Tryon and Charpentier imply that a form of diglossia (two different forms of the same language) is emerging in Vanuatu, dividing Low and High Pidgin speakers along country–town lines. Particularly insidious is the wholesale adoption of technical and abstract English words into Bislama, pidginized terms that remain meaningless for the majority of ni-Vanuatu. Tryon and Charpentier also warn of the fusion of Pidgin and standard English into a country-specific regional English, which would linguistically ghettoize Vanuatu from the Anglophone world.[34]

The above discussion points to a glaring absence of any substantive language planning policy in Vanuatu. While Bislama is enshrined as national language and Bislama, English, and French are official languages, English and French remain the sole media of instruction. Serious language planning in Vanuatu would consist of mechanisms to restrict the Anglicization of Bislama, codification of a single orthography (rather than disparate English, French, and idiosyncratic spellings), creation of an appropriate terminology for new technologies and concepts, and ensuring that Bislama be systematically utilized as the third official lan-

Boundary in Bislish.

guage: in short, language purification, language reform, lexical modernization, and language standardization.[35] The creation of a Bislama Language Board (the example of the Hausa Language Board of the old
Northern Nigeria comes to mind)[36] would represent an important step
in this regard.

A speculative, and admittedly controversial, line of inquiry concerns the psycholinguistic consequences of the creolization of Bislama.
Granting that Bislama "is located between the world of custom and that
of the whites . . . [it is] supra-cultural, belonging to no definite culture,"[37] might not its transformation from pidgin (a non-native lingua
franca) to creole (a foreign-derived first language) entail a loss for ni-
Vanuatu of both linguistic sophistication in addition to cultural (qua
Melanesian) specificity? Without totally embracing the Whorfian paradigm that culture is language and language controls culture, is it not
conceivable that the relative sparseness of the active Bislama lexicon[38] —
especially compared with that of vernacular languages—would constitute a loss in the ability to convey and perpetuate indigenous Melanesian
modes of thought? As Bislama evolves, its functionality will depend on
linguistic borrowings and adaptations. Further "Melanesianization" of
Bislama is unlikely, however; more probable will be its reliance on English (and, to a much lesser degree, French) loanwords.

VERNACULAR LANGUAGES

> "Language is like a door. It unlocks your opportunities to see what is actually behind the scene. When you go through a door to a house, you can find out what is inside—a table, chair, freezer, etc. For any particular country or island, language is the door to the customs and culture."
>
> —Chief Willie Bongmatur, President,
> National Council of Chiefs, interview

The phenomenal spread of Bislama, so important for national unity, is not without its problems. From a cultural perspective its diffusion has come more at the expense of indigenous languages than of European ones. (Joshua Fishman would cast this in terms of the conflict between unification of the nation-state and authentification of preindependence cultures.)[39] With its 113 local languages—and they are distinct languages, not mere dialects—Vanuatu claims the record for the highest number of languages per capita in the world (approximately one per thousand people).[40] Unfortunately, in Vanuatu as throughout the developing world, many indigenous languages with small numbers of speakers are threatened with extinction.

All of Vanuatu's indigenous languages belong to the Malayo-Polynesian or Australasian (Oceanian subdivision) family, which spans from Easter Island to Madagascar. This family includes South Pacific languages except for those of Papua New Guinea. But many of Vanuatu's languages are endangered for want of interlocutors: At last enumeration, 40 percent of them were estimated to have no more than two hundred speakers. Even the most widely spoken languages, those spoken on northeast Ambae and at Whitesands and Lenakel on Tanna, have little more than four thousand parleyers.[41]

The causes of national unity and developmental progress leave the protection of venerable, but vulnerable, languages far behind. As the debate over the appropriateness of teaching only European languages in Melanesian schools goes on, many local languages are dying out. Indeed, five of them (Nasarian and Maragus on Malakula, Sowa on Pentecost, Ura on Erromango, and Aore on Santo), whose speakers numbered fifty, twenty, forty, ten, and one, respectively,[42] may already have become linguistic history.

As a rule, before and throughout most of the condocolonial era only the missionaries bothered to learn and record the indigenous languages of the New Hebrides. Beginning with the Presbyterians who learned and used the language of Aneityum in the first half of the nineteenth century, mastery of the local tongue and translation of the Bible into it were seen as effective if time-intensive proselytizing techniques. About forty indigenous languages were utilized, at one time or another, for evangelical purposes. If any of the archipelago's languages assumed supra-island status, it is because Anglican missionaries employed Mota throughout the northern islands (and even into the southern Solomons) and did the same for Nguna on Efate and in the Shepherds.[43] Eventually, however, even the missionaries decided that Bislama provided the better avenue for propagation of the gospel.[44] Today, only about 8 percent of ni-Vanuatu speak solely an indigenous language.[45]

Although they disagreed about virtually everything else, French and British administrators in the New Hebrides were at one in regarding the plethora of Melanesian languages as a bother to condominial administration. Perhaps the intense competition between English and French, complicated by the existence of an English-derived pidgin Bislama, made the very existence of a whole other range of languages seem like an outright obstruction. Terry Crowley relates how, even after independence, a former French ambassador to Vanuatu could question whether indigenous languages were "real" languages and a senior expatriate (Anglophone) government official could compare intra-Melanesian communication to bird twittering. (Next to these anecdotes, the one about the former French District Agent on Tanna advising a university researcher to study the French language rather than a "rubbish" Tannese one is rather pale.)[46]

Rhetoric in favor of reviving indigenous languages has been strong since independence but action rather limited. Malvatumauri, the Council of Chiefs, has gone on record as being not only in favor of preserving Vanuatu's pluralistic linguistic heritage but including vernaculars in government school instruction.[47] The Christian Council of Vanuatu has also encouraged pride in local languages.[48] The very preamble to the Constitution declares the nation as "cherishing . . . linguistic . . . diversity." Government practice, however, has basically continued to ignore local languages. The Second National Development Plan, while comprehensive in most every other regard, ignores local language development completely. Though traditional arts, *kastom,* and Christianity are highlighted, its chapter on "Culture and Religion" is silent on this question. Only obliquely, in acknowledging "collection of oral traditions" by the Vanuatu Cultural Centre, does the plan intimate that a local language question exists. Even more extraordinary is the absence in the population census of a question to determine mother tongue!

It is not only the small number of speakers, geographical constriction, and lack of written materials that disadvantage local languages in Vanuatu. Competition between English and French, and competition between both European languages with Bislama, seem to have drained energy for local language advocacy. More important, following Brian Weinstein's argument, the absence of any vernacular language elites or "strategists" who might use linguistic discrimination as a political issue further mutes the salience of local language status.[49] Even if Bislama, now classified by linguists as an Austronesian language, is barely Melanesian in its vocabular base, the trifurcation of communication in Vanuatu points to a problematic process: the progressive degradation, in the world's most linguistically pluralistic nation, of indigenous modes of communication in favor of official European languages and a national, largely European-derived, language.

Mutual comprehensibility is a prerequisite of national unity. Colonial-induced linguistic divisions have intensified the importance of Bislama as a factor in national unification. The unfortunate upshot is that the impetus for linguistic national unity has come at the expense of indigenous language integrity. Well-intentioned policies to transcend linguistically based cleavages introduced by condocolonialism have relegated indigenous language survival to a very low priority. This is the paradox of the success of a language movement whose driving force was the achievement of political and cultural integrity.

COMPARATIVE ANGLO-FRENCH BILINGUALISM

As an indigenous society partitioned by competing European languages, Vanuatu serves as comparative reference for many other developing areas divided along English- and French-speaking lines. One of the greatest challenges to African unity, for instance, is the division between so-called Anglophone and Francophone nations. As in Vanuatu, these appellations exaggerate the actual permeation of English and French within African society; yet they do serve as barriers to regional and continental solidarity. Among "Francophone" Africans (whether or not they really speak French) there is an automatic suspicion of Nigerians and Ghanaians (whether or not they really speak English) which easily surpasses that reserved for African strangers from other Francophone lands.

In terms of bridging Anglo-French linguistic boundaries in postcolonial Africa, Cameroon is again the most relevant counterpoint to Vanuatu.[50] With its 225 indigenous languages for fourteen million inhabitants, Cameroon, like Vanuatu, is one of the most polyglot nations in the world. Since its unification in 1961, Cameroon's two official languages have been English and French, making it the sole nation of the African continent to have the same two exoglossic (nonindigenous) official languages as Vanuatu. As in Vanuatu, however, relatively few Cameroonians truly master these European languages. Instead, analogously to Bislama, Cameroonian Pidgin English has become the de facto lingua franca of the nation. But, unlike Bislama for Vanuatu, Pidgin is not a constitutionally recognized national language in Cameroon.

In addition to their significance for domestic communication, the origins of Cameroonian and Vanuatu Pidgins are also similar. Both are derivatives of the English language that emerged from coastally based commercial and missionary interactions during the late precolonial and colonial eras. In both West African and South Pacific cases, the British were more tolerant of Pidgin than were the French, particularly in educational contexts. Both independent Cameroon and Vanuatu have rejected the lingua franca as a language of instruction.

Primary school education in both Cameroon and Vanuatu is either in English or French and still roughly reflects preindependence spatial patterns of European influence. An attempt was made in Cameroon in the 1970s, without parallel in Vanuatu public schools in the 1990s, to introduce English as a subject in Francophone primary schools and vice versa. Bilingualism in secondary schooling was also pursued more aggressively in Cameroon, with French-language examinations required at the end of the fourth year and English-language examinations at the end of the fifth. Model "bilingual" secondary schools in Vanuatu remain institutions where there are distinct tracks for Francophone and Anglophone students; in Cameroon's equivalents, they study both in French and English. On the other hand, curricular unification (referred to in Cameroon as "harmonization") has progressed more rapidly in Vanuatu.

In the postcolonial bilingual world, Cameroon pioneered the use of linguistic centers for adult education, radio programming for distance language learning, and bilingual translators in ministerial and presidential offices. Vanuatu has not availed itself of these first two activities, and its language services departments are understaffed and underfunded.

Cameroonian-Vanuatu contrasts in official language learning are almost mirror images of each other. In Francophone-dominated Cameroon, Anglophones tend to learn French better than Francophones do English. In Vanuatu, where they have been in the minority, Francophones master English much more readily than Anglophones do French.

Motivations to enhance personal language repertoire appear to outweigh intrinsic difficulties in language learning. French may be more grammatically complex a language than English but, given the right political and socioeconomic incentives, is no less apprehensible as a fourth language (following indigenous, pidgin, and dominant official ones).

FUTURE LANGUAGE REPERTOIRES

Both in India and in Africa, multilingual societies that inherited ineradicable colonial languages, David Laitin has identified a 3 ± 1 language outcome for persons hoping to achieve economic and political integration within their wider society. Language No. 1 is the mother tongue, the vernacular. Language No. 2 is the lingua franca, which in some instances will be the same as the vernacular (leading to the 3 - 1 outcome). The colonial language, the official language of government and of international communication, is Language No. 3. A typical resident of Tamil Nadu in southern India, for instance, will learn Tamil as the mother tongue, Hindi as a government-mandated Indian language of instruction, and English as the language of wider communication. If he is not Tamil-born and his family migrated from elsewhere in southern India, Tamil will constitute the fourth (3 + 1) option. In those areas of northern India where Hindi is a first language (as well as the lingua franca), then only two languages are necessary (3 - 1). Similarly, native Kikuyu speakers in Kenya will learn two more languages (Swahili, the lingua franca, plus English) whereas Kamba speakers living among the Kikuyu will learn three more (for they must know Kikuyu), and native Swahili-speakers remaining in the coastal region only one more (English).

When adapted to the Vanuatu case, Laitin's 3 ± 1 model yields a slightly more complicated scenario (see Figure 4).

The critical variable lies less in the relationship between lingua franca and vernacular (as in Laitin's Africa case) and more between the colonial language of initial instruction. For regardless of how long the UMP retains its post-Lini ascendancy, Francophones in Vanuatu will have to learn English: Regional, economic, and demographic reasons ensure this. Australian and New Zealand influence may wax and wane depending on who leads the Vanuatu government, but the paramountcy of these (Anglophone) countries' regional influence in the postcondominial era is unalterable. External private-sector investments and international donor networks will also require some degree of English-language proficiency for persons wishing to be involved in these processes. And

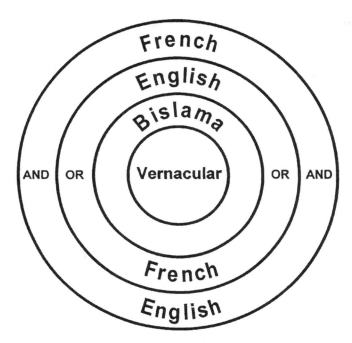

Figure 4. Language Repertoires in Vanuatu

though Bislama will remain the lingua franca between Anglophones and Francophones of all classes, Francophone elites will increasingly require knowledge of English to remain within the "loop" of bilateral business and multilateral development transactions. The converse is not true for English-speaking ni-Vanuatu, even of the elite, no matter how long a Francophone-headed government remains in power. (Such unidirectional bilingualism is the inverse of that which prevailed in Cameroon after independence. There, the minoritarian Anglophones, at least the up-wardly mobile ones, experienced institutional pressures to learn French in a way that Francophones were not for English.)[51]

Consequently, the language repertoire for upwardly mobile ni-Vanuatu will look like this:

$$3[E] - 1[c] \setminus + 1[v] \setminus + 1[F]$$
where E = English language, c = creolization,
v = vernacular, and F = French language.

For most Anglophone ni-Vanuatu, the African 3 ± 1 model will work: one vernacular (e.g., Mota), a lingua franca (Bislama), and an international language (English). If ni-Vanuatu functionaries are posted to, or their youngsters brought up on, an unfamiliar island, a second vernacular language may be acquired (3[E] + 1[v]). As inter-island marriages increase and certain indigenous languages disappear, Bislama will progressively creolize and constitute the mother tongue for some. Such ni-Vanuatu will need to learn only one additional language (3[E] - 1[c]). The model allows for the possibility that some ni-Vanuatu will eventually have a creolized Bislama as their first language and have to pick up a vernacular as an additional language (3[E] - 1[c] + 1[v]). Circumstances that favor creolization (town betrothals among educated couples from different islands) will not make this a common outcome, however. The standard 3[E] (mother tongue vernacular, Bislama, English) will remain the norm for Anglophones.

Because English will increasingly become a prerequisite for economic advancement and political competitiveness, Francophone ni-Vanuatu will generally require a minimum of *four* languages (vernacular, Bislama, English, and French: 3[E] + 1 [F]. This will sometimes be reduced to three on account of creolization (3[E] - 1[c] + 1 [F]; the chronology of learning, of course, is Bislama, then French, then English). Where second vernacular learning is likely (children raised on outer islands with a narrowly spoken maternal vernacular), the outcome will be five languages: 3[E] + 1[v] + 1[F]. To reiterate, the standard repertoire for Anglophones will be three (3[E]) but four (3[E] + 1[F]) for upwardly mobile Francophones.

More than any other mechanism, Bislama allows Francophones and Anglophones to bridge the religious, political, and linguistic boundaries that have separated them as a result of condocolonialism. But this national and linguistic unity comes at a price. While the degree to which English and French will suffer as a result of Bislamization is debatable, there is little doubt that the nation's sundry indigenous languages, the bedrock of Vanuatu's cultural capital, will decline. Bridging mental boundaries is laudable, but there are palpable cultural costs.

CONCLUSION

Condocolonial rivalry in the New Hebrides created linguistic boundaries that separated ni-Vanuatu not along geographical lines, as in the classic colonial model, but along mental ones. The result of dual colonial education was not two kinds of people who could not communicate with one another—for they did share Bislama—but rather two communities whose conception of progress and politics was based on two opposing models of thought, the one (strongly) Gallic, the other (moderately) Anglo-Saxon. Educational policy following independence (i.e., the maintenance of French- and English-medium teaching) has, to a certain degree, perpetuated the language partition.

At the same time, policies of curricular unification and administrative amalgamation have narrowed the social distance between young ni-Vanuatu Anglophones and Francophones. Tensions along linguistic lines still remain among teachers and administrators, yet the rallying cry in Vanuatu education is no longer *Vive la Francophonie,* or "Out With French," but rather "Up With Bilingualism." Bislama, the national language, has made remarkable strides in providing a common basis of communication and bridging colonial-induced gaps between Anglophones and Francophones.

In the absence of any indigenously designed language planning policy, however, there is a danger that the older Anglophone–Francophone dichotomy of mental boundaries will be superseded by another linguistic division. As uninhibited and unstandardized usages of Bislama spread and differentiate urban Bislamaphones from rural ones, and as the developmental gap between town and country widens, there is the real potential of a diglossically divided polity emerging. Coupled with the quasi-total neglect of indigenous languages, ni-Vanuatu may, in the long run, be stratified into High Pidgin-speaking urban residents, who also retain some degree of international language competence, and Low Pidgin-speaking rural dwellers, who both remain isolated from the wider world and are denied development within a stunted and endangered local language context. The prospect that this double linguistic disenfranchisement will eventually translate into significant political opposition is minimal, given the geographically diffuse, politically decentralized, and linguistically marginal status of indigenous Melanesian society.

In the short-to-medium term, linguistic entrepreneurs,[52] particularly Francophone ones, will keep the colonial language dichotomy alive. Beyond the external economic and political rationales for preserving "bilingualism," the Francophone cause constitutes a major cornerstone of political legitimacy for a number of leaders in Vanuatu. Although the UMP has become much more than the party of Francophones, Francophonie still provides, if tacitly, a major raison d'être for that party's existence. More important, it gives French-speaking party leaders, whether of the UMP or not, a support base among the broader pro-Francophonie populace. The *voluntary* nature of the minority linguistic status of Francophones ought to be highlighted, for it distinguishes the case of Vanuatu from the more classical scenario in which linguistic is tied to ethnic minority status. But in Vanuatu, as elsewhere, "linguistic manipulation to locate frontiers between groups affects patterns of access to power and wealth within groups."[53]

Less partisan but no less political, French education represents for true French-speakers (not merely pro-Francophonie elements) a linguistic capital investment whose value can best be protected in the arenas of government activism and policy planning. Even were all parties to concede that French language has no intrinsic value for South Pacific society, those Melanesian families which made a risky investment choice by schooling their children in French must nevertheless protect this investment. Educational portfolio diversification has been one response; electoral politics has been another. Francophone parties arose in part, one might argue, as a response to a "bad" linguistic choice. Those parties have taken on different causes as independence has evolved, but their hard-core leadership and support remain ni-Vanuatu whose personal and family prospects depend on perpetuating the utility and status of French.

In Vanuatu, as in so many other developing nations, language has been bound up with politics and emergent nationalism. In traditional patterns of nationalism, some older, sacred, or kinship-based indigenous language has provided the spur for political or nationalist action. In Vanuatu none of the politicized languages are actually old and indigenous: They are either borrowed from the colonial experience (English and, especially, French) or are nascent and rapidly evolving (Bislama). When Carol Eastman observes that generally "language either demarks [group] boundaries or transcends them,"[54] Vanuatu reminds us that it can do both simultaneously. For whereas the official languages (French, English) continue to demarcate group boundaries, the national language (Bislama) transcends them. Linguistic boundaries are in flux throughout the world. The case of Vanuatu demonstrates just how fluid the bases of linguistic identity can be.

New Boundaries in Space, Time, Law, Gender, and Race

Previous chapters have stressed the mental boundaries separating Anglophone from Francophone, Protestant from Catholic, and *kastom* follower from Christian believer. Nation building has contributed to the blurring of these boundaries and the gradual formation of a ni-Vanuatu identity. However, other boundaries are also shifting—boundaries that are spatial, temporal, economic, legal, sexual, and racial in nature. Successful management of these other boundary shifts are just as important to Vanuatu development as that of the political, linguistic, and religious ones (see Figures 5 and 6).

SPATIAL BOUNDARIES

Social geography impels us to examine the significance of people in space. Despite its being an archipelago, the most profound spatial boundary in Vanuatu life has not been the one separating island from island. Nor has it been the oceanic remoteness of the nation from centers of Australasian and other Western societies. Rather, the most intricate spatial boundaries have been those which demarcate the land and water "roads" along which individuals and groups may travel.[1] In the past, travel off authorized paths (particularly upon sacred or taboo grounds) constituted perilous trespass; today, movement is freer but therefore more uncertain.

Can one climb a mountain, visit a valley, or view a volcano without permission? Today in Vanuatu the extent to which informal "road" boundaries are enforceable is unclear. In theory, freedom of movement throughout the republic is a constitutional right. Yet Pentecost islanders have been warned from unauthorized travel to Santo and villages on Tanna have fought over the right to bring visitors up Yasur hill. In the past the opening of new "roads" required individuals and groups to

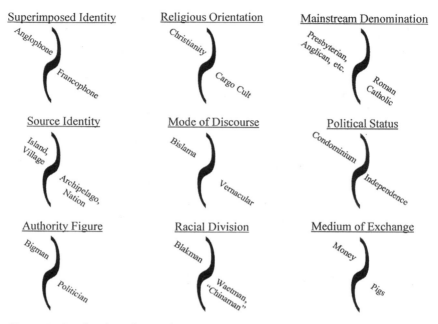

Figure 5. Condocolonial Boundaries

negotiate specific travel rights in the context of reciprocal obligations. Today tacit understandings are being negotiated in the context of the principles of state sovereignty, individual rights of mobility, and customary claims to local "road" boundaries.

Formerly, the most obvious spatial boundary was that separating island highlanders from coastal peoples, the distinction between *manbus* ("bushmen") and *mansolwata* ("saltwater people"). Some islanders did establish settlements on the coast and combined fishing with agriculture for their subsistence. Even these seafaring Melanesians, however, lost the long-distance sailing skills of their ancestors and, unlike their coastal counterparts in Polynesia and Micronesia, limited their oceanic traveling to relatively nearby islands. Though some trade between inland and coastal communities did occur (yams, for example, were exchanged for fish and salt), there was usually more contact between coastal inhabitants of neighboring islands than between coastal and mountain dwellers of the same ones (see Map 4). Participation in grade taking and other ritual ceremonies occasioned some inter-island traffic as well. In the northern islands, spatial movement was correlated with social rank, the men of highest grades traveling the farthest (albeit along specifically

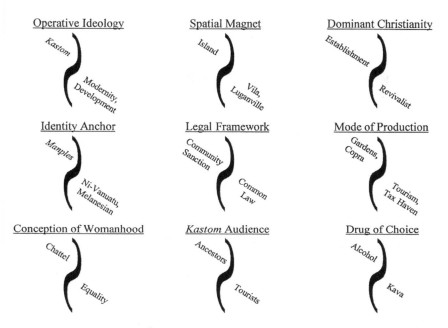

Figure 6. Emerging Boundaries

delineated and predetermined routeways) from home ground.[2] Overall,
however, population mobility (excepting for marriage) was seasonal,
short-term and oscillatory, and generally confined within kinship
groups.[3] Natural disasters, intervillage warfare, and the exhaustion of
farming land constituted the few reasons for permanent relocation.
"[M]ovement between islands in traditional New Hebridean society appears to have been primarily in oscillation, and moves associated with
ceremonies and trading voyages rarely involved Islanders in lengthy ab-
sences from their permanent homes."[4] In the tension between spatial
fixity for security and outward mobility linked to status, a bias toward
territorial immobilism prevailed.

The wedge in worldview between *manbus* and *mansolwata*—the
former inward-, the latter outward-looking—was deepened by evangelical, economic, and condocolonial influences. For purposes of logistical
convenience, missionary stations were established on the coast and the
first converts hailed from communities closest to them. As coastal dwellers converted, evangelization was extended to the mountain regions.
Conversion was conceptualized in quasi-geographical terms: to "come
down" from "on top" meant to join the coastal community and, ergo,

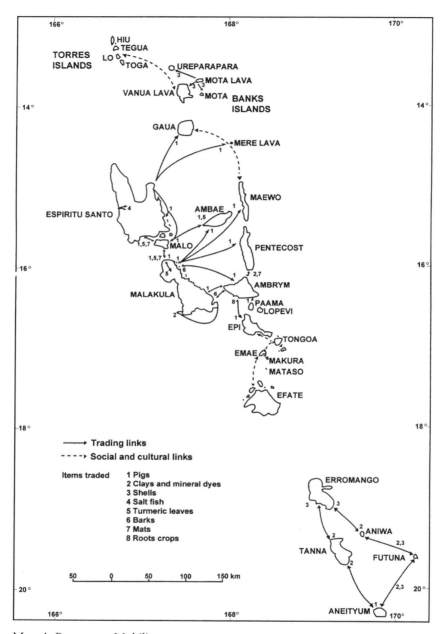

Map 4. Precontact Mobility
Adapted from R. D. Bedford, *New Hebridean Mobility: A Study of Circular Migration* (Canberra, Australian National University, 1973).

Christianity. Hillsmen long remained recalcitrant to the gospel, however, and the "bush" became synonymous with darkness, paganism, and satanism. This view extended from converter to converted.

Trading stations, coconut plantations, and cattle ranches were also situated on or near the "saltwater." Opportunities for wage labor consequently were geographically concentrated along the coast and intensified in the 1880s and 1890s. Circular migration to plantations in Queensland, which affected fifty thousand New Hebrideans and lasted from 1863 to 1904, also induced mountainmen to "come down" and sign up for overseas employment. Though much recruiting conducted by the infamous blackbirders was duplicitous, a good portion of New Hebridean overseas wage employment was indeed voluntary.

Melanesian economy progressively monetized and affected, as Gerald Haberkorn has shown for the small island of Paama, both property rights (through the individuation of landholdings for cash cropping) and marital customs (through the displacement of pigs and giant yams by cash as bride-price).[5] On larger islands with significant mountain communities, however, the overall impact of overseas wage labor movement was anything but progressive: A major incentive for signing up overseas was the opportunity to purchase firearms, thus escalating the level of intervillage violence and making some bushmen communities all the more redoubtable. Indeed, labor-saving technology for everyday activities freed up even more time for discretionary warfare.[6]

As more goods became tradeable, commercial contact between *manbus* and *mansolwata* became more common. During the blackbirding period, there was movement from mountain to frigate for migration, albeit temporary, to Australia, Fiji, Samoa, and New Caledonia. Christian missions in coastal communities encouraged economic autonomy and spatial stability through cash cropping of copra. By the 1890s, virtually all labor recruitment was from mountain communities. Condocolonial penetration, such as it was, was restricted primarily to coastal areas. District headquarters, for example, were invariably near island harbors.

As Christianization, Westernization, monetization, and education (which extended from the missions) advanced along the coast, inland communities increasingly "came down." In mountain communities that possessed neither natural nor medical defenses, epidemics of new diseases also spurred depopulation. Although nineteenth-century predictions of outright extinction mercifully proved wrong, the combination of coastal pull and hilltop push did shift settlement patterns away from indigenous mountain and toward Europeanized missions. Entire villages have disappeared in the process, particularly in Malakula among the Big and Small Nambas, in northeast Santo, and in the interiors of Aneityum and Efate.

World War II marked the definitive rupture with limited spatial movement in the New Hebrides and the eclipse of bush–coastal boundaries by town–country flows. Mandatory wartime conscription by Condominium authorities of adult males to Efate and Santo did not cause ten thousand New Hebrideans to be employed by the U.S. military there; attractive salaries, benefits, and labor conditions—especially compared with plantation work—did. The overnight creation of GI townships was particularly impressive and contributed, as we have seen, to the emergence of cargo cultism. Overall, this "'urban experience' . . . greatly influence[d] employment and mobility patterns in the years following the Second World War. Port Vila and Santo, as potential destinations, had entered the mental maps of most rural ni-Vanuatu, through either their own experience, or that of close kin."[7]

Since the late 1960s and early 1970s, diversification of an urban economy, expansion in civil service, the introduction of offshore banking, copra price collapse, and tourism have all favored the flow of wage-seeking outer islanders to town. Independence, and the ensuing centralization of Vanuatu's political economy, has reinforced this tendency. Even plantation work, which does combine semirural life-style with wage employment, is concentrated on only three islands (Efate, Santo, and Malakula) and even there reinforces periurban clustering.[8] With only two urban centers of significance—Port Vila and Luganville—and the post-Santo rebellion eclipse of the latter, the rural–urban distinction has really translated into a demarcation in outlook and life-style between the capital and the outer islands. Today's critical movement is no longer from hilltop to coast so much as from outer island to urban (or periurban) center. Bush–coast cleavages have not disappeared from the Melanesian mind but are overlaid with discreet insular-to-urban shifts tending toward "permanent rural absenteeism."[9] This is occurring though home "[t]erritory is [still] lived as a space of safety [and even] more deeply as a space of identity."[10]

As the present migration shifts more from (same-island) mountain-coast to (inter-island) district-capital, the relevant spatial boundary moves from *bus-solwata* to *aelan*-Vila. Whereas the older shift was responsible for erosion of the indigenous culture, the newer movement has spawned, particularly among the semieducated young, crime, delinquency, unemployment, alcoholism, and a breakdown in chiefly authority. Attempts to maintain native-island control over outer-island migrants in Vila through urban chiefs in island-clustered neighborhoods is only partially effective. The extent to which social planners in Vila can manage this breaching of island-urban spatial boundaries is crucial to the health not only of Vila but Vanuatu at large.

In addition to inland-coastal and outer island-urban demarcations, there is another critical range of spatial boundaries that divides ni-Vanuatu and demands resolution. This is the incessant and pervasive conflict over property boundaries involving putative *kastom* landowners.

Landownership by foreigners—alienation—had been a major source of political contestation throughout the Condominium: Howard van Trease has justifiably written his valuable, comprehensive history of Vanuatu through the specific lenses of land politics.[11] According to the constitution through which Vanuatu achieved independence, all land in the nation automatically reverted to the "indigenous custom owners and their descendants" (chap. 12, art. 71). Freehold titles by non-Melanesians ceased to exist; non-Melanesians were obliged either to restore to custom owners the lands they had been occupying (receiving a negotiated compensation for any improvement made to it) or to obtain leases for their continued occupation of it. The ministry of lands further distinguished between rural, urban, and public lands, over which latter two the government would own a perpetual lease.

Since independence land reform in Vanuatu has bogged down over identifying the legitimate landholders. "Population decline and movement, plus the fact that many properties had been in European hands for decades, made it extremely difficult to determine who exactly were the true custom owners."[12] In the absence of documentation or unambiguous oral tradition, plantation owners often do not know with whom they should negotiate to obtain leases. Conflict over *kastom* land is endemic throughout the archipelago, and not only between indigenous and non-indigenous litigants. On the island of Tanna, for instance, trying to determine to whom the Yasur volcano "belongs" has been an ongoing dispute, not least because the right to charge tourists access to view the marvel is at stake. Rows between neighboring villages and homesteads—often aggravated by underlying Anglophone-Francophone tensions—regularly occur over claims to land. Land improvement, foreign investment, and general development are often stymied because of such ambiguity of custom ownership. In 1992 Maxime Carlot Korman, then prime minister, was clear on this point: "The land problem is . . . the key to the future. If the custom owners and government do not work hand in hand regarding the land, we won't be able to develop [the country]."[13]

Ambiguity over land has proven to be a major political catalyst as well, as witnessed by the events of May 1988–March 1989. Opposition to the disbanding of the Vila Urban Land Corporation (VULCAN) led to riots and a cycle of partisan and parliamentary challenges to Prime Minister Lini led by Barak Sope. Sope had been a Vanua'aku Pati stalwart in the preindependence era but had subsequently emerged as a rival to Lini within the VP. He was also a representative on the VULCAN board of directors for Ifira, the small islet across the bay from Port Vila whose inhabitants, together with those of the neighboring villages of Erakor and Pango, laid claim to the land of Vila as descendents of its original custom owners. Escalation of tensions and unorthodox attempts to resolve them (presidential dissolution of parliament, the swearing in of an interim government, and threats of foreign intervention) culminated in the 1989 constitutional crisis and the convictions of Sope, President Sokomanu, and future prime minister Carlot. Significantly, the disagreement over the proper disposition of urban land reinforced the seeds of crosscutting cleavages between Carlot's Francophone followers and Sope's Anglophone ones. In at least this one case, land bridged mental and political boundaries formerly riven by language.

Haberkorn's extrapolation that, by the late 1970s, the family origin of over two-thirds of Melanesians resident in Luganville and over half of those in Vila was other than Santo and Efate, respectively,[14] has enormous implications for the politics of identity in Vanuatu. Attachment to land, to *ples,* cannot be as profound for the urban ni-Vanuatu of rural background as it is for their ancestrally rooted insular cousins. Dependence on urban amenities, vacationing in town rather than country, and investment in urban dwellings rather than in prestigious island homes—these findings reflect a public view of Vila as home.[15] *Stamba,* island origin, will necessarily recede in importance for these urbanized ni-Vanuatu. Although the rural–urban boundary is a fluid one, and does not preclude some continuing temporary rural-based circulation, this emotive shift from island to capital points to a novel, demographic basis of Vanuatu identity. Whether the ancestral sense of group self, based on *stamba,* will be replaced by linguistic or national referents is a critical question for the unity of the nation.[16]

Robert Tonkinson's fascinating study of the voluntary diaspora of ni-Vanuatu from southeast Ambrym is of relevance here.[17] For nearly a half-century a portion of the southeast Ambrymese have been settled in the village of Mele-Maat on the island of Efate, now within commuting distance of Port Vila. Identification with and attachment to the homeland on Ambrym have survived, even though gradual economic, cultural, and marital incorporation into their island of adoption has eventually led to "a gradual erosion of cultural boundaries" between southeast Ambrymese and neighboring Efatese.[18] Dual spatial identity of being *from* Ambrym but *of* Efate islands must now also integrate nationhood within "Land Eternal" (Vanuatu). In a society that places such a high premium on place and land as the sources of personhood, migration and nationalism greatly complexify identity. It is difficult enough to combine ancestral identity with adopted home, as for the southeast Ambrymese on Efate; adding the more abstract spatial identity of a sprawling archipelago is all the more challenging. Independence has both accelerated and complicated shifts in the mental mapping of ni-Vanuatu islanders.

Where does one custom owner's property end and his neighbor's begin? Where lies the limit between government-administered public and customary private land? In a democratic state in which *kastom* is glorified, is the urban migrant still bound by the norms of her outer island? Does freedom of movement take precedence over customary "road" restrictions? Will "sophisticated" coastals come to respect the "recalcitrant" bushmen? Can nation rival island or village as a locational source of identity? Such are some of the spatial boundaries challenging Vanuatu unity.

LEGAL BOUNDARIES

> A national of a foreign state or a stateless person may apply to be naturalised as a citizen. . . .
>
> > —Chapter 3, article 12 of the Constitution
> > of the Republic of Vanuatu

> Only *indigenous citizens* of the Republic . . . shall have perpetual ownership of their land. . . .
>
> > —Chapter 12, article 73 of the Constitution
> > of the Republic of Vanuatu (emphasis added)

The centrality of land to the psyche and polity of Vanuatu links spatial to legal boundaries in the young republic. Concern for customary ownership of land has given rise to a constitutional distinction between indigenous and nonindigenous citizens. Whereas the former category of citizen (the Melanesian) can own land in the nation, the nonindigenous citizen (she/he of European, Australian, or Indochinese origin) cannot.

Such distinctions create boundaries between citizens and a challenge to liberal democratic constitutionalism.

The intent of the above constitutional provisions was to prevent foreigners from retaining or acquiring "alienated" real estate, as had been the aggravating case prior to independence. Given that chapter 3, article 13 of the Constitution excludes dual nationality for Vanuatu citizens, the distinction between indigenous and nonindigenous reinforces the ethnic dimension to the legal boundary between indigenous and nonindigenous citizen. So does chapter 6, article 31, which stipulates that only an indigenous citizen may become President of the Republic. The words "and their descendants" were added to the article 71 restriction of landownership to indigenous custom owners because several key members of the Constitutional Planning Committee—the future leaders of the independent republic—themselves had European, Australian, or Polynesian wives.[19] By blurring racial boundaries, *métissage* has complicated the simple nationalist demand of "Vanuatu land to ni-Vanuatu."

In spite of the reputed affinity of Francophone ni-Vanuatu for French language, culture, and society, the boundary between French and ni-Vanuatu citizenship is clearly marked on both sides of the nationality fence. Vanuatu does not recognize dual nationality, and virtually no Francophones, despite the obvious advantages of doing so (e.g., the proximity of New Caledonia with its greater economic opportunities) have sought French citizenship. This clarity in legal boundary between France and former members of the French empire contrasts sharply with that of North Africans and French Indians.

The constitutional distinction between Melanesian and non-Melanesian citizen reflects a much wider, and more ambiguous, legal boundary: that between Western and customary laws and norms. The fundamental rights and duties spelled out in chapter 2 of the Constitution recall those familiar to students of Western European and North American constitutional law: the right to life, liberty, privacy, conscience, religion, and association, and so on, as well as protection from discrimination on the basis of race, national origin, gender, language, and political belief (see Appendix). At the same time, the foundation of the republic, as per the preamble, rests on traditional Melanesian values and Christianity, the former to be promoted by a National Council of Chiefs. Chapter 8 of the Constitution instructs judges, when faced with issues lacking codified legislation, to apply traditional norms. "Thus the Constitution mandates that custom is the principal source in the development of an appropriate underlying law for Vanuatu."[20]

Does the Vanuatu Republic favor individual legal protections or collectivist sectarian values? According to chapter 5, article 28, Vanuatu's forty-six-member unicameral parliament *may* consult with the National Council of Chiefs on any proposed legislation (particularly that which affects custom and tradition), but it is not obliged to. Whereas there operates at one level a recognizable system of jurisprudence in the Anglo-Saxon (and particularly English) mold, at another level *kastom* law prevails. Harmonizing the two legal systems has proven to be more complicated than framers of the post-Condominium judiciary had envisioned.

Ever since the imposition of the Condominium, jurisprudence in the New Hebrides/Vanuatu has been characterized by multiple levels of law. We have seen in Chapter 2 how "justice" during the Condominium was formally dispensed through three judicial systems—that of the British, that of the French, and that of the Condominium per se. In actuality a fourth, unofficial system—*kastom*—flourished beyond the purview of any of the other three.

For islanders subject to "native law," the key to resolution of disputes during the Condominium were the assessors, legal middlemen appointed by the government to resolve such conflicts at the local level and to advise European district agents in court.[21] Assessors were charged with (1) processing and (to the extent possible) resolving local conflicts; (2) reporting major and nonresolvable local offenses to the British (B.D.A.) or French (F.D.A.) District Agent; and (3) advising the European District Agent in native court cases. From a condocolonial perspective, the assessors' most important function was to officiate over an unofficial court (which nevertheless employed formal proceedings) and thereby substantially reduce the number of disputes that required official resolution in a Condominium-convened native court. From the Melanesian viewpoint—and one that echoes indigenous African jurisprudence—unofficial court was preferable, for it aimed toward establishing consensus rather than culpability.

Typically, a division of legal labor arose between the assessor appointed by the Condominium and the chief, bigman, or man-of-rank whose authority issued from strictly indigenous norms. Unlike in Africa, where warrant chiefs appointed by the British and *chefs de canton* installed by the French possessed dubious local legitimacy, assessors in the New Hebrides faced little opposition to their authority.[22] In the politically unstable years preceding sovereignty, the undermining of condocolonial authority and the promulgation of impractical legal reforms spurred some island communities to devise their own systems of justice which, willy-nilly, carried over even after 1980.[23]

Independence has, in principle, brought with it a new legal system in Vanuatu. The position of mediating assessor has been eliminated. Instead, at the local (i.e., regional district) level there is supposed to operate an island court, presided over by three magistrates, exercising criminal or civil jurisdiction as specifically designated. Despite original intent, the island courts lack explicit jurisdiction over *kastom* law and conflict resolution and possess marginal authority to resolve land disputes.[24] During my fieldwork in the early 1990s, the island court system was still in institutional infancy and functioned in few locales as mandated.

Above the island courts stand the magistrates' courts, which exercise some limited jurisdiction over civil and criminal cases. Serious criminal offenses and major civil matters are adjudicated by the supreme court, which also hears cases involving constitutional issues. Two or more supreme court judges officially assembled constitute the court of appeals. For the vast majority of ni-Vanuatu, however, the new legal structure, whether viewed from top or bottom, is as remote as the condocolonial judicial arrangement was. This is not just a condition of legal semiautonomy, as others have noted exists in Oceania and other developing regions. Rather, as William Rodman pointedly observes, much of Vanuatu society consists of "encapsulated" communities which exercise outright autonomy from the state with regard to their legal affairs.[25] Bridging the boundary between community norms and state laws remains a major challenge to Vanuatu nation building.

In large part thanks to Australian and British government aid to the judiciary, the Vanuatu legal system has been effectively (though not officially) Anglicized. Condominium regulations that were not expressly repealed or replaced by parliamentary legislation were to remain in place, as were French and British laws (chap. 15, arts. 93, 94). French was to have equal standing with English as a language of the courts. In fact, the norms and language of British jurisprudence have prevailed since independence. While the secondment of a bilingual chief justice from the United Kingdom helped to rebalance the Anglophone bias in the high court, French jurisprudence and language remain subordinate within the post-Condominium judiciary.[26]

If the language and process of their courts strike most Western laymen as constituting another world, for ordinary ni-Vanuatu their own condocolonially derived legal system must seem like another universe. Few defendants or witnesses are sufficiently conversant in English or

French to dispense with an interpreter, and the Bislama rendition of legal offenses, not to mention statutory definitions, is truncated at best. Nor are the accused guaranteed a Bislama-speaking defense lawyer. Legal proceedings more often resemble a hearing in a headmaster's office than a vigorously argued trial. (There are no juries in the courts of Vanuatu.) It is still the case, as it was a decade before independence, that ni-Vanuatu feel "deep shame, regardless of their guilt or innocence, in answering the questions of a European magistrate in a public forum."[27] Assessing culpability, the aim of Western jurisprudence, skews the process of reaching compromise, the goal in Melanesian dispute resolution. When a foreigner imposes judgment, baldly identifying legal winners and losers, a wedge is driven between local and national notions of justice.

Abolition of the position of assessor who informally mediated between local and national systems of justice has increased the burden on higher levels of Vanuatu's formal legal system. Loss in chiefly authority at the local level, a by-product of decentralization legislation that excluded recognized chiefs from membership on local government councils, has also indirectly contributed to social instability in the outer islands. Deviant members of local communities recognize that, even if they break the law, by opting for trials in the formal courts they can often escape even harsher social sanctions and community pressures. This is particularly the case where the offenses are sexual in nature (i.e., adultery, statutory rape). On the other hand, it has become rather awkward to prosecute for sorcery, even though this is still one of the most deeply feared violations of social norms in Vanuatu society.

One of the most visibly neocolonial images in the postcondocolonial era can be seen at the highest levels of the Vanuatu court system. As late as the mid-1990s a typical criminal case would be prosecuted by a British public prosecutor, defended by an Australian public defense attorney, and presided over by a British judge: The defendant, invariably, would be ni-Vanuatu. A translator, also white, would bridge the linguistic barrier between Bislama and English. Although ni-Vanuatu magistrates and lawyers were being trained and have slowly begun to take up positions within the legal system, fifteen years after independence the Vanuatu High Court still more closely resembled, at least in its outward appearance, the Joint Court of the Condominium than the judiciary of an independent republic.[28] Expatriate jurists claim that ni-Vanuatu do not want the stress, burden, and pressure of having to prosecute and judge their own extended family members and believe that only outsiders can be completely impartial, particularly in political/constitutional

Vila Courthouse.

cases. "During the Condominium ni-Vanuatu were treated like children," repeatedly stated one expatriate magistrate, referring to the legal system. Yet this description, to a significant extent, is still accurate today. Sorcery, homicide, and statutory rape have been particularly thorny cases for the British and Australian legal personnel to deal with, for they constitute indigenous acts over which European jurists have dubious competency. (Spells are also reputedly cast in the courtroom to affect the outcome of cases.) Even at the local level, since independence there has been more confusion about the application of customary law than during condocolonialism.[29]

Assigning to *kastom* the responsibility of law enforcement at the village level is novel, for *kastom* properly referred to social relationships, identification with the land, and the exchange of artifacts, techniques, and artistic creation. In precontact times disputes were settled by negotiation and reparation, not by the application of general rules or formal procedures. (This is why "musket justice" loomed as the ultimate sanction.) When courts were established under condocolonial authority, local adjudication privileged social relationships over individual culpability. Maintaining harmonious community relations prevailed over determining individual guilt or innocence. Within this framework, litigants' emotions and hurt feelings were more important than material damage or loss. Provoking anger was more grave than acting criminally out of anger. Even when resolved in the presence of a Condominium district agent, indigenous norms of justice prevailed over Western ones. Replacement of this modus operandi and the consequent imposition of added legal responsibility to local determiners of ill-defined *kastom* has created, in Larcom's terms, a veritable crisis in legitimation.

In short, the blurring of boundaries between condocolonial and customary law has created jurisprudential schizophrenia in Vanuatu. Although Western, and particularly English-based, law increasingly prevails on the national level, *kastom* is also officially promoted as a basis for regulating social conduct. Poignant indeed is the plight of the convicted ni-Vanuatu who has little understanding of the laws, proceedings, and reasoning of the *waetman* prosecutor and judge. The routine spectacle of ni-Vanuatu leaders submitting to a white expatriate judge for resolution of their political parties' internal squabbles—squabbles that are conditioned, in part, by the distinctively Melanesian form of *jeles* (jealousy)—is another legal phenomenon that still begs for decolonization. Elsewhere in the world, uncertainty over and the contesting of legal boundaries have been sources of societal conflict. Marginalization of traditional authority by newly empowered governments has also created strife in developing nations. That such has not yet been the case in Vanuatu is an encouraging sign, but not one that ought to be taken for granted indefinitely.

GENDER BOUNDARIES

Perhaps the most sensitive boundary still being spanned in Vanuatu today is that between the sexes. Acknowledging women as full human beings rather than reproductive chattels and food producers represents a fundamental shift in the Melanesian worldview. This mental transformation, placing women on the same side of humanity as men, was largely accomplished under missionary (albeit matronizing) tutelage, and consisted of teaching rudimentary literacy and housekeeping skills along with Christian values. The process is by no means complete, however, and remains part of the government's post-Condominium mandate.

Widows are no longer strangled in Melanesia, their social usefulness nullified by virtue of their husbands' deaths. Nor are young women traded for pigs anymore: Mutual affection, not swine value, has become relevant to marriage decisions. Ritual prostitutes no longer initiate young adolescents and young women are no longer sold as future wives for boys. Wife stealing is over, female prostration a relic. Harsh punishment is not visited upon females who transgress the males' *nakamal* (clubhouse) or witness taboo rituals. Female infanticide has virtually disappeared. It is now rare for Melanesian mothers to suckle piglets (an interspecies boundary crossing), and wives invariably possess, as was not previously the case, personal names.

Not all of the above customs were observed everywhere throughout Vanuatu, and some were quite localized. The legacies of such cultural norms linger on, however, and subordination, serviceability, and inequality remain the fate of most ni-Vanuatu women. Collectively, the memory of such practices has created a profound gender distancing between Melanesian men and women. The contested status of polygamy— defended by some (e.g., Nagriamel) as integral to *kastom,* rejected by others (e.g., the Vanuatu Christian Council) as inimical to religion— points up the ambiguity of gender equality in discussions of Vanuatu cultural authenticity. In colloquial terms, men faithful to *kastom* ought to "hold women tight."

It is doubtful that only on Tanna are women part of the "implicit conspiracy which keeps men at the centre of things."[30] Margaret Jolly has demonstrated as much for south Pentecost, adding that *kastom,* as an anticolonial mechanism, has had the perverse effect of intensifying indigenous male control and "immobilizing women in time and in space."[31] That female knowledge (or ideology, as Ron Adams and Lamont Lindstrom would have it) has survived very much intact in many of Vanuatu's microsocieties has not empowered women. The life of woman has been so distinct from the life of man in Vanuatu that closing the gender gap and achieving a modicum of sexual equality would represent an Oceanic revolution. Merely achieving acknowledgment of female contribution to *kastom* has been fraught with difficulty.[32]

To speak of gender boundaries is not metaphorical: With designated locations in and around villages clearly off-limits to females, there is significant overlap between spatial and gender boundaries.[33] Women often have their own meetinghouse, segregated cooking fire, and separate sleeping quarters. In Vanuatu, bridging mental boundaries between males and females will encompass spatial boundary change, and certainly take longer than bridging condocolonial cleavages between Anglophones and Francophones.

The correspondence between female physical movement and gender boundary shifts has been observed in Gerald Haberkorn's meticulous

Table 10 Female Employment by Sector

Occupation Groups	1979	1989
Professional, Administrative, Managerial	29.5%	32.2%
Clerical, Sales & Service Workers	46.3%	51.0%
Agricultural & Related Workers	47.8%	51.3%
Transport, Production & Laborers	1.0%	1.4%

Source: Derived from data in *Vanuatu National Population Census 1989*, p. 52.

analyses of migration throughout the islands of Vanuatu.[34] High female growth rates (6.1 percent) in Vila and Santo throughout the 1970s reflect the interrelationship among gender movement, urbanization, and development and may have been linked to a shift from domestic to more formal-sector work for females. They also account for the important shift from migration to reproduction as the major cause of urban growth.[35] Haberkorn records an 80 percent growth in the female labor force in the twelve years beginning in 1967, and twice that growth rate for women in nonagricultural urban employment. Focusing on the movement of people from one island (Paama) to Vila, he notes almost universal marriage and accompanied spouse rates, and an overall balanced age-sex distribution. Nearly half of Paamese women in town were employed as domestic servants, and another 14 percent in professional or technical work.[36] The shift from a principally single male migration to one including females has changed the economic and social face of urban and periurban Vanuatu.

Census data indicate that, although female participation in the labor force still trails behind that of men, in the decade between 1979 and 1989 there has been a modest but noticeable improvement in every occupational class (see Table 10).

A revised method of occupational classification highlights the prevailing gender gap and women's overall participation in Vanuatu's employment structure more clearly (see Table 11).

Politics and education have modestly expanded the boundaries of female participation in Vanuatu decision making. In its nationalist phase the Vanua'aku Pati included freedom for women as a major plank of its independentist platform, even if a gradualist approach was preferred. According to Walter Lini,

> There is . . . a danger that separate or distinct programmes for the development of women's affairs can lead to a reaction by "custom"—by the

Table 11 Employed Population According to Occupation and Sex, 1989

Occupation Group	Males	Females	Total
Legislators, Senior Officials & Managers	3.4%	0.6%	2.1%
Professionals	4.1%	3.8%	4.0%
Technicians & Associate Professionals	3.1%	0.7%	2.0%
Clerks	2.0%	3.0%	2.5%
Service, Shop and Market Sales Workers	4.6%	2.5%	3.6%
Agriculture and Related Workers	65.5%	81.8%	73.0%
Craft & Related Workers	10.2%	2.1%	6.4%
Plant, Machine Operators & Assemblers	3.5%	0.2%	2.0%
Elementary Occupations	3.6%	5.3%	4.4%
Total Employed	33,468	28,908	62,376

Source: *Vanuatu National Population Census 1989*, p. 53.

men—which could further [cause] division between the people. . . .
[T]here is a danger in concentrating too much on women's affairs and
forgetting that, in our society, men's values need to keep pace with these
things.[37]

Hilda, Father Walter's sister, is a formidable Lini in her own right
and a former cabinet minister. Though now less formally tied to partisan
politics (having been fired as personal secretary to the prime minister in
1990), the poet Grace Molisa has been a gadfly to the powers-that-be
(both during and after condocolonialism) and has been an acerbic critic
of social inequality in Vanuatu. ("Vanuatu is now free of foreign colonial
domination," she has written, "but Ni-Vanuatu women are still col-
onised.")[38] An incipient women's movement, largely grounded in religious organizations, has added a theological dimension to economic processes and political ideology of liberation for women. The Vanuatu
National Council of Women serves as umbrella organization for feminist
politics in a generally nonconfrontational mode.

Although both Hilda Lini and Grace Molisa are Anglophones, outside of Vila the most outspoken and assertive ni-Vanuatu women seem
to be those educated in the Francophone tradition. Whether this is due
to a greater emancipatory pedagogy (and ideology) imparted to girls in
the French system, or merely to a higher level of self-confidence possessed by all pupils educated in Francophone schools, is difficult to say.
Perhaps differentiated condocolonial legacies in the sexual realm still
play a role:

Melanesian matron.

French colonial officials and even French missions were much less devoted to keeping women at home (in both senses), and were more accepting of women both as labourers and as sexual partners on European plantations. British colonial policy forbade the recruiting of
women (at least without the consent of both husband and chief) and
British colonial culture was less open and accepting of sexual and reproductive relations between European men and Ni-Vanuatu women.[39]

Whatever the reason or reasons, the fact that Francophone women in
the islands are less likely than their Anglophone sisters to submit to male
dominance points to intriguing, if as yet understudied, crosscutting
cleavages between language of influence and boundaries of gender under
conditions of condocolonialism.

RACIAL BOUNDARIES

One of the most disconcerting customs the white male encounters in
Vanuatu is being addressed as *Masta* ("Master"). More than a decade
since the formal end of condocolonialism there lingers a racial boundary

marked by deference, if not subordination, vis-à-vis the *waetman* (white-man).[40] This is not an inferiority complex laced with residual fear, as characterizes black-white relations in portions of Africa.[41] Pitting different kinds of whites against each other, most famously the British against the French, practically became a late condocolonial sport in the New Hebrides. In independent Vanuatu this game has been expanded to include a more varied range of players—most notably, Japanese, Australian, Chinese, and New Zealander—in the intramural competition to curry and extend favor through development assistance.

Still, the habit common among nonelite ni-Vanuatu of automatically addressing the whiteman as *Masta* is not merely a linguistic hangover derived from mission and plantation history and devoid of racial significance. It should not be dismissed as a mere mark of Melanesian politeness. A decade of independence has squelched expectations of interethnic economic equality: Expatriates remain a privileged lot. Post-*tufala gavman* economic disappointment (particularly the continuing low level in copra prices) has bred suspicion among a minority of ni-Vanuatu that political sovereignty under fellow *blakman* has only worsened the plight of the people. "When is this independence thing going to be over?" still echoed plaintively in some corners of the archipelago a full decade after the Condominium expired, as if self-government were some kind of experiment that could be abruptly terminated when adjudged unsatisfactory.

Even nationalistic ni-Vanuatu credit (white) missionaries with ending local customs that all local Christians today view as anathema (cannibalism, widow strangling, live burial of twins, etc.) Lesser credit is given to French and British Condominium officials for "pacifying" the New Hebrides. Not only missionaries and condocolonialists are lauded for putting an end to local warfare and violence, however: Itinerant white travelers, including a roving ornithologist, are known to have brought peace to the unruly bush.[42] Except among those groups which have staunchly rejected missionary Christianity (e.g., Nagriamel, Tannese "pagans") there is an inescapable, if uncomfortable, debt to the white world in light of a partially repudiated cultural history.

Boundaries between white and black worlds are not fixed. Through Christianity and modernization, Melanesians can move toward the white world—the world of light—out of the world of darkness. Villagers of Erakor, as "enlightened" natives close to Vila, epitomize an intermediate position between *manbus* and *waetman*. Yet though they may see themselves as materially and spiritually much closer to the white man's universe compared with most outer-islander "bushmen," the Erakor people do not demand identical standards across racial lines. "White people can excuse themselves from going to church now because their forebears did God's work for so long."[43]

Some apprehension about interracial contact still persists as a result of the near extermination of ancestors who contracted *sik blong waetman* (diseases of the white man). On Aneityum, whose population experienced a close brush with extinction in the nineteenth century, a compromise between fear of white contagion and desire for foreign exchange has resulted in the following scenario. Huge cruise ships periodically disgorge hundreds of Australian tourists on a small offshore islet (Inyeug to the Aneityumese, Mystery Island to the tourists), who shop at an artificial market created exclusively for their benefit. By keeping the tourists off the mainland, it is believed, the risk of infection is minimized; at the same time, the revenue accrued from these visits enabled the local development council to purchase a boat that can reexport rice (brought in by the luxury liner *Fairstar*) to neighboring islands at a cheaper rate than from Vila. Although the arrangement is a benign example of the maintenance of racial boundaries for presumed health reasons, it has indirectly intensified local religious boundaries as well. While Catholics and Seventh-Day Adventists will go over to Inyeug even on Sundays if the *Fairstar* has arrived, Presbyterians are prohibited from engaging in such sabbath commerce.

Confining tourists to certain spaces, localities, or paths is entirely consistent with indigenous boundary maintenance: "A person is a proper tourist if he (or she) stays on the correct road." Native enforcement of tourist boundaries goes some way toward restoring the balance of power between Melanesian and European. Yet tourism also reinforces the association of white skin with monetary wealth, including all the predictable consequences. Performing the world-famous land dive *(gol)* ceremony on southwest rather than southeast Pentecost—indeed, shifting it (as was proposed in the 1990s) to another island entirely—highlights the commodification of culture that tourism engenders throughout the photogenic Third World.[44] Objectification of the (invariably white) tourist, viewed as a bearer of foreign exchange, has not reached the proportions in Vanuatu that it has, for instance, in Fiji. That an entire social studies text has been devoted to the subject nevertheless speaks to the growing awareness of interracial contact as an exercise in monetary exchange. For example "The tourist must *pay* for all his needs. He is ready to spend the money which he has brought overseas. There is thus a heap of opportunities so that the local population can extract revenue from the industry of tourism."[45] Elsewhere in the workbook a class exercise in interviewing tourists reminds students to be "smiling and pleasant."

Tannese, known throughout the archipelago for their "strongheadedness," are perhaps most blatant about relying on skin color as a basis for profit strategizing: Transport drivers will unabashedly charge whites seven times the going fare for a ride in a collective taxi. Yet the notion that whites should pay more than Melanesians for certain services extends to even higher levels: The fee scale for access to the national archives, for instance, distinguishes between Melanesians and non-Melanesians, not between Vanuatu citizens and noncitizens.

Familiarity with black peoples beyond Melanesia is limited for most ni-Vanuatu: I once astounded a high school principal on Ambrym by telling him that in the United States live many blacks, most of them descendents of African slaves. "And the government has permitted them to remain?" he asked.

Melanesian cults (Naked Cult, Four Corner Movement, etc.) are generally thought to have originated as reactions against white (missionary and condocolonial) rule. Yet some cargo cultists have appropriated Prince Philip of England as one of their own, maintaining that he is really a *man Tanna* posing as a white.[46] John Frum, too, is portrayed as light-skinned, even though his racial origins remain murky. Cargo itself is invariably associated with the white world. Certainly, cargo cultism represents a marginal phenomenon in contemporary ni-Vanuatu society. But if one acknowledges that, as surely as it may arrive as airborne loot dropping from the sky, cargo may also take the form of grants, loans, gifts, volunteers, and other concessional aid under the guise of international development assistance, then the problematic relationship between recipient and donor, often locally viewed in racial terms, is more prevalent than the exotic term "cargo cultism" implies.

Compounding the ambivalence in racial boundaries is a counterintuitive reaction to developmental help: aid (or cargo) is less a favor than an obligation. Volunteers, missionaries, and professional aid workers throughout the archipelago complain that the so-called beneficiaries of development often act as if they are doing outsiders a favor by accepting their assistance (Tongoa): One hears demands for payment to accept water-borne piping (Malakula); participation in community labor is rejected in favor of individual salaries (Tanna). Perhaps development workers are viewed as saving their own souls through charitable acts and therefore should pay local recipients for the privilege. As in con-docolonial days, efforts on the part of the white world to gain influence through gift giving falls prey to intervillage jealousy and rivalry.

To social scientists, particularly those who reject the biological basis of race, black and white are disreputable categories of group classification. In the Vanuatu context the referents "Melanesian" and "European," though commonly used, are not much better: The former overlooks the Polynesian ancestry of Ambae, Wallis, and Futuna island-ers while the latter ignores the southern-hemispheric specificity of Aus-tralians and New Zealanders.

Even if commonly used to dichotomize the world racially, *waet-man* and *blakman* are not the only relevant racial categories in Vanuatu. Indochinese (particularly Vietnamese) were once prominent laborers on French-owned plantations and in the Forrari manganese mine on Efate. (A well-endowed confidant of Walter Lini, Dinh van Than has played an increasingly visible role in Vanuatu politics.) Capitalist Chinese still dominate the dry goods, general trade, and duty-free shops in Vila and Luganville, while Communist Chinese laborers from the PRC con-structed the present parliament building. Malaysians have provoked controversy by their aggressive logging operations. But the most promi-nent group to encroach on traditional racial boundaries are the Japan-ese. For those ni-Vanuatu who still mistrust Japan on account of World War II, the notion of a Pacific century of Nippon dominance is anath-ema.[47] Nevertheless, as local Japanese investment, particularly in cattle ranching, tourism, and fishing, continues to grow, antiquated mental boundaries that used to divide the political world into black and white, and the white world into English and French, will have to shift to ac-commodate the new realities of an expanding Pacific Rim.

Sensitivity about the demographic diminutiveness of Vanuatu can stunt national self-confidence. Few ni-Vanuatu realize that the entire population of Vanuatu would fit into the Texas Astrodome, but most now do know that for all of the rest of the world their islands are small dots in a large ocean that itself encompasses only part of the globe.

Demographic chauvinism on the part of outsiders can contribute to a lingering paternalism, if not racism, on the part of some old-time planters and expatriates. Some long-established whites do not take seri-ously the notion of an independent republic of Vanuatu, pointing out the lack of educational achievement of government ministers and the inability of the country to function without foreign aid and technical expertise. Alleged corruption on the part of government ministers is another favorite justification for denying the legitimacy of sovereignty. Unintegrated expatriates will smugly refer to ni-Vanuatu as "locals" or "ni-Vans." Even if they stand cosmologically at the center of this world, ni-Vanuatu remain enclosed within racial barriers, which, whether viewed domestically or internationally, require adjustment.

ECONOMIC BOUNDARIES

"Mi stap nomo"—this simple, commonly used phrase speaks volumes about the chasm between a self-subsistence worldview and a developmental one. "I just live" or "I just am," while speaking to a lack of regular employment or occupation, bears no stigma or shame in Vanuatu. He who fishes, she who does garden work, do not think of themselves as holding a job. "Work" is something one is paid to do; living off the sea or the land is just "being." As in the heyday of the plantation, much wage labor is still itinerant. If one works, it is for a designated length of time, or until one has achieved a specific financial goal. Lifetime or career employment is relatively rare. A number of former ni-Vanuatu policemen I happened to meet fit this pattern. But the phenomenon is perhaps best described by a man in his twenties, returning from an afternoon of fishing, whom I encountered on the outskirts of Walaha on West Ambae: "If you want to eat, you just go to the beach and catch a fish. Otherwise, you go to your garden and grow vegetables. You don't need money, just a little to buy soap or kerosene. But if you want to, you can do without. *Mi stap nomo.*"

This man had gone to school for a few years but did not graduate. He exemplified a locally common proclivity for serenity and tranquillity. ("It's good here. It's quiet. No cars, no noise. Nobody bothers you.") He expressed many islanders' contentment with rural life: "I've been to Vila once. It was when I was a boy, for the Arts Festival. I wandered around, I looked at the stores. But if you don't have vatu [money] what's the use?"

In fact, as the earlier discussion on migration and urbanization bears out, increasingly ni-Vanuatu are renouncing the island-paradise caricature and moving to town to "make vatu." Western television, a fairly recent innovation, is also whetting materialist drives. Yet the work ethic, the push for achievement, the developmental model has far from taken hold in Vanuatu. There is residual resistance, often internalized, against an individual getting too far ahead of the group. Melanesian

collectivities still exert an equalizing pull on exceptional accomplishment. Even in school, where the ethos of personal accomplishment is
most systematically taught, students tend to resist submitting home-
work—and taking exams—in isolation from one another. Being singled
out for superior performance is considered more embarrassing than ennobling. If individualism, materialism, and competition are indeed social
prerequisites for economic growth, then the gaps between Melanesian
and Western notions of development, of which growth remains an integral part, remain wide indeed.

Again on the island of Efate, the villagers of Erakor push these
cultural economic boundaries to the limit. Consumerism, upward mobility, and conspicuous consumption have turned this Melanesian settlement into the prototypical suburb.[48] In condocolonial times known as a
bastion of local-level Francophonie, for better or worse Erakor may
represent the future of ni-Vanuatu economic individualism.

On a macroeconomic level, the shift from near-total reliance on a
single primary export commodity to a more diversified and services-ori-
ented market is one that many a developing country has struggled to
make. Vanuatu's economic transformation entails reducing its traditional
dependence on copra in favor of offshore banking and tourist-related
industries. Even if *vatu,* paper money, has practically supplanted tusker
pigs as a medium of exchange, replacing the coconut with the computer
will take many more years to come.

At the conclusion of an interview in August 1992, former Prime
Minister Walter Lini inquired, in a tone of undisguised irony, "Who
invented this development thing?" No matter how prominently economic development figures as an issue in political speeches, there is little
frustration among ni-Vanuatu about being impoverished or underdevel-
oped. Although there are signs that an indigenous ruling class is emerging (one that, for example, sends its children abroad to be educated),
class as such does not yet constitute a major new boundary. There is
little of the sense of relative deprivation that incites other peoples in the
Third World to change, revolution, or violence.[49] Political battles over
symbols—such as that between government officials and John Frummers
over the American flag on Tanna—are no less keen for the paucity of
economic stakes. Even though the economy of Vanuatu has greatly expanded, diversified, and monetized in recent years,[50] wide gulfs still remain between the mind-sets of national development planners and outer
islanders who are still content to *stap nomo.*

TEMPORAL BOUNDARIES

For all the theoretical refinement that the term has undergone since the 1950s, "development" for many practitioners and would-be beneficiaries remains a handmaiden to modernity. But both development and modernity imply a linearity and progression in time that is not consistent with the Melanesian worldview. Bonnemaison makes this point brilliantly in the context of his analysis of the rebellion of Tanna.[51] However, the implications go far beyond that of the 1980 secessionist attempt, for the very notion of a modern state within modern history is at odds with a *kastom* whose temporal referent is neither the lived present or human history. For the real people of *kastom,* the time that counts is mythical history, primordial genesis, sacred time. Construction of a nation-state whose boundaries in no way correspond to experienced pathways of movement has been a formidable challenge. Nationalist engineers overcome the contradiction by melding *kastom* with state, and their success to date has been admirable. Yet as long as indigenous notions of time persist, the nationalist and developmental projects will be diluted.

A more prosaic analysis would contrast "Vanuatu time" with clock time. Private employers in town bemoan workers' unreliability in showing up "on time"; in the outer islands, reliance on watches to coordinate meeting times is an aberration. Chronometric time may indeed be culturally oppressive; it is nevertheless acknowledged as a hallmark of modern society.

In opposition to customary notions of time, eschatological theologies and millenarian sects are beginning to flourish in Vanuatu. For all their emphasis on the end of the world and the end of time, such movements establish outward solidarities and long-lasting continuities with like-minded believers in Europe, Australia, and North America. End-of-worldism, despite its catastrophic outlook, looks forward, not backward. Yet fixation on apocalyptic, no less than mythical, time is at odds with the developmental project of the Vanuatu state and its international donors. Competing concepts of time constitute yet another set of new mental boundaries in Vanuatu, one that parallels a recently noted phenomenon for Melanesia writ large.[52]

BLURRED MEANINGS, BLURRED BOUNDARIES

"Writing up" often forces the social scientist to impose on the subject at hand a structure and a clarity that in the field may be as absent to the informant as it is to the researcher. For those who have not experienced the culture under investigation firsthand, there is the danger that the written structure may be artificial and the clarity misleading.

At several junctures in the course of my fieldwork in Vanuatu—and I am not speaking about kava time—I became uneasily conscious of a certain haziness, indefiniteness, and vagueness regarding the information I was receiving. Contradictory, incomplete, and indeterminant statements (or what I took to be such) periodically punctured whatever gestalt I thought I was imposing on my exposure to local politics and society. Blurred explanations of ongoing and immediately past events seemed to permeate personal conversations, radio broadcasts, and even newspaper articles. It was as if a cognitive fog, a Melanesian haze, had engulfed my brain.

An easy explanation, of course, resides in the oft-assumed inability of an outsider to penetrate and assimilate fully the deep structure of another culture's patterns of thought and reason. But this explanation attributes an impossibility to intercultural communication that my other transcultural experiences bely and fails to address my other observation: that systematic vagueness often characterized communication among ni-Vanuatu themselves. That such dialogic open-endedness was occurring in Bislama, a language not particularly steeped in precision or exactitude, occurred to me more than once.

I might not have admitted to my cognitive vulnerability were it not for the excuse—or comfort—provided by my rereading of the classic texts of the eminent Oceanic anthropologist Jean Guiart. Guiart's books on Espiritu Santo and Tanna are replete with references to the kind of informational imprecision and incompleteness that undermined my own sense of confidence when probing matters of Melanesian import. Descriptions of social and political organization, Guiart found, were mired in the "vague, the approximate" *(du flou, de l'à peu près)*, making it "impossible to describe an orderly and rigorous social system."[53] For Guiart, such vagueness is linked to spatial scattering of community, and both stem from a "social atomism common throughout the archipelago."[54] Chiefs exercise limited authority, territorially as well as jurisprudentially. Some communities have no chiefs at all. In different districts of the same island the criteria for becoming a Moli, high chief, vary considerably. Even the pig-killing ceremony, a venerable institution on some islands, on others became "a superimposed, ill-defined ceremonial pastiche."[55] Atomism, acephalism, dispersal, and localism all contribute to a lack of consistency, frustrating the Cartesian desire for rationality and order.

Yet a more trenchant explanation for the boundaries of meaning and comprehension may be derived from William Rodman's insight into "hidden talk" (*qaltavalu* in the language of Longana, Ambae). *Qaltavalu* encompasses implicit meanings, rhetorical devices, and parabolic instruction. Yet it is more than just parable, another culturally revered mode of discourse in Vanuatu. (Indeed, President Léyé has long been known as "Parable Man," and Chief Willie Bongmatur, former head of the Malvatumauri, was also a master of the analogy.) When "indirection [is] raised to the level of a fine art,"[56] insider and outsider alike may be excused for not always "getting it." A man asks a woman for rice, though it is not food he is seeking; a teacher responds to his student's question, not with an answer, but a puzzle to work through.

Beyond social atomism and hidden talk there is, perhaps, an underlying Melanesian worldview that, even when adapted to the modern spheres of politics and media communications, refuses categorization of reality and the indiscriminate revealing of accurate information. Several mental explorers of Melanesia, including Joan Larcom and Lamont Lindstrom, have proposed that, in indigenous society, knowledge is both a commodity and a manifestation of power and is not freely shared or given away. For all the rhetoric of a "Pacific way" and a "Melanesian way," there remain within Vanuatu alone multiple understandings of the world and its processes. The monotheistic uniformity imposed by Christianity and the Western rationalization wrought by condocolonialism have been far from complete. Boundaries between Anglophone and Francophone worldviews, between Protestant and Catholic versions of theology, between indigenous and pidgin modes of communication, between Melanesian and condocolonial constructions of the world—all these have contributed to a lack of common perception and expression.

Video and television are now blurring perceptual meaning in new ways. Although government censorship of cinematic imports goes back to condocolonial days, there is no longer any effective control over the local distribution of videotapes. Indeed, until 1988, "VCR-television-generator packages were common favour-currying 'development' donations from High Commissions and Embassies . . . and remain popular 'pork-barrel' gifts from politicians."[57] A tradition of unchallenged acceptance of Western instruction makes for rather uncritical viewing of Western films and videos. Cinematically unsophisticated villagers do not know "how to separate the instructional information from the dramas, the facts from the fiction."[58] In the mind of many a ni-Vanuatu viewer, video fantasy and existential reality are one. Even for the bookishly educated, the most science-fictional violence portrayed by Hollywood can be true.

Given the limited circulation of videos, their misinformational impact on ni-Vanuatu perceptions of Western society was relatively contained. It was television that represented the floodgate to hypermedia exposure, and Prime Minister Walter Lini kept that gate closed. Convinced of the need to shield the nation from the influences of Western consumerism and inappropriate social models, Lini put a moratorium on television.[59] Upon his election as prime minister, Maxime Carlot reversed the ban and, with French government funding, introduced television to Vanuatu in July of 1992. Carlot viewed television as a way to "open up to the world," as an expression of national sovereignty, as a tool for education and development, and as a method for churches to demonstrate "that Vanuatu is a constitutionally Christian country."[60] The first televised broadcasts were images from the summer Olympics in Barcelona, but soon they included such prime-time favorites as *The Simpsons* and *Bugs Bunny*. New Zealand joined France as a source of free programming.

In a society where dream time coexists with real time, where cargo cults suddenly erupt and then melt away, where John Frum is as real as Jacques Chirac, where video is taken for reality, it is perhaps inevitable that misunderstanding periodically prevails over understanding and that minds blur rather than meet.

CHAPTER 6

Global Boundaries in the Microcosm

Boundaries are an essential component of a recognizable and coherent identity. Whether the borders in question are territorial, ideological, religious, economic, social, cultural, or amalgams thereof, their erosion or dissolution is likely to be traumatic.

—Ken Jowitt, "The New World Disorder"

Islands are always fragments torn, the ends of the route, the shores of anxiety; the harmony of the world dissolves in their confined spaces, as do certainties of the soul, with the breaching of borders.

—Joël Bonnemaison, "The Metaphor of the Tree and the Canoe"

Writing about the new world disorder that has succeeded the disintegration of the Soviet Union and the end of global East–West bipolarity, Ken Jowitt stresses the fragility of those familiar borders and identities that germinated during the Cold War. Particularly for the Third World, geographical boundaries, ideological identities, and directions of foreign aid were a by-product of the struggle between the U.S.A. and the U.S.S.R. Wars over would-be annexation in the Persian Gulf and ethnic borders in the former Yugoslavia show how unsettling the dissipation of these old frames of reference and demarcations (capitalist West versus communist East, with a putatively nonaligned South in between) has already been.

It would be aggrandizing folly to suggest a parallel between the impact of the end of the Condominium in the New Hebrides and the end of the Cold War upon the Third World at large. Or would it? Although there is indisputably no comparison between the stakes involved in the two cases (except, of course, for the people of Vanuatu themselves), the process of dismantling entrenched mental boundaries is really not so very different. In both cases competing ideologies and mind-sets superimposed by rival great powers tended to split apart smaller and weaker peoples who were caught in the middle. In both cases, donors used development assistance as an inducement to create and solidify alliances to further their respective national interests. No matter that the master puppeteers were American and Soviet in the one case and French and British in the other; nor that the global struggle pitted capitalism against communism while the Melanesian contest was between condocolonialism and independence. It is more significant that in both cases the grand patrons managed to avoid fighting each other directly, leaving the spilling of blood (mercifully limited in Vanuatu) to civil wars and internecine conflicts among their clients.

To nations coping with the uncertainties of boundary collapse — whether of ideologies, territories, or identities — Vanuatu may serve as a beacon. Though facing past legacies and problems still in the making, Vanuatu has emerged from its one secessionist crisis with surprisingly few scars. Ever since, it has been moving, however cumbersomely, toward transcending the institutional and psychological effects of the Condominium. Unfortunately, as in so many other nations long subject to European rule, decolonization in Vanuatu has consisted essentially of nationalizing and adapting those institutions inherited from the overlords. Rarely have decolonized nations had the luxury of deciding from scratch which institutional forms and policies are truly necessary or appropriate for them.

One prime example of institutional inertia in Vanuatu is the lack of a full-blown language policy. The government needs to take into account the perils facing the vernacular tongues and the ambiguity of having a national language (Bislama) officially ignored in the schools. There is also the unchallenged persistent hegemony of two European languages in the educational system. Another sector demanding institutional decolonization is the legal system. Citizens deserve a relevant and autochthonous system of criminal justice to replace the currently incongruous one which applies emphatically non-Melanesian rules and principles of jurisprudence to ni-Vanuatu defendants.

For all its religious referents, Vanuatu (and in this it differs little from most developing nations) has not yet exploited its independence as an opportunity for consummate re-creation. "[I]n a turbulent, dislocating, traumatic Genesis environment the dissolution of existing boundaries and identities can generate a corresponding potential for the appearance of genuinely new *ways of life*."[1] Though the boundaries dividing ni-Vanuatu have not totally disappeared, and a new Melanesian Eden is far from realization, the goal of forging a progressive *and* indigenous polity, one that is truly Melanesian in its institutions as well as its discourse, can still be attained.

The legacy of condocolonialism may be clearly seen in the contrast between two nearby institutions in the heart of Port Vila. Up on a hill, at the "Law Court," as Anglophones call it (*Tribunal* for the Francophones), proceedings are conducted in a freshly painted, wood paneled chamber, cooled with ceiling fans. The case—a civil one—is quite complicated. After twenty minutes the observer can barely fathom the gist of it. There are references to a corporation with a branch in Arizona, investment in a racehorse (Total Departure), and other wheelings and dealings of high finance. The chamber is empty except for the litigants, all of whom are not even present.

Although we are in the Republic of Vanuatu, a sovereign nation in the South Pacific, these civil proceedings might just as well be taking place in London. The sitting magistrate is a blond English lady. The examining lawyer wears a black judicial gown. The witness on the stand—and he is standing—wears long sleeves and a tie. The plaintiff sports a three-piece suit; the stylishly made-up woman at his side is also blond. The men wear shoes: closed, polished, leather footwear, worn on a South Pacific island principally to score some social or political point, as if to say, "My feet will *not* be exposed to you!" The accents, the participants, the judicial language—all are quintessentially English. The magistrate is very keen on distinguishing documents as being originals, copies, and annotated copies. Other than the colonial tropical architecture and the view of Vila Bay, the only reminder that we are not in Great Britain is the sole black person present, the *greffier,* or scribe, who is following events with an air of interested befuddlement. Criminal proceedings in Vanuatu are invariably "black"; but civil cases are "white."

The visitor manages to absent himself from the excruciatingly boring proceedings because of a previous appointment. He walks down the hill, a mere fifty paces, to the Ecole Publique. Here, business is being conducted in French. All participants are natives of the country. Here, too, a language foreign to the average ni-Vanuatu is used. The teachers (with few exceptions middle-aged women) are teaching the children French verbs, conjugations, sayings, and songs. Though this is probably the best-supported Francophone public primary school in the country, the *directeur* complains of neglect. One is drawn, once again, to the issue of footwear: a pile of thongs, some with the proprietors' name etched on the plastic, lies outside each classroom. Flip-flops are the national footwear, and they should be removed before entering someone's home, or the classroom.

Are these not legacies of the Condominium? Emerging from the Ecole Publique one looks upward to the Law Court, where the high-finance, corporate multinational, Old Bailey–like proceedings are continuing. *This* is where the money that counts, the interests of the outside world, are decided, in English, by and among whites. Below, at the school, the *directeur* bemoans the marginalization of French education in the former Nouvelles Hébrides. In neither place is ordinary speech, the national language Bislama, to be heard. Three languages, one country, two worlds, fifty paces.

There is growing recognition that, for the world at large, political space must be "reimagined."[2] Classical distinctions between domestic and international politics must be rethought. "[G]lobalization challenges the assumptions of the bounded sovereign state. . . . [A]s definer of political boundaries and the boundaries of political space" the state is in flux. At the same time, it behooves us to acknowledge that, just as colonialism had disproportionate effects on the colonized vis-à-vis the colonizer, so will globalization affect the North and South quite differently. "The state may be in transition, but the specific nature of this transition varies from a Western to a postcolonial environment."[3]

Decolonization and nation building require the simultaneous dismantling and reconstruction of boundaries. Juridical and cognitive barriers to solidarity with colonially divided neighbors must be broken down. At the same time, the creation of a sense of nationhood requires that new contours of identity be erected. Managing both processes successfully in an age of informational and economic globalization requires visionary management of boundaries. Developmental success hinges on the ability of leaders and policymakers to recognize both the psychological and the territorial dimensions of the boundary.

Yet even the most visionary leadership must be sensitive to geohistorical constraints. For autonomous garden-plot growers throughout much of the archipelago the government of the sovereign Republic of Vanuatu will continue to mean little more than the politics of Port Vila. Their mental maps will not change. Beyond periodic symbolic displays, such as elections, the state remains at best remote from the consciousness and daily life of a good many ni-Vanuatu. For others, the democratic polity borders on the nonsensical. "Whiteman elections are no good here," one Tannese informed me. "You constantly have to elect your chief over and over again. Why? With us, we choose a leader once and for all and are done with it. *That's* the way we know how to do things." For a political scientist, the functional irrelevance of the state remains one of the most startling aspects of life in this postcondocolonial nation.

Vanuatu epitomizes the five dimensions of globalization.[4] Increased interdependence, the first dimension, is part of the independent nation's fate. No longer can these Melanesian islands be considered "the ends of the earth," cocooned by patronizing European condocolonizers. A prominent stance in national liberation and antinuclear debates at the United Nations is one example of Vanuatu's connectedness; so too, unfortunately, is the need for AIDS prevention posters even on the outer islands. Nor is Vanuatu immune from informal imperialism (the second dimension). Newer, more proximate regional powers are replacing the original British and French empires through patterns of economic domination and developmental dependency. Development workers, particularly at the grass-roots level, bemoan the rampant expectations of donor aid that undermine community self-reliance. Cultural homogenization, the third dimension, does not bypass Vanuatu, particularly now that videos and television are becoming part of the national diet. A personal example: One lad in Luganville knew the players of the Boston Celtics better than I, though I occupy the same municipal space as the basketball team. A simultaneous increase in uniformity and diversity, the fourth dimension, recalls the byword of "unity in diversity," so often invoked in speeches by Vanuatu's leaders. Anticolonialism and Third World national liberation were almost a stock formula for political change by the time they came to the New Hebrides; *kastom,* the Melanesian Way, and Melanesian socialism, in contrast, are unique (if ambiguous) expressions of an otherwise familiar form of nationalist politics. Space–time collapse, the fifth dimension, will also engulf Vanuatu, now that Telecom Vanuatu has linked local computer users to the World Wide Web. (Real time, televised transmission of the Barcelona Olympics to Vila in 1992, was a watershed with respect to transcending temporal discontinuity.)

Such electronic transcendence of boundaries will do little to reduce the cognitive distance between outer islanders and the Vanuatu state. In the North, the computer revolution has already begun to create a wedge between the electronic elite and the informational proletariat. For Third World nations in general, the overshadowing of primary nation building by technological globalization will create even wider domestic, knowledge-based boundaries.

FOREIGN POLICY AND FRANCE

Major reorientations in international relations since independence have entailed a mental remapping of the world for ni-Vanuatu leaders (see Map 5). In condocolonial days France and Britain were the primary

Television comes to Vanuatu; viewing the Barcelona Olympics.

external actors influencing New Hebridean society. Missionary and trad-ing interests extended to Australia a secondary power role, while World War II conferred on the United States significant, if fleeting, influence. Geographical regional realities counted for little, except for the tempo-rary menace of Japan.

International relations for the New Hebrides were triangulated. As they engaged in a "rivalry-in-partnership" with each other, Britain and France competitively flexed their condocolonial muscles vis-à-vis the New Hebrideans. But these muscles, because of the clumsiness of Condomin-ium, were flabby and uncoordinated. New Hebrideans consequently adopted a counter-condocolonial response of "divide-though-con-quered." In the 1960s and 1970s local communities keenly played the French and British residencies off against each other, just as they had previously done with competing missionary denominations. Lacking po-litical and national unity, though, New Hebrideans remained subordinate players in the condocolonial game. This accounts for their lowest position in the pictorial representation of New Hebrides triangulation (see Figure 7). With independence, the two former condocolonial powers receded in prominence, giving way to other regional and ideological partners. In the case of the British, early believers in Pacific decolonization, withdrawal

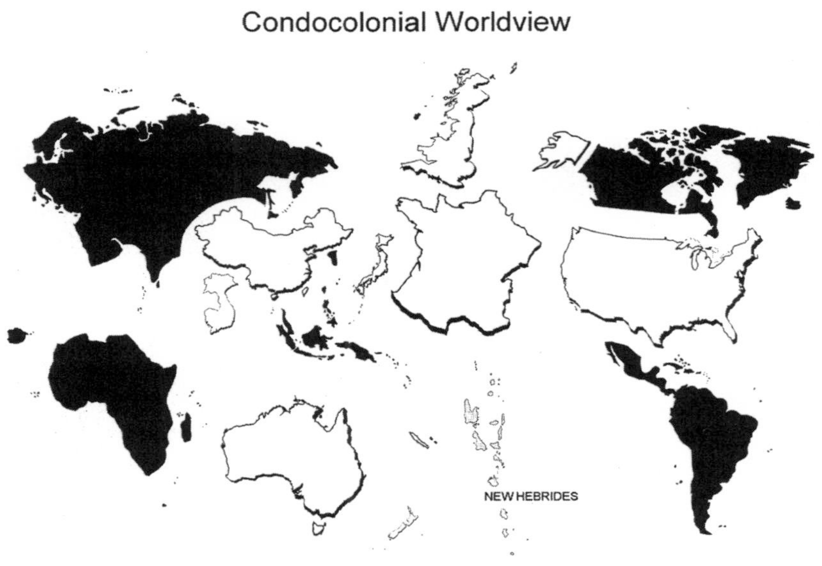

Condocolonial Worldview

NEW HEBRIDES

Map 5. Changing Mental Maps

of influence was largely voluntary. For France, the debacle of the Santo rebellion, and the ensuing Francophobic policies of the Lini government, meant that her eclipse was undesired but unavoidable.

New Hebridean triangulation in international relations has been superseded by more pluralistic and centripetal dynamics, which accounts for the Vanuatu "hub-wheel" constellation (see Figure 8). Australia and New Zealand, economic and strategic powerhouses of the South Pacific, have naturally filled the vacuum left by France and Britain. But there has been no mere replacement of European condocolonial powers by Oceanic regional ones. In its first decade Vanuatu underscored its decolonization and sovereignty by establishing diplomatic relations with Cuba (an early supporter of independence), moving closer to Libya (although the circumstances were ultimately embarrassing to the Lini government), and signing a major fishing treaty with the U.S.S.R. Although not much came of plans to adopt the Tanzanian model of socialism to Vanuatu, a greater consciousness of Africa emerged from such ideological musings, as it did from diplomatic representations on behalf of the South West African People's Organization (SWAPO) and the African National Congress (ANC).

Independent Worldview

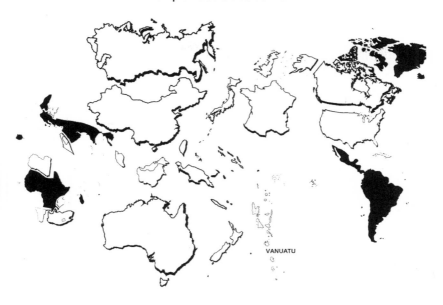

As an active member of the Melanesian Spearhead Group, formed in 1986 in part to lobby for Kanaky independence in New Caledonia, Vanuatu has privileged the most proximate partners in her emerging regional identity. Yet, however attractive Melanesian identity may be ideologically, it will not prove as significant economically. In the long run, more distant Pacific Rim superpowers will become increasingly significant external actors in Vanuatu's polity and economy. (An interesting exception to this tendency is the Netherlands, which in recent years has become the most significant market for Vanuatu's export commodities; See Table 12.) Neocondocolonialism in Vanuatu will not arise from resurgent political rivalries between Britain and France; it might, however, result from expanded economic rivalry between China and Japan.

As an independent republic, Vanuatu is a member of a host of international, regional, and developmental organizations, such as the United Nations (UN), the South Pacific Commission (SPC), the South Pacific Forum (SPF), the Asian Development Bank (ADB), and the Economic and Social Commission for Asia and the Pacific (ESCAP). As a former Anglo-French Condominium that is officially bilingual, Vanuatu enjoys the distinction of belonging to both the British Commonwealth and its French equivalent, the Agence de Coopération Culturelle et Technique (ACCT).

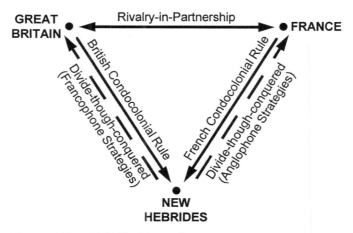

Figure 7. New Hebrides Triangulation

Notwithstanding their lack of French, in the 1980s Prime Minister Walter Lini and, in 1991, Prime Minister Donald Kalpokas represented Vanuatu in meetings of the Conférence des Chefs d'Etat et de Gouvernment des pays ayant en commun l'usage du français (Conference of heads of state and government of countries which have in common the use of French), more colloquially referred to as the Summit of Francophonie.

The mercurial nature of its relations with France presents the greatest challenge in attempts to map Vanuatu's international profile. In the early 1980s Vanuatu's foreign policy was largely premised on opposition to French sovereignty in New Caledonia and, on account of nuclear testing, in Polynesia. French ambassadors were almost regularly expelled, and domestic Francophonie was accordingly endangered. Mental boundaries between ni-Vanuatu Anglophones and Francophones automatically hardened as a result of these diplomatic roils.

Table 12 Vanuatu's Principal Trading Partners, 1990

Imports		Exports	
Australia	(37%)	Netherlands	(26%)
Japan	(12%)	Japan	(18%)
New Zealand	(10%)	Australia	(12%)
Fiji	(9%)	New Caledonia	(8%)
France	(8%)	France	(7%)

Source: Compiled from data in *The Europa Yearbook,* Europa Publications, 1995.

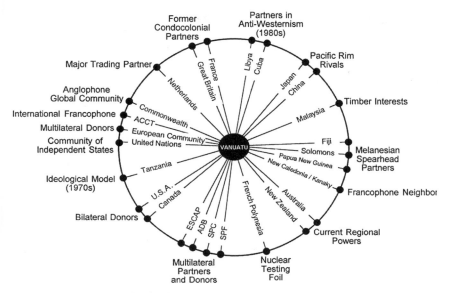

Figure 8. Vanuatu Hub-wheel

With the election of Maxime Carlot as prime minister in 1991, France enjoyed a considerable reversal in Pacific fortune. So did ni-Vanuatu Francophones, though not to the degree hoped for. Official opposition to French sovereignty over New Caledonia was muted (though this was in part due to the Matignon Accords), and French economic aid to Vanuatu increased significantly. Indeed, in 1996 official French per-capita aid to Vanuatu (equivalent of $10 million for 165,000 inhabitants) was the highest in the world.[5] Visits from a French warship, parachuting paratroopers on independence day, the return of previously deported immigrants, compensation for erstwhile rebels—all these drew Vanuatu and France much, much closer.[6] As a kind of symbolic capstone, in late 1995 Prime Minister Maxime Carlot Korman was awarded one of the highest distinctions in Francophonie: decoration as Grand Officer in the Order of the Legion of Honor. Not unexpectedly, such Franco-Vanuatu rapprochement elicited the accusation from the opposition, and especially Walter Lini, that the UMP had been "selling" Vanuatu to France. Reporting by influential English-language publications, such as *The Economist* and *Pacific Islands Monthly*, reinforced the suspect and almost unnatural image of a France returning to the former Condominium. (British and Australian activity, in contrast, is usually taken for granted.) Electoral defeat of the UMP in 1998 may well cool this renewed French ardor for Vanuatu.

Rapprochement with France notwithstanding, international relations in the postcondocolonial period have been characterized by an unprecedented opening up to and diversification of multiple foreign interests. Nevertheless, it is in the realm of foreign policy that the mental boundaries between Anglophone and Francophone ni-Vanuatu are perhaps the least susceptible to dismantling.

ENVIRONMENT AS BOUNDARY BRIDGE

Perhaps no other phenomenon more cogently challenges the control exercised by conventional boundaries than does the environment: Pollution scorns sovereignty. Even though it does not eliminate the relevance of political divisions, ecological interconnectedness seriously limits their power. Denuclearization and deforestation are two environmental issues that illustrate, not only for Vanuatu but for the Pacific at large, the overlap of environmental and mental boundaries.

Under the guidance of Walter Lini, Vanuatu was one of the most vocal small-island advocates of a nuclear-free Pacific. Closely allied with New Zealand on this point, the U.S. nuclear-powered submarine was *machina non grata* in Vanuatu waters. Signatory to the 1985 Rarotonga treaty for a South Pacific Nuclear Free Zone (SPNFZT)—indeed, having held out for an even stronger version—the Lini government joined other South Pacific nations in denouncing French nuclear testing in the Murora atoll, located several thousand miles to the east of Vanuatu.

Under the leadership of Prime Minister Maxime Carlot Korman, Vanuatu backed off from its earlier unequivocal condemnation of French nuclear testing. When, shortly after his election as president in 1995, Jacques Chirac announced the end of the Mitterrandist moratorium on nuclear testing in French Polynesia, Vanuatu became the sole respite in the Pacific from unmitigated outrage. While never outrightly endorsing Chirac's stance, Vanuatu exhibited "moderate opposition with a will to maintain political dialogue with Paris."[7] Indeed, Vanuatu's rapprochement with France under Carlot Korman may have created a slight nuclear wedge between the umbrella South Pacific Forum (fifteen members, including Australia and New Zealand) and the regional Melanesian Spearhead Group (Vanuatu, Papua New Guinea, the Solomon Islands, and the FLNKS party of New Caledonia). Whereas the former organization expressed "extreme outrage" in its September 1995 summit meeting in Madang, Papua New Guinea, over the resumed testing, the latter's August meeting on Malakula resulted in the somewhat more conciliatory Lakatoro Declaration, which voiced opposition but called for continuing discussion of the issue with France.[8]

Sandalwood was nearly eradicated from the New Hebrides in the early nineteenth century. Toward the end of the twentieth, Vanuatu has again attracted overseas interest in its forests. Timber-hungry logging companies, mostly from Malaysia, have resumed tree cutting on Erromango, Santo, and other islands. On this environmental issue Carlot Korman gradually moved toward a more hard-line defense of his nation's hardwood heritage, instituting a ban on the export of round logs—a ban that his successor repealed. Whether any independent but financially vulnerable government can indefinitely resist external economic pressure to permit profit-earning strip clearing remains to be seen. Problematic trade-offs between essential revenues and precious ecosystems are hardly unique to Vanuatu. Given the state's relative weakness in monitoring business and enforcing the law throughout the archipelago, Vanuatu's environment may be more vulnerable than apparent at first glance.

CONDOMINIAL CAUTION

From time to time, the idea of a condominium is proposed as a solution to seemingly intractable problems of competing national sovereignties. In recent times, Jerusalem, the object of competing Israeli and Palestinian claims of sovereignty, has been suggested as a candidate for a condominial solution. International lawyer John Whitbeck has developed the idea of a condominium ("joint sovereignty over an undivided city") as the only workable and inspirational solution to the most incorrigible site of Middle Eastern conflict.[9] Whitbeck twice invokes the New Hebrides (including its mixed court) as a precedent relevant to his optimistic assessment of the "condominium solution."

Cool-headed reassessment of the experience in the New Hebrides, where animus between the competing powers was much less than it is in the Middle East, should instill caution. A condominium does not reduce rivalry but merely displaces it within a complex and riven structure subject to manipulation. Far from institutionalizing cooperation, a condominium can become a new sphere of competition and conflict. Jurists charged with interpreting multijurisdictional codes, not to mention policemen responsible for enforcing divergent, contending sets of laws, may often find themselves at a loss. For the administered themselves, the arrangement might really mean, as the old saw went in the New Hebrides, not condominium but pandemonium.

Of course, the Middle East is not the South Pacific. One could argue that it was its mode of operation, not its intrinsic structure, which caused the Condominium to fail in the New Hebrides. It is nevertheless incumbent on planners of Jerusalem's sovereignty to grasp fully the true outcomes of condominial rule before endorsing Vanuatu's past as a model for Jerusalem's future. At the very least, they need to weigh D. P. O'Connell's judgment that, from the perspective of international law, "the concept of Condominium is unstable and incongruous."[10]

OVERCOMING CONDOCOLONIALISM

It is not easy to reverse in a short time the divisions created by over three generations of joint colonialism. As long as ni-Vanuatu have to choose between being educated in English or in French, and as long as their political leaders are regarded as either Anglophone or Francophone, the challenge of building national unity will remain. Ceremonial reconciliation requires undergirding at every level, national as well as local, psychic as well as political.

There is one benefit of the condocolonial legacy, which should not be overlooked. It is true that the Condominium divided the South Pacific islanders of Vanuatu into two camps. However, because each colonial power was checked by the other, neither France nor Britain achieved undue influence anywhere in the archipelago. Ironically, having two competing colonial powers protected the New Hebrides from being overly colonized by either one of them. Though missionizing did eradicate indigenous life-styles on some islands, overall condocolonial neglect preserved a critical mass of traditional customs that otherwise might have been lost. Even those of the once-endangered *kastom* dances that are revived for public performance exude a spirit of authenticity that their New Caledonian counterparts, perhaps more fetching for their carefully rehearsed choreography, do not. Indigenous customs, ideologically recuperated and recast into nationalistic *kastom,* enabled the nation to enter independence with a viable sense of Melanesian identity and Vanuatu nationalism.

The challenge of independence will be to unite the insular peoples of Vanuatu by overcoming the long-standing indigenous, superimposed condocolonial, and emerging mental boundaries that divide them. Only then will the efforts to secure a more prosperous economic future be developmentally meaningful. One serious risk is that reliance on outside donors and the penetration of Western consumer society, as they have done in so many other developing nations, will compromise Vanuatu's cultural and political integrity. Vanuatu's trump card, practiced from playing off condocolonial powers against each other, is its strategic ability to counterbalance bilateral and multilateral donors alike.

During and throughout the Condominium, the people of the New Hebrides, partitioned not by territory but by ideology, were offered two basic Western models from which to choose. Independence, regionalism, and globalism have greatly increased and complexified the choices now open to the citizens of Vanuatu. The implications are no less portentous for the microcosmic setting. For as Vanuatu goes, so goes much of the developing world.

APPENDIX A: EXCERPTS FROM THE CONVENTION ESTABLISHING THE NEW HEBRIDES CONDOMINIUM

Signed in London, 27th February, 1906.

PROTOCOL.

The Undersigned, Eldon Gorst, Assistant Under-Secretary of State for Foreign Affairs, Knight Commander of the Most Honorable Order of the Bath; Hugh Bertram Cox, Assistant Under-Secretary of State for the Colonies, Companion of the Most Honorable Order of the Bath; Marcel Saint-Germain, Senator, President of the Council of Administration of the Colonial Office at the Ministry of the Colonies, Officer of the Order of Public Instruction, Holder of the Colonial Medal; Edouard Picanon, Inspector-General of the Colonies of the First Class, Governor of French Guiana, Officer of the Legion of Honour, Officer of the Order of Public Instruction, delegated respectively by the Government of His Britannic Majesty and by the Government of the French Republic, in order to draw up, in conformity with the Declaration of the 8th April, 1904, concerning the New Hebrides, an arrangement which shall put an end to the difficulties arising from the absence of jurisdiction over the natives of the New Hebrides and settle the disputes of their respective nationals in the said islands with regard to landed property, have agreed to the following provisions, which they have resolved to submit for the approval of their respective Governments:

PREAMBLE.

The Government of his Britannic Majesty and the Government of the French Republic, being desirous of modifying, as far as the New Hebrides are concerned, the Convention of the 16th November, 1887, respecting the New Hebrides and the islands leeward of Tahiti, in order to secure the exercise of their paramount rights in the New Hebrides and to assure for the future the better protection of life and property in the Group, have agreed on the following Articles:

GENERAL PROVISIONS.

ARTICLE I.
Status.

(1) The Group of the New Hebrides, including the Banks and Torres Islands, shall form a region of joint influence, in which the subjects and citizens of the two Signatory Powers shall enjoy equal rights of residence, personal protection, and trade, each of the two Powers retaining jurisdiction over its subjects or citizens, and neither exercising a separate control over the Group. . . .

ARTICLE VIII.
Native Administration.

(1) In the present Convention, "native" means any person of the aboriginal races of the Pacific who is not a citizen or subject or under the protection of either of the two Signatory Powers.

(2) No native, as defined above, shall acquire in the Group the status of subject or citizen or be under the protection of either of the two Signatory Powers.

(3) The High Commissioners and their Delegates shall have authority over the native Chiefs. They shall have power to make administrative and police regulations binding on the tribes, and to provide for their enforcement.

(4) They shall respect the manners and customs of the natives, where not contrary to the maintenance of order and the dictates of humanity. . . .

ARTICLE XVIII.
Official Languages.

Either the English or French language may be employed in proceedings before the Joint Court. In a suit between British subjects and French citizens, the proceedings shall be interpreted and the judgements shall be drawn up in both languages. The registers of the Court shall be kept in both languages. . . .

PROVISIONS RELATING TO LAND.

ARTICLE XXII.
Land Suits between Non-natives and Natives.

(1) In land suits, the rights of non-natives may be proved either by occupation or by title-deeds establishing the sale or grant of the land in question.

(2) When occupation is made of sole ground of a claim to ownership, visible and material proofs must be forthcoming, such as building, plantations, cultivation, cattle-rearing, improvements, clearing or fencing. Occupation must be bona fide, and have been continuous during three years at least. . . .

Appendix B: Excerpts from the Constitution of the Republic of Vanuatu

PREAMBLE

WE the people of the New Hebrides,
PROUD of our struggle for freedom,
DETERMINED to safeguard the achievement of this struggle,
CHERISHING our ethnic, linguistic and cultural diversity,
MINDFUL at the same time of our common destiny
HEREBY proclaim the establishment of the united and free Republic of the New Hebrides founded on traditional Melanesian values, faith in God, and Christian principles,
AND for this purpose give ourselves this Constitution.

CHAPTER 1

THE STATE AND SOVEREIGNTY

1. The Republic of the New Hebrides is a sovereign democratic state.
2. The Constitution is the supreme law of the New Hebrides.
3. (1) The national language of the Republic is Bislama. The official languages are Bislama, English, and French. The principal languages of education are English and French.
   (2) The Republic shall protect the different local languages which are part of the national heritage, and may declare one of them as a national language.
4. (1) National sovereignty belongs to the New Hebridean people which they exercise through their elected representatives.
   (2) The franchise is universal, equal and secret. Subject to such conditions or restrictions as may be prescribed by Parliament, every citizen of the New Hebrides who is at least 18 years of age shall be entitled to vote.
   (3) Political parties may be formed freely and may contest elections. They shall respect the Constitution and the principles of democracy.

CHAPTER 2

FUNDAMENTAL RIGHTS AND DUTIES

Part 1: Fundamental Rights

5. (1) The Republic of the New Hebrides recognizes, that, subject to any restrictions imposed by law on non-citizens, all persons are entitled to the following fundamental rights and freedoms of the individual without discrimination on the grounds of race, place of origin, religious or traditional beliefs, political opinions, language or sex but subject to respect for the rights and freedoms of others and to the legitimate public interest in defense, safety, public order, welfare and health:
   (a) life;
   (b) liberty;
   (c) security of the person;
   (d) protection of the law;
   (e) freedom from inhuman treatment and forced labour;
   (f) freedom of conscience and worship;
   (g) freedom of expression;
   (h) freedom of assembly and association;
   (i) freedom of movement;
   (j) protection for the privacy of the home and other property and from unjust deprivation of property; . . .

Part 2: Fundamental Duties

7. Every person has the following fundamental duties to himself and his descendants and to others:
   (a) to respect and to act in the spirit of the Constitution;
   (b) to recognize that he can fully develop his abilities and advance his true interests only by active participation in the development of the national community;
   (c) to exercise the rights guaranteed or conferred by the Constitution and to use the opportunities made available to him under it to participate fully in the government of the Republic;
   (d) to protect the New Hebrides and to safeguard to the national wealth, resources and environment in the interests of the present generation and of future generations;
   (e) to work according to his talents in socially useful employment and, if necessary, to create for himself legitimate opportunities for such employment;
   (f) to respect the rights and freedoms of others and to cooperate fully with others in the interests of interdependence and solidarity;
   (g) to contribute, as required by law, according to his means, to the

revenues required for the advancement of the Republic and the attainment of national objectives;

(h) in the case of a parent, to support, assist and educate all his children, legitimate and illegitimate, and in particular to give them a true understanding of their fundamental rights and duties and of the national objectives and of the culture and customs of the people of the New Hebrides;

(i) in the case of a child, to respect his parents. . . .

CHAPTER 3

CITIZENSHIP

9. On the day of Independence the following persons shall automatically become citizens of the New Hebrides:

(a) a person who has or had 4 grandparents who belong to a tribe or community indigenous to the New Hebrides and

(b) a person of New Hebridean ancestry who has no citizenship, nationality or the status of an optant. . . .

CHAPTER 12

LAND

71. All land in the Republic belongs to the indigenous custom owners and their descendants.

72. The rules of custom shall form the basis of ownership and use of land in the Republic.

73. Only indigenous citizens of the Republic who have acquired their land in accordance with a recognized system of land tenure shall have perpetual ownership of their land. . . .

Persons Interviewed

Titles and affiliations are those of February 1991–August 1992.

GOVERNMENT OFFICIALS AND ELECTED REPRESENTATIVES

James Adin, president of Ambae/Maewo local government council
George Andrew, chief of planning, statistics, and implementation
Selwyn Arutungai, secretary of Ambae/Maewo local government council
Raymond Aupy, language services consultant
Tom Bakeo, director of local government
Chief Willy Bongmatur Maldo, president of Malvatumauri
Vincent Boulekone, member of parliament (Pentecost)
Gaetano Bulewok, member of parliament (Pentecost)
Frank Dadza, regional development planning adviser
Osman dan Ladi, regional planning officer
Job Delaisa, director of public service
John Dickenson, president of Banks/Torres local government council
Isabelle Donald, deputy secretary of Epi local government council
Gerald Haberkorn, national planning and statistics officer
Paul Hakwa, mayor of Luganville
Lonsdale Hinge, treasurer of Ambae/Maewo local government council
Anatole Hymak, parliamentary clerk
John Bill Ierogen, superintendent of prisons
Louisette Issachar, language services director
Joe Joseph, secretary of Santo/Malo local government council
Maxime Carlot Korman, prime minister of the republic
Jean-Marie Léyé, president of TAFEA local government council
Walter Lini, member of parliament (Pentecost); former prime minister
Joseph Natuman, first secretary to prime minister
Kalo Nial, member of parliament (Santo/Mal)
Jean-Pierre Nirua, National Planning and Statistics Office
Chief Jimmy Noankikam, member of parliament (Tanna)
Chief John Peter, president of Malakula local government council
Sethy Regenvanu, cabinet minister
Jean Sésé, ministry of foreign affairs
Philip Shing, secretary of TAFEA local government council
Cecil Sinker, member of parliament (Banks and Torres)

John Solomon, secretary of Shepherds local government council
Merilyn Tahi, Vanuatu Centre for International Relations
Martin Tete, financial officer, directorate of local government
Fred Timakata, president of the republic
Samuel Turget, president of Santo/Malo government council
K. Usamoli, president of Shepherds government council
Serge Vohor, minister of foreign affairs

MEMBERS OF THE JUDICIARY

Dawn Barcinski, senior magistrate
Jonathan Baxter-Wright, public prosecutor
Edwin Goldsbrough, senior magistrate
Silas Hakwa, attorney general
Charles Vaudin d'Imecourt, chief justice
Vincent Lunabek, court clerk
Michael Purcell, public solicitor
Tagar Wycliffe, Santo magistrate

CHIEFS/BIGMEN/NOTABLES/CULTURAL CENTRE FIELDWORKERS

Ambae

Chief Johnson Bihu, Walaha
Chief Pastor Amos Fira, Walaha
Chief James Gwero, Nabangahake (interviewed in Saranambuka)
Chief Willie Levu, Walaha
Chief Moïse, Lolopuépué
Chief Rupert Ngarae, Atavoa
Chief James Tambe, Lolovenué
Chief Jackson Tarifolo, Natakaro

Ambrym

Dalili Andrew, Port Vato
Hamliplip, Port Vato
Cyprien Mermer
Daniel Naros, Sanesup
Abraham Talis, Sanesup
Taso Wilson aka Baïap, Yeleviak

Aneityum

Robert Nasave, Aniplithai
Chief Nawlita, Anelghowat
Chief David Yotaya, Umej
Tom Yowie, Anelghowat

Epi

Willie Kora, Nikaura
Chief Marcel, Mapvilao
John Morrison, Matel
Jimmy Simon (interviewed in Vila)
Chief Timothy (Nikaura)
Chief Mansik Vavatu, Burumba
Jack Waiwo, Laman Island
Atis Willy, Burumba

Hiu

Edward Pilis, Yakwana (interviewed in Yeu Gavigamena)
Pelam Mwayuraka, Yeu Gavigamena
Leonard Sorinyoy, Yeu Gavigamena

Lo

Chief Isaac, Rinuha
Peter Wotekwo, Lungharigi

Maewo

Cyril Aru, Gaiowo
Steven Aru, Lalafaru (interviewed in Nafénfene)
Kaiowo, Nafénfene
Chief Mark Meliu, Tanemeitu (interiewed in Nakoro)
Jona Tali, Nasawa
Jeffrey Uli, Gara Bay

Malakula

Benjamin Emile, Lamap
Ignace Liatlatmal, Walarano
David Remy, Maë
Chief Philip Talei, Levetbao (interviewed in Ronivié)
Tomé, Orap
Christophe Tulili, Unmet
Rémy Tusai, Unmet
David William aka Apia, Tautu (interviewed in Norsup)

Mota Lava

Chief Albi, Nerenigman
Fox Eldat, Queremandé
Chief Willie Lilip, Queremandé
Norman Wilson, Avar

Pentecost

Mark Gamali Ala, Abwantantora
Chief Luk Bulukolo, Loltong
Chief Willie Garae, Amatbobo
Charlot Gihiala, Latano
Richard Leona, Loltong
Chief Silas Narileo, Labultamata (interviewed in Abwantantora)
Charley Tor, Panlimsi (interviewed in Pangi)
Graham Tema Tor, Ronbatur
Chief Vital, Baravet (interviewed in Melsisi)
Pierre Vuty, Latano

Santo

Chief Tari Buluk, Fanafo
Chief Kufu Kevin, Hog Harbor (interviewed in Luganville)
Chief Liza, Forsinelli
Andy Moli, Fanafo
Pierre Naliupis, Port Olry
Dominique Raopepe, Port Olry
Moli Jimmy Stephens, Vila and Fanafo
Chief Tangus, Fanafo
Timothy Willis, Fanafo

Tanna

Chief Kiel Johnson, Lawliyuliyu
Chief Jonah, Yénémaha
Chief Kowia, Yarkei
Kissel Lop, Yakukak
Chief Tom Mweles, Ipeukel
Chief Jack Naiva, Yaohonan
Chief Namu, Yénémaha
Peter Poita, Ipeukal
Chief Samuel, Launapunga
Chief Seymo, Yarkei
Chief Tuk Numuau, Yakukak
Jack Usamoli, Bethel
Isaac Wan, Ipeukal

Toga

Chief Elton, Litao
Harry Palmer, Likwal
Paton, Litao

Tongoa

Alick Ben, Euta
Chief Tom Tipoloamata (interviewed in Vila)

Vanua Lava

Chief David, Mossina

EDUCATION OFFICIALS

(Unless noted otherwise, interviewed in Vila)
Billy Bakokoto, regional education officer
Susan Bareleo, principal, Vanuatu Teachers' College
Romain Batick, minister of education
Jean-Pierre Bulebanban, Melsisi Junior Secondary (Pentecost)
Jacques Gédéon, headmaster, Lycée Bougainville (Santo); acting director,
    TAFEA Junior Secondary (Tanna)
Michael Kihi, headmaster, Nivutiriki Junior Secondary School (Ambae)
Bob Kuau, president, teachers' union
Georges Kuse, director, Catholic educational system (DEC)
John Lanne, principal education officer for secondary schools
Sandy-Robson Maniuri, principal, Institut National de Technologie
Brother Marius, headmaster, Collège de Montmartre (Santo)
James Murray, headmaster, Malapoa College
Charles Niederhauser, department of education planner
Georges (Bob) Noel, headmaster, Laman Bay Junior Secondary (Epi)
Manwo Paul, director, Francophone Protestant educational system (FELP)
    (Malakula)
Jean-Louis Rousse, Francophone secondary school planner
Jacques Sésé, curriculum development centre
David Slimming, science adviser, ministry of education
Serge Soufflé, adviser, Lycée Bougainville
Peter Tarakoto, director general of education
Hollingsworth Tari, regional education officer (Ambae)
Olga Tari, headmaster, Collège de Santo (Santo)
George Worek, headmaster, Arep Secondary School (Mota Lava)
Barry Wrick, headmaster, Rensarie Junior Secondary School (Malakula)

PRIMARY SCHOOLS VISITED

Arep public (Vanua Lava)
Colardeau French government (Vila)
Craig Cove Catholic mission (Ambrym)
Erakor public (Efate)

Ere public (Tongoa)
Fali Catholic mission (Ambrym)
Iapilmai public (Tanna)
Ienaula/Louiapeng public bilingual (Tanna)
Ioahnanen public *kastom* (Tanna)
Itakoma public (Tongoa)
Katundaula public (Tongoa)
King's Cross public (Tanna)
Lamap Catholic mission (Malakula)
Lautapunga Catholic mission (Tanna)
Lemboroe public (Tongoa)
Lolopuépué Catholic mission (Ambae)
Loltong Catholic mission (Pentecost)
Lumbukuti public (Tongoa)
Maë Catholic mission (Malakula)
Melsisi Catholic mission (Pentecost)
Naboutariki public (Ambae)
Namaram Catholic mission (Pentecost)
Nottage public (Tongoa)
Nuguhu public (Lo)
Port Olry Catholic mission (Santo)
Port Vato public (Malakula)
St. Jeanne d'Arc Catholic mission (Efate)
Sesivi Catholic mission (Ambrym)
Tautu public (Malakula)
Telhei public (Mota Lava)
Umej Catholic mission (Aneityum)
Unmet Catholic mission (Malakula)
Vila public (Efate)
Vilakalaka public (Ambae)
Walarano Catholic mission (Malakula)
Wonesky public (Mota Lava)

PASTORS/PRIESTS

Father John Cecil, Loltano (Pentecost)
Father Esuva Din, Mossina (Vanua Lava)
Father Paul Donoghue, Walarano (Malakula)
Father Derek Finlay, Melsisi (Pentecost)
Pastor Amos Fira, Walaha (Ambae)
Bishop Francis Lambert, Luganville (Santo)
Father Gérard Leymang, Port Vila
Father Paul Monnier, Port Vila

Pastor Nawayang, Lowniel (Tanna)
Dr. Titus Path, Hog Harbor (Santo)
Pastor Dean Polinghorne, Walaha (Ambae)
Father Jean Rodet, Port Vila
Father Albert Sacco, Port Gilla
Father Bertrand Soucy, Lamap (Malakula)

DIPLOMATS

David Ambrose, Australian High Commissioner
Philip Guérin, French chargé d'affaires
Charles Louis le Guern, French cultural attaché
Robert Van Lierop, Vanuatu ambassador to the United Nations
M. Pain, French chargé de nationalité
John Thompson, British High Commissioner

MEDIA

Patrick Decloitre, *Pacific Islands Monthly*
François Isave, broadcaster for Radio Vanuatu
Godwin Ligo, director of Radio Vanuatu
Ambong Thompson, program supervisor of Radio Vanuatu and the *Vanuatu Weekly*

CONDOMINIUM AGENTS AND RESIDENCY OFFICIALS

Paul Gardissat, French education
Gordon Norris, British district agent
Jean-Jacques Robert, French inspector general
Dominique Vian, French district agent

PLANTERS AND SETTLERS

M. and Mme. Bienvenu
Max and Robert Chabot
Peter Colmar
Georges Cronsteadt
Charles Graziani
Gabriel Grilhault des Fontaines
Marie-Stella Laurent-Simonsen
Gilbert and Mère Leeman
Mimi Le Roi
Arthur Métois
Peter Morris
Henri Russet

Roy and Edwin Sarginson
Denis Savoie
Jeffrey Seggoe
Mme. Stegler

OTHERS

Charles Denjean, local director of Caisse Centrale de Coopération Economique
Graham Kalsakau, former chief minister of self-government
Aime Maléré, former UMP activist
Henri Ramirez, director of Vanitel
Ati George Sokomanu, former president of the republic

NOTES

PREFACE

1. Ron Crocombe, "The Continuing Creation of Identities in the Pacific Islands: Blood, Behaviour, Boundaries and Belief," in David Hooson, ed., *Geography and National Identity* (Oxford: Blackwell Publishers, 1994), p. 313.

2. Helen Hintjens and Malyn Newitt, eds., *The Political Economy of Small Tropical Islands: The Importance of Being Small* (Exeter, U.K.: University of Exeter Press, 1992).

3. See, for example, his *Sovereignty and Survival: Island Microstates in the Third World.* Research Monograph No. 3, Department of Geography, University of Sydney, 1988.

INTRODUCTION

1. It is for this reason that I extend my sympathy to specialists of the erstwhile Soviet Union who, as a result of its breakup, have been forced to become experts about an additional fourteen independent republics.

2. G. Raymond Babineau, "The Compulsive Border Crosser," *Psychiatry* 35 (1972): 283.

3. Avner Falk, "Border Symbolism Revisited," in Howard F. Stein and William G. Niederland, *Maps from the Mind: Readings in Psychogeography* (Norman: University of Oklahoma Press, 1989), p. 157.

4. For a geographical analysis of such phenomena, see Mark W. Corson and Julian V. Minghi, "Reunification of Partitioned Nation-States: Theory versus Reality in Vietnam and Germany," *Journal of Geography* 93 (1994).

5. William F. S. Miles, *Hausaland Divided: Colonialism and Independence in Nigeria and Niger* (Ithaca, NY: Cornell University Press, 1994).

6. William F. S. Miles, *Elections and Ethnicity in French Martinique: A Paradox in Paradise* (New York: Praeger, 1986).

7. William F. S. Miles, *Imperial Burdens: Countercolonialism in Former French India* (Boulder, CO: Lynne Rienner Publishers, 1995).

8. Conventionally, independent polities with populations of less than one million have been designated *ministates,* whereas *microstates* are those with fewer than a half-million inhabitants. Except for the former Soviet republics and con-

stituent parts of Yugoslavia, virtually all independences since that of Vanuatu have been those of microstates, most of them insular: Belize (1981), Antigua and Barbuda (1981), St. Kitts and Nevis (1983), Brunei Darusalaam (1984), the Marshall Islands (1991), the Federated States of Micronesia (1991), and Palau (1994). In the early 1990s, four long-standing independent ministates—Liechtenstein, San Marino, Andorra, and Monaco—also joined the United Nations. By the mid-1990s a full one-fifth of the UN was composed of member states of less than one million. If one raises the demographic threshold of "ministatehood," as global population growth logically demands, to, say, 1.5 million, then nearly one-quarter (45 out of 185) of the UN has come to include ministates.

9. Ron Crocombe, "The Continuing Creation of Identities in the Pacific Islands: Blood, Behavior, Boundaries and Belief," in David Hooson, ed., *Geography and National Identity* (Oxford: Blackwell Publishers, 1994), p. 326.

10. Carol M. Eastman, *Language Planning: An Introduction* (San Francisco: Chandler and Sharp, 1983), p. 49.

11. I have also made this point with reference to Israeli and Palestinian French-speakers. See William F. S. Miles, "Minoritarian Francophonie: The Case of Israel, with Special Reference to the Palestinian Territories," *International Migration Review* 29 (1995).

12. Fredrik Barth, ed., *Ethnic Groups and Boundaries: The Social Organization of Culture Difference* (Boston: Little, Brown, 1969).

13. A. I. Asiwaju, *Partitioned Africans: Ethnic Relations across Africa's International Boundaries, 1884–1984* (New York: St. Martin's Press, 1985).

14. Peter Sahlins, *Boundaries: The Making of France and Spain in the Pyrenees* (Berkeley: University of California Press, 1989).

15. Claude Raffestin, *Pour une géographie du pouvoir* (Paris: Librairies Techniques, 1980).

16. For a comprehensive treatment of Vanuatu history and politics from the perspective of the unfolding conflict over land, see Howard van Trease's excellent *The Politics of Land in Vanuatu: From Colony to Independence* (Suva: University of the South Pacific, 1987).

17. B. Hours, "Un Mouvement politico-religieux Néo-Hébridais: Le Nagriamel," *ORSTOM* 11 (1974): pp. 230–231.

18. Author's interview with Prime Minister Carlot Korman, 1992.

19. For my treatment of political geography, I have relied on Martin Ira Glassner, *Political Geography* (New York: John Wiley and Sons, 1992); Jean Gottman, *The Significance of Territory* (Charlottesville: University of Virginia, 1973); Peter M. Slowe, *Geography and Political Power: The Geography of Nations and States* (London: Routledge, 1990); and Peter Taylor, *Political Geography: World-Economy, Nation-State and Locality,* 3d ed. (Essex: Longman Scientific and Technical, 1993).

20. Roger Downs and David Stea, *Maps in Minds: Reflections on Cognitive Mapping* (New York: Harper and Row, 1977).

21. Ibid., p. 6.

22. Peter Gould and Rodney White, *Mental Maps,* 2d ed. (Boston: Allen and Unwin, 1986), pp. 96–119.

23. Geographical convention divides the Pacific Ocean into three major zones: Micronesia (the "small islands") located north of the equator and falling principally under U.S. tutelage; Polynesia (the "many islands") in the southeast Pacific, which includes Tonga, Kiribati, and the French overseas territories of Tahiti, and Wallis and Futuna; and Melanesia (the "black [peopled] islands"), of Papua New Guinea, the Solomons, Vanuatu, and Fiji (the latter overlapping Melanesia and Polynesia). The term "Oceania" includes Australia and New Zealand among the smaller Pacific islands inhabited by indigenous peoples.

24. Approximately one-fifth of these are Australian, followed by British and French (11% each), New Caledonians (8%), and New Zealanders (6%).

25. David B. Knight, "People Together, Yet Apart: Rethinking Territory, Sovereignty, and Identities," in George J. Demko and William B. Wood, eds., *Reordering the World: Geopolitical Perspectives on the Twenty-first Century* (Boulder, CO: Westview Press, 1994), pp. 76–77; emphasis added.

26. J. Anderson, "Nationalist Ideology and Territory," in R. Johnson, David Knight, and E. Kofman, eds., *Nationalism, Self-Determination and Political Geography* (London: Croon Helm, 1988), pp. 18–39.

27. Downs and Stea, *Maps in Minds,* p. 146.

28. Ibid., p. 148; emphasis in original.

29. Joël Bonnemaison, "The Metaphor of the Tree and the Canoe," *Pacific Arts,* July 1994, p. 22. This is an extract from the first volume of Bonnemaison's *Les Fondements d'une identité: Territoire, histoire et société dans l'archipel de Vanuatu (Mélanésie). (Essai de géographie culturelle),* trans. Peter Crowe.

30. For works detailing with the globalization of the world, see: Benjamin Barber, *Jihad vs. McWorld* (New York: Random House, 1995); Richard J. Barnet and John Cavanagh, *Global Dreams: Imperial Corporations and the New World Order* (New York: Simon and Schuster, 1994); Mike Featherstone, *Global Culture: Nationalism, Globalization and Modernity* (London: Sage Publications, 1990); and Zdravko Mlinar, ed., *Globalization and Territorial Identities* (Aldershot: Avebury, 1992). An early inquiry into globalization that uses the boundary as springboard is Peter Brown and Henry Shue, eds., *Boundaries: National Autonomy and Its Limits* (Totowa, NJ: Rowman and Littlefield, 1981).

31. Charles Beitz, "Democracy in Developing Countries," in Brown and Shue, eds., *Boundaries,* p. 177. In its entirety, this book explores philosophical and normative questions relating to the relativity of national boundaries. The fact that such a volume was under preparation precisely when the New Hebrides was acceding to independence underscores the coincidence of Vanuatu national sovereignty with scholarly appreciation of international boundary permeability.

32. See Taylor, *Political Geography,* for an excellent, neo-Wallersteinian survey of the discipline.

33. As the focus of this book is on Vanuatu since independence, readers wishing a comprehensive account of the history of the New Hebrides should consult the following works. For the "discovery" of the archipelago and early explorations thereof, Andrew Sharp, *The Discovery of the Pacific Islands* (Oxford: Clarendon Press, 1960). For the trading period leading up to the establishment of the Condominium, Dorothy Shineberg's *They Came for Sandalwood: A Study of the Sandalwood Trade in the South-West Pacific 1830-1865* (Melbourne: Melbourne University Press, 1967) is a classic. So, for the historical context leading up to the Anglo-French agreement, is Deryck Scarr's *Fragments of Empire: A History of the Western Pacific High Commission 1877-1914* (Canberra: Australian National Press, 1967). Jeremy MacClancy's *To Kill a Bird with Two Stones: A Short History of Vanuatu* (Vila: Vanuatu Cultural Centre, 1980) is indeed a concise and valuable work, but it is unfortunately difficult to obtain. Excellent treatments of the New Hebrides/Vanuatu from the French perspective but in the English language are: Robert Aldrich, *The French Presence in the South Pacific, 1842-1939* (London: Macmillan, 1990), and Stephen Henningham, *France and the South Pacific: A Contemporary History* (Honolulu, University of Hawai'i Press, 1992. For the major works in the French language, see the entries in the Bibliography for Joël Bonnemaison and Jean Guiart.

34. Circular boar canines, acquired through an intricate process of strategic tooth removal and painstaking hand-feeding, remain the highest status symbols in the islands. See William F. S. Miles, "Pigs, Politics and Social Change in Vanuatu," *Society and Animals* 5 (1997).

35. Howard Van Trease, *The Politics of Land in Vanuatu: From Colony to Independence* (Suva: University of the South Pacific, 1987), pp. 155-156.

36. See John Beasant, *The Santo Rebellion: An Imperial Reckoning* (Honolulu: University of Hawai'i Press, 1984); David Robie, "Vanuatu: Beyond Pandemonium," in his *Blood on Their Banner: Nationalist Struggles in the South Pacific* (London: Zed Books, 1989); Richard Shears, *The Coconut War: The Crisis on Espiritu Santo* (Melbourne Cassell Australia, 1980).

37. Robert's role is denounced in Jean Leder, *Les Cent Jours au bout du monde (autopsie d'une tragédie)* (Nouméa: Impriméries Réunies de Nouméa, 1981). In an interview with me in 1992, however, Monsieur Robert categorically denied the charge of connivance in the rebellion:

> It is absolutely false! First of all, I am not about to lead my own personal policy. I am a representative of the French government and . . . my minister, who was . . . energetic . . . and strict, would have thrown me out in the hours which followed. . . . Had I wanted to mount an operation in Santo . . . believe me, I would have. But it did not happen that way. . . .

38. See Ralph Premdas, "Vanuatu: Melanesian Socialism and Political Change," *The Round Table* 304 (1987); idem, "Melanesian Socialism: Vanuatu's

Quest for Self-Definition," *Journal of Commonwealth and Comparative Politics* 25 (1987).

39. See, for example, Ralph R. Premdas and Jeffrey S. Steeves, "Vanuatu: The Politics of Anglo-French Cooperation in the Post-Lini Era," *Journal of Commonwealth and Comparative Politics* 32 (1994), in which the authors characterize Vanuatu as "bifurcated," a society of "two communities" riven by "Anglophone/Francophone divisions." Uncritical acceptance of government statistics indicating that 88 percent of ni-Vanuatu actually speak English or French helps to explain the oversimplification that ensues.

40. William F. S. Miles, "Francophonie in Post-Colonial Vanuatu," *The Journal of Pacific History* 29 (1994).

CHAPTER 1. MENTAL RIVALRIES AND CONDOCOLONIALISM

1. Edward Jacomb, *France and England in the New Hebrides: The Anglo-French Condominium* (Melbourne: George Robertson, 1914), p. 195.

2. Tom Harrisson, *Savage Civilisation* (London: Victor Gollancz, 1937), pp. 181, 299.

3. A. J. Marshall, *The Black Musketeers: The Work and Adventures of a Scientist on a South Sea Island at War and in Peace* (London: William Heinemann, 1937), p. 228.

4. Interview with Jean-Jacques Robert, September 1992.

5. J. MacClancy, "*Kastom* and Politics," *International Journal of Moral and Social Studies* 3 (1988): 95.

6. Grace Molisa, Nikenike Vurobaravu, and Howard Van Trease, "Vanuatu: Overcoming Pandemonium," in *Politics in Melanesia*, (Suva: University of the South Pacific, 1982), p. 85.

7. D. P. O'Connell, "The Condominium of the New Hebrides," *British Yearbook of International Law 1968–1969* (London: Oxford University Press, 1970), pp. 76, 91–92. O'Connell's French counterpart in legal scholarship, Hubert Benoist, is considerably more indulgent regarding the New Hebrides cosovereign experiment and the theoretical possibility of a successful Condominium. While admitting the legitimacy of criticism toward it, Benoist maintains that circumstances continuously intervened to prevent the Condominium from operating the way it was meant to. See Hubert Benoist, *Le Condominium des Nouvelles-Hébrides et la Société Mélanésienne* (Paris: Editions A. Pedone, 1972), esp. pp. 212–213.

8. Edwin Ardener, "The Nature of the Reunification of Cameroon," in Arthur Hazlewood, ed., *African Integration and Disintegration: Case Studies in Economic and Political Union* (London: Oxford University Press, 1967), p. 330.

9. Sanford Ungar, *Africa: The People and Politics of an Emerging Continent* (New York: Simon and Schuster, 1986), p. 355.

10. O'Connell, "The Condominium of the New Hebrides," p. 72.

11. See Milton Forman Goldman, "Origins and Development of the Colonial Conflicts Resolved by the Anglo-French Entente of 1904," Ph.D. diss., The Fletcher School of Law and Diplomacy, Medford, MA, 1964.

12. O'Connell, "The Condominium of the New Hebrides," p. 76.

13. It is worth noting that neither the Protocol of 1914 nor the Convention of 1906 actually called the Anglo-French arrangement a "Condominium," though supplementary and subsequent documents did. Even the term "Protocol," according to international standards of treaty drafting, is misleading: By supplanting (not merely amending or interpreting) the 1906 accord, the 1914 agreement was itself a Convention. See O'Connell, pp. 77, 92.

14. Deryck Scarr, *Fragments of Empire: A History of the Western Pacific High Commission 1877–1914* (Canberra: Australian National University, 1967), pp. 230-235.

15. The statelessness of the indigenous New Hebrideans was not an oversight. Written clarifications to the Convention (Article VIII [2]) specifically prohibited them from becoming either British subjects or French citizens, or even acceding to the unilateral legal protection of Britain or France.

16. O'Connell, p. 106.

17. Ibid., p. 122.

18. Jacomb, *France and England in the New Hebrides,* pp. 23–34.

19. Ibid., pp. 158–159.

20. Marshall, *The Black Musketeers,* pp. 287–288.

21. Ibid., pp. 26–27.

22. This is my somewhat free translation of "Pour les Nouvelles-Hébrides l'Angleterre ne tirera pas le canon. Elle se contentera de tirer des traites. Avec elle, les affaires commencent par la Bible et se terminent par une facture."

23. Pierre Benoit, *Océanie Française* (Paris: Editions Alpina, 1933), pp. 56–57.

24. Ibid., pp. 35, 66.

25. Ibid., p. 37.

26. Interview with Jimmy Stephens, August 1992. For a poignant treatment of this issue, see Michael Young, "Gone Native in Isles of Illusion, in James G. Carrier, ed., *History and Tradition in Melanesian Anthropology* (Berkeley: University of California Press, 1992).

27. For example, Hausa living on both sides of the border between Niger and Nigeria concur that the French practiced a *mulkin zahi,* a "hot" or "fiery rule," while the British regime in Nigeria was characterized by *sauki,* relative ease. William F. S. Miles, "Colonial Hausa Idioms: Toward a West African Ethno-Ethnohistory," *African Studies Review* 36 (1993). A. I. Asiwaju comes to similar conclusions for colonial Yorubaland, in his *Western Yorubaland under European Rule, 1889–1945* (Atlantic Highlands, NJ: Humanities Press, 1976).

28. Miles, "Colonial Hausa Idioms"; Pierre Alexandre, "Chiefs, Commandants, and Clerks: Their Relationship from Conquest to Decolonisation in French West Africa," in Michael Crowder and Obaro Ikime, eds., *West African*

Chiefs: Their Changing Status under Colonial Rule and Independence (New York: Africana, 1970).

29. The following narrations distill over one hundred interviews, mostly from community leaders throughout the outer islands. See the list of interviews, especially under the subheading "Chiefs/Bigmen/Notables/Cultural Centre Fieldworkers."

30. President Timikata expressed this sentiment in a slightly different way. "When I am asked if my country was ready to become independent, I reply, 'Did you know at your wedding if you were ready to be married?'"

31. For a readable account of the Marist missionaries, see Paul Monnier, *One Hundred Years of Mission 1887–1987: The Catholic Church in Vanuatu* (Port Vila, 1987).

32. For a good account of evangelical competition in the New Hebrides, see chapter 4 ("L'Evangile et le Royaume") of Joël Bonnemaison's *La Dernière Ile* (Paris: Arléa/Orstom, 1986).

33. Maurice Delauney, *Kala-Kala: De la grande à la petite histoire. Un ambassadeur raconte* (Paris, 1986), p. 119. Delauney gives the respective numbers of pupils in British versus French schools as eight thousand and two thousand.

34. Gamali Mark, "Post-Primary Education in the New Hebrides: Problems and Prospects," M.A. thesis, University of Leeds, 1979.

35. Jean-Michel Charpentier, *Le Pidgin Bislama(r) et le multilinguisme aux Nouvelles-Hébrides* (Paris: Société d'Etudes Linguistiques et Anthropologiques de France, 1979), p. 102.

36. Ibid., p. 104.

37. Delauney, *Kala-Kala,* pp. 153–154; my translation.

38. A comparison of 1980 and 1986 enrollments in the *Second National Development Plan, 1987–1991* offers a slightly different picture: In 1980, according to Table 23.02, "Primary School Enrolments in 1980 and 1986" (p. 409), overall Francophone enrollment actually exceeded Anglophone enrollment by 148, or 50.3 percent versus 49.7 percent. The ostensible difference between these two data sets is that the *Development Plan* explicitly "refers to Government supported schools and Seventh-Day Adventist schools only" and also excludes French vocational training. Yet this data set gives an absolute *higher* number of combined primary enrollments than that given in Ministry of Education figures for 1980. More intriguing, in 1980, according to the *Development Plan* figures, the Francophone proportional advantage, such as it was, was attributable to the numbers of *female* Francophone pupils, who outnumbered female Anglophones by 329; Anglophone males outnumbered Francophone males by 181.

39. From data provided by Mark, "Post-Primary Education in the New Hebrides," p. 20.

40. Résidence de France, *Rapport Mensuel,* April 1976, p. xvii; Robert Aldrich, *France and the South Pacific since 1940* (Honolulu: University of Hawai'i Press, 1993), p. 227.

Table 13 1980 Primary School Enrollments in Vanuatu
Alternative Data Set

	# Male	# Female	% Male	% Female	Total
Francophone	6,108	5,348	53.3	46.7	11,451
Anglophone	6,284	5,019	52.2	44.8	11,303
Total	12,387	10,367	54.4	45.6	22,754

Source: *Republic of Vanuatu Second National Development Plan;* source of data listed as "Ministry of Education and Sport."

41. Certainly grammar and diction were, and are, more strongly stressed in Francophone education. In French school, one teacher assured me, pupils will be taught that "pom-me" is a two-syllable noun; in English, they'll just learn "apple." The implication is that Anglophones will swallow the pronunciation as surely as the fruit.

42. Charpentier, *Le Pidgin Bislama(r)*, pp. 96–97, 110.

43. Ibid., p. 109.

44. Ibid., p. 110.

45. Ibid.

46. Ibid., p. 128.

47. William Miles, "Anachronistic Antagonisms: Britain versus France in the New Hebrides, 1966–1977," *Proceedings of the Nineteenth Meeting of the French Colonial Historical Society, Providence, R.I. May 1993* (Cleveland, OH: Cleveland State University, 1994). A full examination of the *Synthèses Mensuelles* is also to be found in Howard van Trease's three-part series in *Pacific Islands Monthly* (July, August, September 1982).

CHAPTER 2. NATIONALISM, KASTOM, AND OTHER BOUNDARIES

1. This simple but concise summary of the colonial national experience is consistent with the major accounts on nationalism of the last generation, which include, in addition to the specific ones below: John Breuilly, *Nationalism and the State* (Chicago: University of Chicago Press, 1993 [1982]); Ernest Gellner, *Nations and Nationalism* (Oxford: Oxford University Press, 1983); Elie Kedourie, ed., *Nationalism in Asia and Africa* (London: Widenfeld and Nicholson, 1971); and Anthony D. Smith, *Theories of Nationalism,* 2d ed. (New York: Holmes and Meier, 1983).

2. Tom Harrisson's *Savage Civilization* (1937), a popular account of his trek through Santo bush in the 1930s, went far toward fashioning this image of the New Hebrides.

3. See, for instance, Professor Connor's "The Nation and Its Myth," in *International Studies in Sociology and Social Anthropology* 50 (1992).

4. Benedict Anderson, *Imagined Communities: Reflections on the Origins and Spread of Nationalism* (London: Verso Books, 1983). In the context of the Pacific, where ethnicity is less salient than culture, Alain Babadzan refers to "imaginary mono-ethnism" as the "fictive construction" of nationalism. Alain Babadzan, "*Kastom* and Nation-Building in the South Pacific," in Remo Guidieri, Francesco Pellizzi, and Stanley J. Tambiah, eds., *Ethnicities and Nations: Processes of Interethnic Relations in Latin America, Southeast Asia, and the Pacific* (Austin: University of Texas Press, 1988), p. 216.

5. I use "nationalize" in the sense of politicizing people for specifically nationalist ends. Surprisingly, there is no common verb that otherwise connotes this historically significant process.

6. E. J. Hobswawm, *Nations and Nationalism since 1780* (Cambridge University Press, 1990), p. 11. This is particularly true in Pacific societies, "where individuals are likely to possess multiple, nested affiliations in a conceptual hierarchy." Jocelyn Linnekin and Lin Poyer, "Introduction," in their edited volume, *Cultural Identity and Ethnicity in the Pacific* (Honolulu: University of Hawai'i Press, 1990), p. 11.

7. It is a pity that Hobswawm is dismissive of what other scholars, without being deprecatory, label "microstates." He fixes what seems to be an arbitrary threshold of one million before a community can be taken seriously as a nation, regardless of its own claims to nationhood. Insular and pelagic peoples therefore labor under insurmountable logistical prerequisites: With whom else can they bond to achieve a critical mass for nationhood? Are they condemned, by reasons of geography and demography, to remain nationless? Must Barbados really think less of itself as a nation than Burma, Fiji less than Finland? Hobswawm has missed a theoretical opportunity by not taking seriously small and insular communities, the most recent candidates for statehood *and* nationhood, in his otherwise magisterial study of nationalism.

8. Professor Smith makes this point most directly in his introductory review chapter "Ethnicity and Nationalism," in *International Studies in Sociology and Social Anthropology 50* (1992). But see also his *National Identity* (Reno: University of Nevada Press, 1991), and *Theories of Nationalism* (New York: Harper and Row, 1971).

9. Not even the Vila branch of the University of the South Pacific felt comfortable hosting a farewell lecture that would touch on the colonial past. "The Condominium is still too sensitive a topic," I was told. "You may talk about your research elsewhere, but not in Vanuatu." (In the end, I did deliver the lecture, at the Vila Centre for International Relations.)

10. Howard van Trease, *The Politics of Land in Vanuatu* (Suva: University of the South Pacific, 1987), pp. 128–131; Jean Guiart, *Espiritu Santo (Nouvelles Hébrides)*, (Paris: Librairie Plon, 1958), pp. 198–204.

11. Guiart, *Espiritu Santo,* pp. 76–78, 198–202.

12. Van Trease, *Politics of Land in Vanuatu,* p. 138.

13. From the memorial erected in his memory, Lumbukuti village, Tongoa.

14. David Hilliard, *God's Gentlemen: A History of the Melanesian Mission, 1849-1942* (St. Lucia: University of Queensland Press, 1978), p. 287.

15. For the rural Hausa of Nigeria, I have documented this in *Elections in Nigeria: A Grassroots Perspective* (Boulder, CO: Lynne Rienner Publishers, 1988).

16. See, for instance, the chapters in Adu Boahen, ed., *General History of Africa VII: Africa under Colonial Domination 1880-1935* (UNESCO and University of California Press, 1985).

17. Van Trease, *The Politics of Land in Vanuatu,* p. 139. According to John Beasant's version (p. 17n.), *nagria* represents both peace and the body of the Santo people.

18. Ibid., pp. 159-160, 163.

19. John Beasant, *The Santo Rebellion: An Imperial Reckoning* (Honolulu: University of Hawai'i Press, 1984), p. 21.

20. Interview with author, August 1992.

21. Van Trease, *The Politics of Land in Vanuatu,* p. 164.

22. Interview with author, July 1991.

23. Interview with author, August 1992.

24. Though not without friction: One dispute over a dress code (customary penis wrappers and grass skirts versus standard shorts, tee shirts, and Mother Hubbards) threatened to split the community in the early 1990s.

25. Jeremy MacClancy, "*Kastom* and Politics," *International Journal of Moral and Social Studies* 3 (1988): 96.

26. Ibid., p. 103.

27. Peter Taurakoto relates how his supervisors would wink and turn a blind eye to his using the education department's mimeograph machines to run off nationalist tracts. Interview with author, 1991.

28. For a critical assessment of arts festivals throughout Oceania, and the inauthenticity of the *kastom* movement in general, see Babadzan, "*Kastom* and Nation-Building in the South Pacific," pp. 208, 212-216. Babadzan views public displays of *kastom* as a combination of "folkloristic reification" and "Western fetishism of merchandise."

29. Eric Hobswawm and Terence Ranger, eds., *The Invention of Tradition* (Cambridge University Press, 1983).

30. Lamont Lindstrom, "Leftamap Kastom: The Political History of Tradition on Tanna, Vanuatu," *Mankind* 13 (1982).

31. Margaret Jolly, "Birds and Banyans of South Pentecost: Kastom in Anti-Colonial Struggle," *Mankind* 13 (1982).

32. William L. Rodman and Margaret Rodman, "Rethinking Kastom: On the Politics of Place Naming in Vanuatu," *Oceania* 55 (1985).

33. Joan Larcom, "The Invention of Convention," *Mankind* 13 (1982).

34. Robert Tonkinson, "Church and Kastom in Southeast Ambrym," in Mi-

chael Allen, ed., *Vanuatu: Politics, Economics and Ritual in Island Melanesia* (Toronto: Academic Press, 1981).

35. Lynne Hume, "Church and Custom on Maewo, Vanuatu," *Oceania* 56 (1986).

36. Robert Tonkinson, "Vanuatu Values: A Changing Symbiosis," *Pacific Studies* 5 (1982): 58.

37. Margaret Jolly, "Custom and the Way of the Land: Past and Present in Vanuatu and Fiji," *Oceania* 62 (1992).

38. Robert Norton, "Culture and Identity in the South Pacific: A Comparative Analysis," *Man* 28 (1993).

39. William Miles, "Traditional Rulers and Development Administration: Chieftaincy in Niger, Nigeria, and Vanuatu," *Studies in Comparative International Development* 28 (1993).

40. Robert Tonkinson, "Vanuatu Values: A Changing Symbiosis," *Pacific Studies* 5 (1982): 45.

41. Jean-Marc Philibert, "The Politics of Tradition: Toward a Generic Culture in Vanuatu," *Mankind* 13 (1982): 9.

42. Babadzian, "*Kastom* and Nation-Building in the South Pacific," p. 212.

43. Interview with Chiefs James Adin, Cyril Aru, and Jeffrey Uli of Maewo island.

44. Lamont Lindstrom, "Kava, Cash, and Custom in Vanuatu," *Cultural Survival Quarterly* 15 (1991): 31.

45. But do see the letter to the editor reported in Lamont Lindstrom, "Traditional Cultural Policy in Melanesia *(Kastom Polisi long Kastom)*, in Lindstrom and White, eds., *Culture, Kastom, Tradition*, pp. 79–80.

46. Even in this context, the term "indigenous" is relative. Imported calico, hardly an indigenous product, is used to fashion male loincloths.

47. The traditionally clothed children are taught in English. Here is one response to an in-class writing exercise that was assigned at my request.

NEWS

Yesterday after school i went home and i took my bow and arrows and i went to the bush i shot one bird after shoting the birds i went to the house i went to the nakamal i chewed my faters kava after chewing my fathers kava i went to the house. i had my supper after having my supper then i went to bed.

Sam, class 3, Iohnanen Custom School, Tanna Island

48. Communication of Chief Tuk.

49. In Pentecost *kastom* villages such as Bunlap, *nambas* is still daily normal wear for most men.

50. Some expatriate development workers nevertheless claimed that, even into the early 1990s, some unnationalized and dissatisfied outer islanders were still asking, "When will this independence thing be over?"

51. Ron Crocombe, "The Continuing Creation of Identities in the Pacific Islands: Blood, Behaviour, Boundaries and Belief," in David Hooson, ed., *Geography and National Identity* (Oxford: Blackwell Publishers, 1994), p. 328.

52. It is noteworthy in this respect that the most extensive and popular Bislama dictionary, published on the tenth anniversary of Vanuatu's independence (Terry Crowley's *An Illustrated Bislama-English and English-Bislama Dictionary* [Vila: University of the South Pacific, 1990]), did not yet carry a local language entry for Melanesian, though both *Inglis man* (Britisher) and *Franis man* (and even the archaic *man Wiwi*) were included. The omission should not be taken as an oversight but rather as conforming to the upper-limit standard for lexical inclusion: "used systematically in informal contexts by people with primary level education in towns . . . except for the more formal and anglicised registers of the best educated anglophone ni-Vanuatu" (pp. 4, 8). As an English-language term, Melanesian is proffered as a definition for *blakman, manples,* and, for New Caledonian, *Kanak.* Throughout Oceania more widely, "the terms *Micronesian, Melanesian,* and *Polynesian* . . . are only occasionally used . . . [as] significant ethnic designations" (Alan Howard, "Cultural Paradigms, History, and the Search for Identity in Oceania," in Jocelyn Linnekin and Lin Poyer, eds., *Cultural Identity and Ethnicity in the Pacific* (Honolulu: University of Hawai'i Press, 1990), p. 277).

53. Alan Howard, "Cultural Paradigms, History, and the Search for Identity in Oceania."

54. Howard, p. 262.

55. William F. S. Miles, "Anachronistic Antagonisms: France versus Britain in the New Hebrides, 1966–1977," in James Pritchard, ed., *Proceedings of the Nineteenth Meeting of the French Colonial Historical Society, Providence, R.I. May 1993* (Cleveland, OH: FHCS, 1994), pp. 210–213.

56. Joël Bonnemaison, "The Metaphor of the Tree and the Canoe," *Pacific Arts,* July 1994, p. 21.

57. See, for example, Bernard Nietschmann, "The Fourth World: Nations versus States," in George Demko and William Wood, *Reordering the World: Geopolitical Perspectives on the Twenty-first Century* (Boulder, CO: Westview Press, 1994).

58. Anthony King, "Introduction: Spaces of Culture, Spaces of Knowledge," in his edited *Culture, Globalization and the World-System: Contemporary Conditions for the Representation of Identity* (Binghamton: SUNY, 1991), p. 8.

59. King, "Spaces of Culture, Spaces of Knowledge," p. 16.

60. Not until the 1940s, however: "Though one must dislike the Condominium for the abuses it tolerates," wrote Tom Harrisson in 1937, "at the same time one must be grateful to it for tolerating things which we have put down as abuses in other colonies. Only under a Condominium could cannibalism thrive a few miles from a Government officer, radio and hospital" (*Savage Civilisation,* p. 310).

CHAPTER 3. RELIGIOUS BOUNDARIES CONSTRUCTED AND BRIDGED

1. Joël Bonnemaison, *La Dernière Ile* (Paris: Orléa/Orstom, 1986), p. 239.

2. Jean Guiart, "Culture Contact and the 'John Frum' Movement on Tanna, New Hebrides," *Southwestern Journal of Anthropology* 12 (1956): 109.

3. Bonnemaison, *La Dernière Ile*, p. 108.

4. Paul Monnier, *One Hundred Years of Mission: The Catholic Church in New Hebrides-Vanuatu 1887-1987*, p. 26; Bonnemaison, *La Dernière Ile*, p. 115. In my blending of these two versions, I have taken liberties with punctuation and my translation of the Bislama.

5. Monnier, *One Hundred Years of Mission*, p. 33.

6. National Archives of Vanuatu, received by Ministry of Home Affairs, May 1, 1985.

7. Born in Lawrence, Massachusetts, in 1921, Francis Lambert served in Vanuatu from 1948 until 1997. He was consecrated archbishop in 1977. Of Québecois family background, Bishop Lambert was perfectly fluent in French as well as Bislama.

8. The original uses the word "pere," a term that has entered Bislama from the French *père* (father).

9. Illustrative is the case of the completely non-Francophone New Zealander priest on the island of Pentecost who was forced to learn the French liturgy by rote in order to perform service. Educated Catholics in the outer islands are particularly disappointed by the prospect of having a "pere" with whom they cannot communicate in French.

10. Interview, August 9, 1992.

11. Interview, May 1992.

12. The civil religion paradigm is best associated with Robert Bellah, who developed it in the context of American Protestantism. It has since been applied to a number of other societies where religion has been integrated into the national psyche and political culture.

13. Gérard Leymang, "Reviser la Constitution Vanuatuane, c'est célébrer l'Amour," *Eklesia* 89 (July 1990): 1.

14. A contemporary account of the disruption in social life occasioned by sexual liberation on Aneityum in the mid-nineteenth century is worth recording in this context: "The tables are now turning. Those men who embrace Christianity must give up their barbarous practices and treat their wives with humanity and kindness. Some of the women begin to take advantage of the altered state of things and to retaliate on their husbands. . . . In some instances they have gone so far as to beat their husbands. . . ." John Geddie, *Geddie's Journals 1848-1857;* quoted in Mathew Spriggs, "A School in Every District: The Cultural Geography of Conversion on Aneityum, Southern Vanuatu," *The Journal of Pacific History* 20 (1985): 36.

15. Margaret Jolly, "Sacred Spaces: Churches, Men's Houses and Households

in South Pentecost, Vanuatu," in Margaret Jolly and Martha Macintyre, *Family and Gender in the South Pacific: Domestic Contradictions and the Colonial Impact* (Cambridge University Press, 1979). Jolly fears a "new spectre of [sexual] segregation" on account of Vanuatu Christianity. While celebrating the wifehood and maternity of women, such churches "strip . . . away those sacred aspects of human kinship which gave women a crucial if subordinated place in the ancestral religion" (p. 235).

16. Brian Macdonald-Milne and Pamela Thomas, eds., *Yumi Stanap: Leaders and Leadership in a New Nation* (Pacific Churches Research Centre, 1981). The main title is derived from the motto of the Republic of Vanuatu, *Long God Yumi Stanap* (With God We Stand). George Kalsakau, assistant superintendent in the British division of the New Hebrides Constabulary until chosen first chief minister of the Representative Assembly, relates how he came to choose the motto:

> [W]hen the two High Commissioners of Great Britain and France handed over the reins of Government to me, in Parliament in Port Vila, I thought back over the years and remembered those words which were told to me at the Australian Police College . . . exactly three years [before]. . . .
>
> We had just started our training [when the] Senior Detective Superintendent of the Srilankan Police Force . . . came up to me and asked me if I would let him read my palm.
>
> I did not know him very well [but] I showed him my hands; this is what he read out to me: "God has written into your hand that in three years time, the people of your country will elect you as their Prime Minister." I laughed at him and said how come . . . I am [but] a policeman. . . . I went back home, but I . . . never gave any thought to his words, because I did not believe them. . . .
>
> He said God had written into the palm of my hand . . . so it is important that we should know that God exists and he is guiding us today. This is why I chose the motto "Long God Yumi Stanap."
>
> (G. K. Kalsakau, "How God's Plan?" in his *History of the Three Flags: New Hebrides' Changeover to the Republic of Vanuatu* [Port Vila, 1980], p. 68)

17. MacDonald-Milne and Thomas, *Yumi Stanap*, p. 99.

18. David Hilliard, *God's Gentlemen: A History of the Melanesian Mission 1849–1942* (St. Lucia: University of Queensland Press, 1978), p. 198, quoting from Walter Durrad, "The Depopulation of Melanesia," in W. H. R. Rivers, ed., *Essays on the Depopulation of Melanesia* (Cambridge University Press, 1922).

19. Bonnemaison, *La Dernière Ile*, p. 98.

20. *One Hundred Years of Mission*, p. 23.

21. Father Walter Lini, interview, August 9, 1992.

22. The last officially documented case of cannibalism occurred in 1942. There is an understandable reticence among informed persons residing in Vanuatu to comment or speculate about more recent instances.

23. Walter Lini, interview, August 8, 1992.

24. Gérard Leymang, "Reviser la Constitution Vanuatuane, c'est célébrer l'Amour," p. 1.

25. Kava is traditionally served in a coconut shell (*sel* in Bislama), the standard unit of consumption.

26. *The Story of Our Islands, Part II: The People and Government* (Vanuatu Teachers College, 1983), p. 123

27. Etymology of the cult founder's name is uncertain. Some say it is a simplification of "John [from] America." Others say Frum derives from "broom": He will sweep away the white man.

28. Jean Guiart, "John Frum Movement in Tanna," *Oceania* 22 (1952): 175.

29. Jean Guiart, "Forerunners of Melanesian Nationalism," *Oceania* 22 (1951): 81.

30. Bonnemaison, *La Dernière Ile,* chap. 13.

31. In addition to the scholarly accounts mentioned above, John Frum has also been explored in more rhapsodic and popular works by, respectively: Edward Rice, *John Frum He Come: A Polemical Work about a Black Tragedy* (Garden City, NY: Doubleday and Company, 1974), and Michael Krieger, *Conversations with the Cannibals: The End of the Old Pacific* (Hopewell, NJ: The Ecco Press, 1994). Lamont Lindstrom's chapter in *Cargo Cult: Strange Stories of Desire from Melanesia and Beyond* (Honolulu: University of Hawai'i Press, 1993) straddles the two.

32. Bonnemaison, *La Dernière Ile,* p. 293.

33. Guiart, "John Frum Movement," p. 174.

34. John Beasant, *The Santo Rebellion: An Imperial Reckoning* (Honolulu: University of Hawai'i Press, 1984), p. 20.

35. Bonnemaison, *La Dernière Ile,* p. 124.

36. *Vanuatu National Population Census, 1989,* p. 38. In terms of overall religious affiliation (i.e., counting "other," "none," or "unstated"), this represents an increase from 6.1 to 8.2 percent.

37. It was at one such revival meeting in Luganville that I encountered a ni-Vanuatu high-schooler quite excited by meeting someone from Boston: His hero was Larry Byrd of the Celtics basketball team, whose picture he had posted on the wall of his room!

38. Lynne Hume, "Church and Custom on Maewo, Vanuatu," *Oceania* 56 (1986): 310.

39. The religious situation in the United States in the nineteenth century, when Catholics constituted a growing but disenfranchised minority, comes to mind here. A milestone were the 1843 riots in Philadelphia, provoked by conflict

over which version of the Bible (Catholic versus Protestant) was to be employed in city classrooms.

40. Sex education in Vanuatu thus comes under the rubric of religious education. It is interesting to note how premarital sex is treated in Vanuatu high schools:

Why is sex before marriage wrong?

(a) Those who have sex outside marriage are doing it 'for fun'; they are using another person. It is not a true expression of love and real concern for the other person's welfare.

(b) An unwanted child may result. Children need a stable and loving home and the guidance of both parents to develop their personalities. Children born of unmarried parents sometimes do not receive enough love and attention.

(c) It makes you feel guilty and spoils your relationship with Jesus. Anxiety can lead to mental illness later in life.

(d) There is shame and disgrace when other people find out.

(e) There is a danger of contracting serious diseases.

(f) If you are 'secondhand' when you marry will your partner trust you?

(g) It can spoil your school work, which should be the main concern of people lucky enough to have a secondary or university place.

41. Writing well before the historic Israel–PLO agreement of 1993—and the fundamentalist attempts on both sides to sabotage it—Arthur Hertzberg observed, "Wise state officials still have the opportunity to use the pervading fear of messianic politics as reason for them to work together. They can have order and stability at home only by accommodating, and thus sustaining, one another." Obviously, the stakes of religious accommodation are much greater in the Middle East than in the South Pacific; it is the similarity of process that captures our attention. Arthur Hertzberg, "The Religious Right in Israel," *The Annals of the American Academy of Political and Social Science,* special issue on *Religion and the State: The Struggle for Legitimacy and Power,* January 1986, pp. 91–92.

CHAPTER 4. LANGUAGE, EDUCATION, AND NATIONAL IDENTITY

1. Karl Deutsch, *Nationalism and Social Communication* (Cambridge, MA: MIT Press, 1966).

2. Joshua Fishman, *Language and Nationalism: Two Integrative Essays* (Rowley, MA: Newbury House Publishers, 1972).

3. Joshua Fishman, *Bilingual Education: An International Sociological Perspective* (Rowley, MA: Newbury House Publishers, 1976).

4. Brian Weinstein, "Language Planning in Francophone Africa," *Language Problems and Language Planning* 4 (1980): 55.

5. Brian Weinstein, *The Civic Tongue: Political Consequences of Language Choices* (New York and London: Longman, 1983).

6. James E. Jacob and William R. Beer, eds., *Language Policy and National Unity* (Totowa, NJ: Rowman and Allanheld, 1985).

7. David Laitin, *Language Repertoires and State Construction in Africa* (Cambridge University Press, 1992), pp. 5, 18.

8. Carol M. Eastman, *Language Planning: An Introduction* (San Francisco: Chandler and Sharp Publishing, 1983), p. 46.

9. Another explanation might lie in survey language. Census takers posed the question (no. 33): "Wanem kaen skul yu go long hem, inglis o franis?" Even though this followed question no. 29 on church affiliation, my own experience indicates that the intended meaning of the question still may have been ambiguous to the respondent. Depending on context and personal usage, *skul* can connote religious instruction (independent of language) rather than formal education per se. *Skul inglis,* for example, might mean attending Anglican church meetings without studying the English language per se.

10. The perspective of a metropolitan French adviser posted to the Vanuatu Ministry of Education before the UMP victory is interesting in this regard. This informant did not believe that anti-Francophone discrimination was practiced at the higher levels of his ministry. At the level of middle-level management, however, mundane administrative decisions taken on an ad hoc basis (such as the decision to supply School A rather than School F with requested notebooks) tapped Anglophone networks of solidarity to the (relative) detriment of Francophone institutions and personnel.

11. "Table 23.10: Performance in 1985 Primary Leaving Examination," *Second National Development Plan,* p. 417.

12. Résidence de France, *Rapport Mensuel,* April 1976, p. xvi.

13. Ibid.

14. James C. Scott, *The Moral Economy of the Peasant: Rebellion and Resistance in Southeast Asia* (New Haven and London: Yale University Press, 1976), pp. vii, 24. The classic text in this genre of "peasant thinking" research is Edward Banfield, *The Moral Economy of a Backward Society* (New York: The Free Press, 1958). Banfield explains peasant behavior (in a southern Italian village) in terms of amoral familism, the "inability to concert activity beyond the immediate family" (p. 10).

15. Samuel L. Popkin, *The Rational Peasant: The Political Economy of Rural Society in Vietnam* (Berkeley, Los Angeles, and London: University of California Press, 1979).

16. Field notes from West Ambrym.

17. Larry Bowman, *Mauritius: Democracy and Development in the Indian Ocean* (Boulder, CO: Westview Press, 1991), pp. 53–57.

18. An unknown number of ni-Vanuatu Francophones apparently shifted to an English-language track for the express purpose of attending university. See Terry Crowley, "Language Issues and National Development in Vanuatu," in István Fodor and Claude Hagège, eds., *Language Reform: History and Future*, (Hamburg: Helmut Buske Verlag, 1989), p. 134.

19. Unification aside, standards within the Francophone system have deteriorated according to one educator at the Walarano Catholic Mission school on Malakula: "During the Condominium, there was lots of memorization in the lessons—pupils were made to develop their memory. But with the new system, we try to impart everything in the classroom."

20. See, for example, Brian Weinstein, "Francophone: A Language-based Movement in World Politics," *International Organization* 30 (1976): 485–507.

21. Michel Tétu, *La Francophonie: Histoire, problématique et perspectives* (Paris: Hachette, 1988); and Jean-Philippe Thérien, "Co-operation and Conflict in la Francophonie," *International Journal* 48 (1993): 492–526.

22. Here is the TV listing for Monday, August 9, 1993:

6:00 P.M.   *Clip blong Pasifik* (Bislama)
6:05 P.M.   *Sesame Street* (English)
6:32 P.M.   *Les moomies* (French)
7:00 P.M.   *The Simpsons* (English)
7:23 P.M.   *La fête à la maison - Quoi d'neuf Doc?* [What's Up, Doc?]
             (French)
8:10 P.M.   *Just the Ten of Us* (English)
8:33 P.M.   *Les incorruptibles* [The Untouchables] (French)
9:20 P.M.   *Foreign Correspondent*

23. The validity of this observation struck home like a hammer when I joined a group of secondary school teachers at a headmaster's home on Epi and viewed (thanks to a fuel-pumped generator in the nonelectrified village) a disturbingly bizarre and violent video film. I later gathered that it was *Robo Cop*.

24. The genesis of Bislama lies with seafarers in the early nineteenth century who, in addition to combing the Pacific for whales and sandalwood, sought *bêches-de-mer* (sea slugs) for export to China.

25. Jean-Michel Charpentier, *Le Pidgin Bislama(r) et le multilinguisme aux Nouvelles-Hébrides* (Paris: Société d'Etudes Linguistiques et Anthropologiques de France, 1979).

26. Darrell Tryon, *Bislama: An Introduction to the National Language of Vanuatu* (Canberra: Australian National University, 1987), p. 3.

27. Stephen Wurm, "Papua New Guinea Nationhood: The Problems of a National Language," in Joshua Fishman, Charles Ferguson, and Jyotirindra Das

Gupta, eds., *Language Problems in Developing Countries* (New York: John Wiley and Sons, 1968), p. 355.

28. Crowley, "Language Issues and National Development in Vanuatu," p. 119.

29. This paradigm is borrowed from Herbert C. Kelman, "Language as an Aid and Barrier to Involvement in the National System," in Joan Rubin and Björn Jernudd, *Can Language Be Planned? Sociolinguistic Theory and Practice for Developing Nations* (Honolulu: University Press of Hawai'i, 1971). The extension and development of Bislama confirms the more general proposition that "language planning in a developing nation needs to pay particular attention to how both the instrumental attachment to the nation may be achieved and how sentimental attachment may be shifted from one's group to one's country by means of language" (Eastman, *Language Planning*, p. 44).

30. See Brian Weinstein, ed., *Language Policy and Political Development* (Norwood, MA: Ablex Publishing Corporation, 1990), p. 6.

31. Charpentier, *Le Pidgin Bislama(r)*, pp. 137-139, 143-144.

32. Figure 14.6 and Table B61 of the 1989 *Vanuatu National Population Census* indicate that 63.7 percent of Vanuatu over age six claim to speak Bislama; but from Table B62 of that same census one extrapolates a figure of 82 percent.

33. This figure is derived from extracting the non-ni-Vanuatu population enumerated in Table B18 from the percentage of residents speaking only a local language provided in Table B61.

34. Tryon and Charpentier, "Linguistic Problems in Vanuatu," p. 17. See also Crowley, "Language Issues and National Development in Vanuatu," p. 131.

35. Eastman, *Language Planning*, passim, 1983.

36. See Anthony Kirk-Greene, "The Hausa Language Board," *Afrika und Ubersee* 47 (1963): 187-203.

37. Charpentier, *Le Pidgin Bislama(r)*, p. 121.

38. The Bislama-English section of Terry Crowley's splendid dictionary (Vila: University of the South Pacific, 1990) contains an impressive 224 pages of entries. In the absence of widespread nonliturgical literature, Bislama nevertheless remains a predominantly oral language containing a virtually nonexistent passive vocabulary.

39. Joshua A. Fishman, "The Impact of Nationalism on Language Planning," in Joan Rubin and Bjorn H. Jernudd, eds., *Can Language Be Planned?* (Honolulu: University Press of Hawai'i, 1971), pp. 3-5.

40. D. T. Tryon and J.-M. Charpentier, "Linguistic Problems in Vanuatu," *Ethnies: Droits de l'homme et peuples autochtones* 4 (1989): 14.

41. Ibid., p. 14.

42. Ibid.

43. Crowley, "Language Issues and National Development in Vanuatu," p. 118.

44. Tryon and Charpentier, "Linguistic Problems in Vanuatu," p. 16.

45. Derived from Table B61 of 1989 *Vanuatu National Population Census,* p. 127.

46. Terry Crowley, "Language Issues and National Development in Vanuatu," p. 117.

47. Ibid., p. 122.

48. Tryon and Charpentier, "Language Issues and National Development in Vanuatu," p. 15.

49. Brian Weinstein, "Language Strategists: Redefining Political Frontiers on the Basis of Linguistic Choices," *World Politics* 31 (1979).

50. My account of Anglo-French bilingualism in Cameroon is based heavily on Beban Sammy Chumbow, "Language and Language Policy in Cameroon," in Ndivia Kofele-Kale, *An African Experiment in Nation Building: The Bilingual Cameroon Republic since Reunification* (Boulder, CO: Westview Press, 1980). See also Renaud Santerre, "Linguistique et Politique au Cameroun," *Journal of African Languages* 8 (1969). DeLancey's chapter on "Society and Culture" in his 1989 book, *Cameroon: Dependence and Independence* (Boulder, CO: Westview Press, 1989), is also very informative.

51. Chumbow, "Language and Language Policy in Cameroon," pp. 298, 307n.–308n.

52. This is a variation on Crawford Young's analysis of cultural entrepreneurs, in his classic *The Politics of Cultural Pluralism* (Madison: University of Wisconsin Press, 1976). Young acknowledges that "[l]anguage is a crucial expression of identity and will command much of [the cultural entrepreneur's] attention" (p. 46). In Vanuatu, where relationship to imported language has been *the* relevant marker within the political class, "linguistic entrepreneur" is more apt.

53. Weinstein, "Language Strategists," p. 362.

54. Eastman, *Language Planning,* p. 49. I have slightly altered Eastman's statement by replacing "ethnic" with "group" boundaries to make it more congruent with the Vanuatu reality of nonethnic linguistic division.

CHAPTER 5. NEW BOUNDARIES IN SPACE, TIME, LAW, GENDER, AND RACE

1. Joël Bonnemaison, "The Tree and the Canoe: Roots and Mobility in Vanuatu Societies," *Pacific Viewpoint* 25 (1984).

2. Joël Bonnemaison, "Territorial Control and Mobility within Ni-Vanuatu Societies," in Murray Chapman and R. Mansell Prothero, *Circulation in Population Movement: Substance and Concepts from the Melanesian Case* (London: Routledge and Kegan Paul, 1985).

3. R. D. Bedford, *New Hebridean Mobility: A Study of Circular Migration* (Canberra: Australian National University, 1973), pp. 14, 20; Gerald Haberkorn, "Temporary versus Permanent Population Mobility in Melanesia: A Case Study from Vanuatu," *International Migration Review* 26 (1992): 808.

4. Bedford, *New Hebridean Mobility,* pp. 16, 20.

5. Haberkorn, "Temporary versus Permanent Population Mobility in Melanesia," pp. 817–820.

6. Dorothy Shineberg, *They Came for Sandalwood,* p. 162.

7. Gerald Haberkorn, *Port Vila: Transit Station or Final Stop? Recent Developments in Ni-Vanuatu Population Mobility* (Canberra: Australian National University, 1989), pp. 8–9.

8. Ibid., p. 5.

9. Haberkorn, "Temporary versus Permanent Population Mobility in Melanesia," p. 810.

10. Bonnemaison, "Territorial Control and Mobility within Ni-Vanuatu Societies" p. 59.

11. Howard van Trease, *The Politics of Land in Vanuatu: From Colony to Independence* (Suva: University of the South Pacific, 1987).

12. Ibid., p. 261.

13. Interview with Prime Minister Carlot Korman, May 1992.

14. Haberkorn, *Port Vila,* p. 14.

15. Ibid., p. 152.

16. I cannot resist drawing a parallel between the Melanesian concept of *stamba* and the Hausa equivalent of *asali.* In Hausaland, ancestral origin can go back several generations without being lost to family memory. It will be intriguing to know if future generations of Santo and Vila dwellers will recall their *stamba* as assiduously.

17. Robert Tonkinson, "Forever Ambrymese? Identity in a Relocated Community, Vanuatu," *Pacific Viewpoint* 25 (1984).

18. Ibid., p. 148.

19. Van Trease, *The Politics of Land in Vanuatu,* p. 238, citing Bernard Narokobi, "Land in the Vanuatu Constitution," in Peter Larmour, ed., *Land, People and Government* (Suva: Institute of Pacific Studies of the University of the South Pacific, 1981), p. 151.

20. David Weisbrot, "Custom, Pluralism, and Realism in Vanuatu: Legal Development and the Role of Customary Law," *Pacific Studies* 13 (1989): 74.

21. William Rodman, "Gaps, Bridges and Levels of Law: Middlemen as Mediators in a Vanuatu Society," in William L. Rodman and Dorothy Ayers Counts, eds., *Middlemen and Brokers in Oceania* (Lanham, MD: University Press of America, 1983). My discussion of assessors and Condominium-era jurisprudence relies heavily on Rodman's account.

22. The classic treatment of African chieftaincy under colonial rule is Michael Crowder and Obaro Ikime, eds., *West African Chiefs: Their Changing Status under Colonial Rule and Independence* (New York: Africana, 1970). For a comparative treatment of the role of Vanuatu bigmen and African chiefs, see William Miles, "Traditional Rulers and Development Administration: Chieftaincy in Niger, Nigeria, and Vanuatu," *Studies in Comparative International Development* 28 (1993).

23. William Rodman, "'A Law unto Themselves': Legal Innovation in Ambae, Vanuatu," *American Ethnologist* (1985).

24. Weisbrot, "Custom, Pluralism, and Realism," pp. 80–81.

25. William Rodman, "The Law of the State and the State of the Law in Vanuatu," in Victoria Lockwood et al., *Contemporary Pacific Societies: Studies in Development and Change* (Englewood Cliffs, NJ: Prentice-Hall, 1990).

26. One highly placed expatriate member of the bar asserted, without concealing his displeasure, that those litigants who insist on their right to speak French in court do so merely to obstruct the proceedings.

27. William Rodman, "Gaps, Bridges and Levels of Law," p. 82.

28. Judicial postings have since experienced significant localization and some controversy. In mid-1996 Vincent Lunabek (a Francophone) and Kalkot Mataskelekele (an Anglophone) became the nation's first ni-Vanuatu judges, with a ni-Vanuatu taking over from the British public prosecutor. Later that year Prime Minister Vohor dismissed the chief justice of Vanuatu, Charles Vaudin d'Imecourt of the United Kingdom, although his contract had been renewed but a few months previously.

Vanuatu is not unique in having foreigners highly placed in its legal system long after independence; several members of the Commonwealth still have recourse to British jurisprudence and judges at the appellate and supreme court levels. In the Seychelles judges and state lawyers hail from Mauritius, Sri Lanka, and Tanzania.

29. This discussion relies on Joan Larcom, "Custom by Decree: Legitimation Crisis in Vanuatu," in Jocelyn Linnekin and Lin Poyer, eds., *Cultural Identity and Ethnicity in the Pacific* (Honolulu: University of Hawai'i Press, 1990). Though Larcom limits her discussion and conclusions to the Mewun people of Malakula, it is not abusive to extrapolate to the larger context of customary versus Western legal boundaries in Vanuatu.

30. Ron Adams, "Homo Anthropologicus and Man-Tanna," *Journal of Pacific History* 22 (1987): 13.

31. Margaret Jolly, *Women of the Place: "Kastom," Colonialism and Gender in Vanuatu* (Chur, Switzerland: Harwood Academic Publishers, 1994), pp. 10, 257.

32. Lissant Bolton, "*Bifo Yumi Ting Se Samting Nating:* The Women's Culture Project at the Vanuatu Cultural Centre," in Lamont Lindstrom and Geoffrey M. White, eds., *Culture, Kastom, Tradition: Developing Cultural Policy in Melanesia* (Suva: University of the South Pacific, 1994).

33. See Margaret Jolly, "Sacred Spaces: Churches, Men's Houses and Households in South Pentecost, Vanuatu," in Margaret Jolly and Martha Macintyre, eds., *Family and Gender in the Pacific: Domestic Contradiction and the Colonial Impact* (Cambridge University Press, 1989).

34. Haberkorn, *Port Vila,* and "Temporary versus Permanent Population Mobility in Melanesia." Haberkorn built on the solid foundation established by R. D. Bedford, *New Hebridean Mobility.*

35. Haberkorn, *Port Vila,* pp. 13–14 passim.

36. Haberkorn, "Temporary versus Permanent Population Mobility in Melanesia," p. 823.

37. Walter Lini, *Beyond Pandemonium: From the New Hebrides to Vanuatu* (Suva: University of the South Pacific, 1980), p. 34.

38. Quoted in Margaret Jolly, "The Politics of Difference: Feminism, Colonialism and Decolonisation in Vanuatu," in Gill Bottomley, et al., eds., *Intersexions. Gender/class/culture/ethnicity* (London: Allen and Unwin, 1991).

39. Jolly, "The Politics of Difference," p. 69.

40. Those familiar with the *stronghed* mentality of *man Tanna* will rightly take exception to this observation. Extensive cultural and locational diversity among the indigenous cultures of Vanuatu will temporize almost all generalizations relating to national character, belief, and custom.

41. See, for example, William F. S. Miles, "Colonial Hausa Idioms: Toward a West African Ethno-Ethnohistory," *African Studies Review* 36 (1993): esp. 24–25.

42. Jean Guiart, *Espiritu Santo* (Paris: Librairie Plon, 1958), p. 97. The specific reference is to Tom Harrisson.

43. Jean-Marc Philibert, "Social Change in Vanuatu," in Albert Robillard, ed., *Social Change in the Pacific Islands* (London: Kegan Paul, 1992), p. 122. The quote is from one of Philibert's informants.

44. For a detailed analysis of the larger implications of the land dive, see Margaret Jolly, "*Kastom* as Commodity: The Land Dive as Indigenous Rite and Tourist Spectacle in Vanuatu," in Lamont Lindstrom and Geoffrey M. White, eds., *Culture, Kastom, Tradition.*

45. Margaret Toukone, Mildred Sope, and Charles Pierce, *Le Tourisme à Vanuatu: Sciences Sociales 8.2.2.* (Vila: Ministry of Education, 1987), p. 25; my translation, emphasis in original. In presenting and encouraging student discussion on the potential negative cultural impact of tourism, the textbook is highly meritorious.

46. Interview with Chief Tuk, Yakukak, Tanna, March 1991.

47. As an American, I was hard-pressed to justify the perceived inequity of the present closeness of relations (particularly economic) between the United States and Japan, two former enemies, and the comparative neglect by the United States of Vanuatu, a former ally in the Pacific Theater. A more contemporary military analogy concerned the Gulf War, which was under way during my initial research in Vanuatu. Ni-Vanuatu easily drew parallels between Desert Storm, understood as an effort by the United States to protect a weak ally threatened by invasion, and the similar deployment of American forces in the New Hebrides during the Second World War.

48. Philibert, "Social Change in Vanuatu," pp. 124–126. First fieldwork impressions may carry disproportionate weight, but my first auditory memory in Vanuatu comes squarely from Erakor: the maddeningly familiar suburban drone of several lawnmowers.

49. Ted Gurr, *Why Men Rebel* (Princeton, NJ: Princeton University Press, 1970).

50. Mark Sturton and Andrew McGregor, *Vanuatu: Toward Economic Growth* (Honolulu: East-West Center, 1991).

51. Joël Bonnemaison, "Un Certain Refus de l'état: Autopsie d'une tentative de sécession en Mélanésie," *International Political Science Review* 6 (1985): 230-247.

52. See the articles following, and Bronwen Douglas' own introduction to "Fracturing Boundaries of Time and Place in Melanesian Anthropology," *Oceania* 66 (1996).

53. Jean Guiart, *Un siècle et demi de contacts culturels à Tanna. Nouvelles Hébrides* (Paris: Musée de l'Homme, 1956), p. 107.

54. Ibid., p. 115.

55. Guiart, *Espiritu Santo*, p. 164.

56. William Rodman, "When Questions Are Answers: The Message of Anthropology, According to the People of Ambae," *American Anthropologist* 93 (1991): 429.

57. S. Combs, "Will Television Really Spoil the South Pacific?" unpublished manuscript, 1995.

58. Rob Ferguson, "Paradise Lost, or On Sale Now?" *The Globe and Mail* (Toronto), November 17, 1993, p. A20.

59. Interview, August 1992.

60. Interview, May 1992.

CHAPTER 6. GLOBAL BOUNDARIES IN THE MICROCOSM

1. Ken Jowitt, "The New World Disorder," in Larry Diamond and Marc F. Plattner, eds., *The Global Resurgence of Democracy* (Baltimore: The Johns Hopkins University Press, 1993), p. 251; emphasis in original.

2. Joseph A. Camilleri, Anthony P. Jarvis, and Albert J. Paolini, eds., *The State in Transition: Reimagining Political Space* (Boulder, CO: Lynne Rienner, 1995), represents an important crossover of international politics with political geography.

3. Anthony Jarvis and Albert Paolini, "Locating the State," pp. 7, 15, 17.

4. Colin H. Williams, "Towards a New World Order: European and American Perspectives," in his edited *The Political Geography of the New World Order* (London: Belhaven Press, 1993).

5. Patrick Decloitre, "Chirac Rewards Carlot," *Pacific Islands Monthly*, December 1995, pp. 13-14.

6. Anna Buckley, "Return of the French," *Pacific Islands Monthly*, March 1992, p. 34.

7. Decloitre, "Chirac Rewards Carlot," p. 13.

8. Ibid.

9. John Whitbeck, "The Road to Peace Starts in Jerusalem: The Condominium Solution," *Middle East Policy* 3 (1994). Whitbeck credits former Undersecretary of State George Ball with having advanced the idea of an Arab-Israeli condominium in his 1992 book *The Passionate Attachment*. Without using the term "condominium," Ian Lustick has proposed as much in "Reinventing Jerusalem," *Foreign Policy* 93 (1993). Among Israeli legal scholars, Ruth Lapidot has invoked the condominium in her comparative research on Jerusalem.

10. D. P. O'Connell, "The Condominium of the New Hebrides," *British Yearbook of International Law 1968-1969* (London: Oxford University Press, 1970), p. 81.

BIBLIOGRAPHY

Adams, Ron. "Homo Anthropologicus and Man-Tanna: Jean Guiart and the Anthropological Attempt to Understand the Tannese." *Journal of Pacific History* 22 (1987): 3–14.

Aldrich, Robert. *France and the South Pacific since 1940.* Honolulu: University of Hawai'i Press, 1993.

Allen, Michael R. "Elders, Chiefs, and Big Men: Authority Legitimation and Political Evolution in Melanesia." *Ethnologist* 11 (1984): 20–41.

———. "The Establishment of Christianity and Cash-Cropping in a New Hebridean Community." *The Journal of Pacific History* 3 (1968): 25–46.

———. "Innovation, Inversion and Revolution as Political Tactics in West Aoba." In *Vanuatu: Politics, Economics and Ritual in Island Melanesia,* pp. 105–134. Sydney: Academic Press, 1981.

Anderson, Benedict. "Imagined Communities: Reflections on the Origins and Spread of Nationalism. London: Verso Books, 1983.

Anderson, J. "Nationalist Ideology and Territory." In R. Johnson, David Knight, and E. Kofman, eds., *Nationalism, Self-Determination and Political Geography.* London: Croon Helm, 1988.

Ardener, Edwin. "The Nature of the Reunification of Cameroon." In Arthur Hazlewood, ed., *African Integration and Disintegration: Case Studies Economic and Political Union.* London: Oxford University Press, 1967.

Asiwaju, A. I. *Partitioned Africans: Ethnic Relations across Africa's International Boundaries, 1884–1984.* New York: St. Martin's Press, 1985.

———. *Western Yorubaland under European Rule, 1889–1945.* Atlantic Highlands, NJ: Humanities Press, 1976.

Babadzan, Alain. "*Kastom* and Nation-Building in the South Pacific." In Remo Guidieri, Francesco Pellizzi, and Stanley J. Tambiah, eds., *Ethnicities and Nations: Processes of Interethnic Relations in Latin America, Southeast Asia, and the Pacific,* pp. 199–228. Austin: University of Texas Press, 1988.

Babineu, G. Raymond. "The Compulsive Border Crosser." *Psychiatry* 35 (1972): 281–290.

Banfield, Edward. *The Moral Basis of a Backward Society.* New York: The Free Press, 1958.

Barber, Benjamin R. *Jihad vs. McWorld.* New York: Random House, 1995.

Barnet, Richard J., and John Cavanagh. *Global Dreams: Imperial Corporations and the New World Order.* New York: Simon and Schuster, 1994.

Barth, Fredrik, ed. *Ethnic Groups and Boundaries: The Social Organization of Culture Difference.* Boston: Little, Brown and Company, 1969.

Beasant, John. *The Santo Rebellion: An Imperial Reckoning.* Honolulu: University of Hawai'i Press, 1984.

Bedford, R. D. *New Hebridean Mobility: A Study of Circular Migration.* Canberra: Australian National University, 1973.

Beer, William R., and James E. Jacob, eds. *Language Policy and National Unity.* Totowa, NJ: Rowman and Allanheld, 1985.

Benoist, Hubert. *Le Condominium des Nouvelles-Hébrides et la Société Mélanésienne.* Paris: Editions A. Pedone, 1972.

Benoit, Pierre. *Océanie Française.* Paris: Editions Alpina, 1933.

Bevan, Stuart. *Vanuatu: 10 Yia Blong Independens.* Rozelle, Australia: Other People Publications, 1990.

Bolton, Lissant. "*Bifo Yumi Ting Se Samting Nating:* The Women's Culture Project at the Vanuatu Cultural Center." In Lamont Lindstrom and Geoffrey M. White, eds., *Culture, Kastom, Tradition: Developing Cultural Policy in Melanesia,* pp. 147–160. Suva: University of the South Pacific, 1994.

Bonnemaison, Joël. "Un Certain Refus de l'état: Autopsie d'une tentative de sécession en Mélanésie." *International Political Science Review* 6 (1985): 230–247.

———. "Circular Migration and Uncontrolled Migration in the New Hebrides: Proposals for an Effective Urban Migration Policy." *South Pacific Bulletin,* 4th quarter (1976), pp. 7–13.

———. *Circulation in population movement: Substance and concepts from the Melanesian case,* pp. 57–79. London: Routledge and Kegan Paul, 1985.

———. *La Dernière Ile.* Paris: Arléa/Orstom, 1986.

———. "The Impact of Population Patterns and Cash-Cropping on Urban Migration in the New Hebrides." *Pacific Viewpoint* 18 (1977): 119–132.

———. "The Metaphor of the Tree and the Canoe." *Pacific Arts,* July 1994, pp. 21–24. Translated by Peter Crowe.

———. "Passions et misères d'une société coloniale: Les plantations au Vanuatu entre 1920 et 1980." *Société des Océanistes,* 82–83 (1986), pp. 65–84.

———. "Territorial Control and Mobility within niVanuatu Societies." In Murray Chapman and R. Mansell Prothero, eds., *Circulation in Population Movement: Substance and concepts from the Melanesian Case.* London: Routledge and Kegan Paul, 1985.

———. "The Tree and the Canoe: Roots and Mobility in Vanuatu Societies." *Pacific Viewpoint* 25 (1984): 117–151.

Bowman, Larry. *Mauritius: Democracy and Development in the Indian Ocean.* Boulder, CO: Westview Press, 1991.

Breuilly, John. *Nationalism and the State.* Chicago: University of Chicago Press, 1993 (1982).

Brown, Peter, and Henry Shue, eds. *Boundaries: National Autonomy and Its Limits.* Totowa, NJ: Rowman and Littlefield, 1981.

Brunton, Ron. *The Abandoned Narcotic: Kava and Cultural Instability in Melanesia.* Cambridge University Press, 1989.

———. "Kava and the Daily Dissolution of Society on Tanna, New Hebrides." *Mankind* 12 (1979): 93–103.

———. "The Origins of the John Frum Movement: A Sociological Explanation." In Michael Allen, ed., *Vanuatu: Politics, Economics and Ritual in Island Melanesia,* pp. 357–377. Sydney: Academic Press, 1981.

Charpentier, Jean-Michel. "La Francophonie en Mélanésie: Extension et avenir." *Anthropologie et Sociétés* 6 (1982): 107–126.

———. Le Pidgin Bislama(r) et le multilinguisme aux Nouvelles-Hébrides. Paris: Société d'Etudes Linguistiques et Anthropologiques (SELAF), 1979.

Cheesman, Evelyn F. R. E. S. *Camping Adventures on Cannibal Islands.* New York: Medill McBride, 1950.

Chumbow, Beban Sammy. "Language and Language Policy in Cameroon." In Ndiva Kofele-Kale, ed., *An African Experiment in Nation Building: The Bilingual Cameroon Republic since Reunification,* pp. 281–311. Boulder, CO: Westview Press, 1980.

Conforti, Joseph M. "The Cargo Cult and the Protestant Ethic as Conflicting Ideologies: Implications for Education." *The Urban Review* 21 (1989): 1–14.

Connell, John. *Sovereignty and Survival. Island Microstates in the Third World.* Sydney: Department of Geography, Research Monograph No. 3, University of Sydney, 1988.

Connor, Walker. *Ethnonationalism: The Quest for Understanding.* Princeton, NJ: Princeton University Press, 1994.

Corson, Mark W., and Julian V. Minghi. "Reunification of Partitioned Nation-States: Theory versus Reality in Vietnam and Germany." *Journal of Geography* 93 (1994): 125–131.

Crocombe, Ron. "The Continuing Creation of Identities in the Pacific Islands: Blood, Behavior, Boundaries and Belief." In David Hoosan, ed., *Geography and National Identity,* pp. 311–330. Oxford: Blackwell Publishers, 1994.

Crowder, Michael, and Obaro Ikime, eds. *West African Chiefs: Their Changing Status under Colonial Rule and Independence.* New York: Africana, 1970.

Crowley, Terry. *An Illustrated Bislama-English and English-Bislama Dictionary.* Vila: University of the South Pacific Pacific Languages Unit, 1990.

———. "Language Issues and National Development in Vanuatu." In István Fodor and Claude Hagège, eds., *Language Reform: History and Future,* 4:111–139. Hamburg: Helmut Buske Verlag, 1989.

Deacon, Bernard. *Malekula: A Vanishing People in the New Hebrides.* London: George Routledge and Sons, 1934.

Decornoy, Jacques. "Grandes puissances et micro-états dans le Pacifique sud." *Le Monde Diplomatique,* December 1986, p. 9.

DeLancey, Mark W. *Cameroon: Dependence and Independence.* Boulder, CO: Westview Press, 1989.

De La Rue, E. Aubert. "Aux Nouvelles Hébrides: La colonisation et le régime du Condominium." *La Géographie* 68 (1937): 193-207.

Delauney, Maurice. *Kala-Kala: De la grande à la petite histoire un ambassadeur raconte.* Paris: Editions Robert Laffont, 1986.

Delpech, Christiane, and Félix Bellaïche. *Hier les Nouvelles-Hébrides.* Arles: Perrin, 1987.

Deutsch, Karl. *Nationalism and Social Communication.* Cambridge, MA: MIT Press, 1966.

Dorian, Nancy. "Introduction." In Nancy C. Dorian, ed., *Investigating Obsolescence: Studies in Language Contraction and Death,* pp. 1-7. Cambridge University Press, 1989.

Douglas, Bronwen. "Introduction: Fracturing Boundaries of Time and Place in Melanesian Anthropology." *Oceania* 66 (1996): 177-188.

Downs, Roger, and David Stea. *Maps in Minds: Reflections on Cognitive Mapping.* New York: Harper and Row, 1977.

Drilhon, Freddy. *Le Peuple inconnu.* Paris: Amiot, 1955.

Eastman, Carol M. *Language Planning: An Introduction.* San Francisco: Chandler and Sharp, 1983.

Falk, Avner. "Border Symbolism Revisited." In Howard F. Stein and William G. Niederland, eds., *Maps from the Mind: Readings in Psychogeography.* Norman: University of Oklahoma Press, 1989.

Featherstone, Mike, ed. *Global Culture: Nationalism, Globalization and Modernity.* London: Sage Publications, 1990.

Ferguson, Rob. "Paradise Lost, or On Sale Now?" *The Globe and Mail* (Toronto), November 17, 1993, p. A20.

Fishman, Joshua A. *Bilingual Education: An International Sociological Perspective.* Rowley, MA: Newbury House Publishers, 1976.

————. *Language and Nationalism: Two Integrative Essays.* Rowley, MA: Newbury House Publishers, 1972.

Fishman, Joshua A., Charles A. Ferguson, and Jyotirindra Das Gupta, eds. *Language Problems of Developing Nations.* New York: John Wiley and Sons, 1968.

Forster, R. A. S. "Vanuatu: The End of an Episode of Schizophrenic Colonialism." *The Round Table* 280 (1980): 367-373.

Gédéon, Jacques. "Le Condominium des Nouvelles-Hébrides." *Société d'Etudes Historiques de Nouvelle Calédonie* 9 (1991): 61-80.

Gellner, Ernest. *Nations and Nationalism.* Oxford: Oxford University Press, 1983.

Ghai, Yash. "Vanuatu." In Peter Larmour and Ropafe Qalo, eds. *Decentralisation in the South Pacific: Local, Provincial and State Government in Twenty Countries,* pp. 43–73. Suva: University of the South Pacific, 1985.

Giles, H., R. Y. Bourhis, and D. M. Taylor. "Towards a Theory of Language in Ethnic Group Relations." In Howard Giles, ed., *Language, Ethnicity and Intergroup Relations,* pp. 307–347. London: Academic Press, 1977.

Glassner, Martin Ira. *Political Geography.* New York: John Wiley and Sons, 1992.

Goldman, Milton Forman. "Origins and Development of the Colonial Conflicts Resolved by the Anglo-French Entente of 1904." Ph.D. diss., The Fletcher School of Law and Diplomacy, Medford, MA, 1964.

Gottmann, Jean. "The Political Partitioning of Our World: An Attempt at Analysis." *World Politics* 4 (1952): 512–519.

———. *The Significance of Territory.* Charlottesville: University of Virginia Press, 1973.

Gould, Peter, and Rodney White. *Mental Maps.* 2d ed. Boston: Allen and Unwin, 1986.

Gourguechon, Charlene. *Journey to the End of the World: A Three-Year Adventure in the New Hebrides.* New York: Charles Scribner's Sons, 1977.

Grundy-Warr, Carl, and Richard N. Schofield. "Man-Made Lines That Divide the World." *The Geographical Magazine* 62 (1990): 10–15.

Guiart, Jean. "Culture Contact and the 'John Frum' Movement on Tanna, New Hebrides." *Southwestern Journal of Anthropology* 12 (1956): 105–116.

———. *Espiritu Santo (Nouvelles Hébrides).* Paris: Librairie Plon, 1958.

———. "Forerunners of Melanesian Nationalism." *Oceania* 22 (1951): 81–90.

———. "John Frum Movement in Tanna." *Oceania* 22 (1952): 165–177.

———. "Le mouvement 'Four Corner' à Tanna." *Océanistes* 46 (1975): 107–111.

———. *Un siècle et demi de contacts culturels à Tanna, Nouvelles Hébrides.* Paris: Musée de l'Homme, 1956.

Guidieri, Remo, and Franceso Pellizzi. "Introduction: 'Smoking Mirrors'—Modern Polity and Ethnicity." In Remo Guidieri, Francesco Pellizzi, and Stanley J. Tambiah, eds., *Ethnicities and Nations: Processes of Interethnic Relations in Latin America, Southeast Asia, and the Pacific,* pp. 7–38. Austin: University of Texas Press, 1988.

Haberkorn, Gerald. *Port Vila: Transit Station or Final Stop? Recent Developments in Ni-Vanuatu Population Mobility.* Canberra: Australian National University, 1989.

———. "Temporary versus Permanent Mobility in Melanesia: A Case Study from Vanuatu." *International Migration Review* 26 (1992): 806–842.

Harrisson, T. H. "Living in Espiritu Santo." *The Geographical Journal* 90 (1938): 243-261.

———. "Living with the People of Malekula." *The Geographical Journal* 88 (1936): 97-127.

———. "The New Hebrides People and Culture." *The Geographical Journal* 88 (1936): 332-341.

———. *Savage Civilisation.* London: Victor Gollancz, 1937.

Henningham, Stephen. *France and the South Pacific: A Contemporary History.* Honolulu: University of Hawai'i Press, 1992.

———. "Pluralism and Party Politics in a South Pacific State: Vanuatu's Ruling Vanua'aku Pati and Its Rivals." *Conflict* 9 (1989): 171-195.

Hilliard, David. *God's Gentlemen: A History of the Melanesian Mission, 1849-1942.* St. Lucia: University of Queensland Press, 1978.

Hintjens, Helen, and Malyn Newitt, eds. *The Political Economy of Small Tropical Islands: The Importance of Being Small.* Exeter, U.K.: University of Exeter Press, 1992.

Hobsbawm, E. J. *Nations and Nationalism since 1780: Programme, Myth, Reality.* 2d ed. Cambridge University Press, 1990.

Hobsbawm, Eric, and Terence Ranger, eds. *The Invention of Tradition.* Cambridge: Cambridge University Press, 1983.

Hours, B. "Leadership et cargo cult: L'Irresistible Ascension de J.T.P.S. Moïse." *Océanistes* 51-52 (1976): 207-231.

———. "Un Mouvement politico-religieux Neo-Hébridais: Le Nagriamel." *Cahiers ORSTOM, Série Sciences Humaines* 11 (1974): 227-242.

Howard, Alan. "Cultural Paradigms, History, and the Search for Identity in Oceania." In Jocelyn Linnekin and Lin Poyer, eds., *Cultural Identity and Ethnicity in the Pacific,* pp. 259-279. Honolulu: University of Hawai'i Press, 1990.

Huffer, Elise. *Politique extérieure blong Vanuatu 1980-1989.* Nouméa: OR-STOM, 1989.

Hume, Lynne. "Church and Custom on Maewo, Vanuatu." *Oceania* 56 (1986): 304-313.

Jackson, A. L. "Current Developments in the Pacific: Towards Political Awareness in the New Hebrides." *Journal of Pacific History* 7 (1972): 155-162.

Jacomb, Edward. *France and England in the New Hebrides: The Anglo-French Condominium.* Melbourne: George Robertson, 1914.

———. *The Joy Court (Comédie Rosse).* London: Braybook and Dobson, 1929.

Jarvis, Anthony P., and Albert J. Paolini. "Locating the State." In Joseph A. Camilleri, Anthony P. Jarvis, and Albert J. Paolini, *The State in Transition: Reimagining Political Space.* Boulder, CO: Lynne Rienner Publishers, 1995.

Johnson, R. J., David B. Knight, and Eleonore Kofman, eds. *Nationalism, Self-Determination and Political Geography.* London: Croon Helm, 1988.

Jolly, Margaret. "Birds and Banyans of South Pentecost: Kastom in Anti-Colonial Struggle." *Mankind* 13 (1982): 338-356.

―――. "Custom and the Way of the Land: Past and Present in Vanuatu and Fiji." *Oceania* 62 (1992): 330-354.

―――. "The Forgotten Women: A History of Migrant Labour and Gender Relations in Vanuatu." *Oceania* 58 (1987): 119-139.

―――. "*Kastom* as Commodity: The Land Dive as Indigenous Rite and Tourist Spectacle in Vanuatu." In Lamont Lindstrom and Geoffrey M. White, eds., *Culture, Kastom, Tradition: Developing Cultural Policy in Melanesia,* pp. 131-144. Suva: University of the South Pacific, 1994.

―――. "Sacred Spaces: Churches, Men's Houses and Households in South Pentecost, Vanuatu." In Margaret Jolly and Martha Macintyre, eds., *Family and Gender in the Pacific: Domestic Contradiction and the Colonial Impact,* pp. 213-234. Cambridge University Press, 1989.

―――. *Women of the Place: "Kastom," Colonialism and Gender in Vanuatu.* Chur, Switzerland: Harwood Academic Publishers, 1994.

Jolly, Margaret, and Nicholas Thomas. "The Politics of Tradition in the Pacific." *Oceania* 62 (1992): 241-248.

Jowitt, Ken. "The New World Disorder." In Larry Diamond and Marc F. Plattner, eds., *The Global Resurgence of Democracy,* pp. 247-256. Baltimore: The Johns Hopkins University Press, 1993.

Jupp, James. "Custom, Tradition, and Reform in Vanuatu Politics." *The Politics of Evolving Cultures in the Pacific Islands,* February 1982, pp. 143-158.

―――. "The Development of Party Politics in the New Hebrides." *Journal of Commonwealth and Comparative Politics* 3 (1979): 263-282.

―――. "Elections in Vanuatu." *Political Science* 35 (1983): 1-15.

Jupp, James, and Marian Sawer. "The New Hebrides: From Condominium to Independence." *Australian Oulook* 33 (1979): 15-25.

Kalsakau, G. K. *History of the Three Flags: New Hebrides' Changeover to the Republic of Vanuatu.* Vila: I.P.V. Printers, 1978.

Kedourie, Elie, ed. *Nationalism in Asia and Africa.* London: Widenfeld and Nicholson, 1971.

Keesing, Roger M. "Creating the Past: Custom and Identity in the Contemporary Pacific." *The Contemporary Pacific* 1 (1989): 19-42.

Keller, Janet D. "Woven World: Neotraditional Symbols of Unity in Vanuatu." *Mankind* 18 (1988): 1-13.

King, Anthony, D. "Introduction: Spaces of Culture, Spaces of Knowledge." In Anthony D. King, ed., *Culture, Globalization and the World-System: Contemporary Conditions for the Representation of Identity.* Binghamton: State University of New York Press, 1991.

Kirk-Greene, Anthony. "The Hausa Language Board." *Afrika und Ubersee* 47 (1963): 187-203.

Knight, David B. "Identity and Territory: Geographical Perspectives on Nationalism and Regionalism." *Annals of the Association of American Geographers* 72 (1982): 514-531.

———. "People Together, Yet Apart: Rethinking Territory, Sovereignty, and Identities." In George J. Demko and William B. Wood, eds., *Reordering the World: Geopolitical Perspectives on the Twenty-first Century,* pp. 71-86. Boulder, CO: Westview Press, 1994.

———. "Territory and People or People and Territory? Thoughts on Postcolonial Self-Determination." *International Political Science Review* 6 (1985): 248-272.

Laitin, David D. "The Game Theory of Language Regimes." *International Political Science Review* 14 (1993): 227-239.

———. *Language Repertoires and State Construction in Africa.* Cambridge University Press, 1992.

Lane, R. B. "The Melanesians of South Pentecost, New Hebrides." In P. Lawrence and M. J. Meggitt, eds., *Gods, Ghosts and Men in Melanesia: Some Religions of Australian New Guinea and the New Hebrides,* pp. 250-279. Melbourne: Oxford University Press, 1965.

Lapidoth, Ruth. "Jerusalem: Past, Present and Future." Unpublished article prepared for the Jerusalem Institute for Israel Studies.

Larcom, Joan. "Custom by Decree: Legitimation Crisis in Vanuatu." In Jocelyn Linnekin and Lin Poyer, eds., *Cultural Identity and Ethnicity in the Pacific,* pp. 175-190. Honolulu, University of Hawai'i Press, 1990.

———. "Following Deacon: The Problem of Ethnographic Reanalysis, 1926-1981." In George W. Stocking, ed., *Observers Observed: Essays on Ethnographic Fieldwork,* pp. 175-195. Madison: University of Wisconsin, 1983.

———. "The Invention of Convention." *Mankind* 13 (1982): 330-337.

Larmour, Peter, ed. *Land Tenure in Vanuatu.* Suva: University of the South Pacific, 1984.

Leder, Jean. *Les Cent Jours du bout du monde.* Nouméa: Impriméries Réunies de Nouméa, 1981.

Lepage, Sylvie. "Vanuatu: Rivalités post-coloniales aux antipodes." *Le Monde,* April 21, 1994, p. 6.

Levy, Françoise P., and Segaud, Marion. *Anthropologie de l'espace.* Paris: Centre Georges Pompidou, 1983.

Leymang, Gérard. *Political Utopia of the Year 2000.* Vila, 1991.

Lindstrom, Lamont. "Big Men as Ancestors: Inspiration and Copyrights on Tanna (Vanuatu)." *Ethnology* 29 (1990): 313-326.

———. *Cargo Cult: Strange Stories of Desire from Melanesia and Beyond.* Honolulu: University of Hawai'i Press, 1993.

———. "Cult and Culture: American Dreams in Vanuatu." *Pacific Studies* 4 (1981): pp. 101-123.

———. "Cultural Politics: National Concerns in Bush Arenas on Tanna

(Vanuatu)." In *The Politics of Evolving Cultures: The Pacific Islands*, pp. 232-246. Institute for Polynesian Studies Conference Proceedings, 1982.

———. "Kava, Cash, and Custom in Vanuatu." *Cultural Survival Quarterly* 15 (1991): 28-31.

———. "Knowledge of Cargo, Knowlege of Cult: Truth and Power on Tanna, Vanuatu." In G. W. Trompf, ed., *Cargo Cults and Millenarian Movements: Transoceanic Comparisons of New Religous Movements*, pp. 239-261. Berlin: Mouton de Gruyter, 1990.

———. "Leftamap Kastom: The Political History of Tradition on Tanna, Vanuatu." *Mankind* 13 (1982): 316-329.

———. "Say What? Language and Political Boundaries on Tanna (Vanuatu)." *Anthropological Linguistics* 25 (1983): 387-403.

———. "Speech and Kava on Tanna." In Michael Allen, ed., *Vanuatu: Politics, Economics and Ritual in Island Melanesia*, pp. 379-393. Sydney: Academic Press, 1981.

———. "Spitting on Tanna." *Oceania* 50 (1980): 228-334.

———. "Traditional Cultural Policy in Melanesia *(Kastom Polisi long Kastom)*." In Lamont Lindstrom and Geoffrey M. White, eds., *Culture, Kastom, Tradition: Developing Cultural Policy in Melanesia*, pp. 66-81. Suva: University of the South Pacific, 1994.

Lindstrom, Lamont, and Geoffrey M. White. "Cultural Policy: An Introduction." In Lamont Lindstrom and Geoffrey M. White, eds., *Culture, Kastom, Tradition: Developing Cultural Policy in Melanesia*, pp. 1-18. Suva: University of the South Pacific, 1994.

Lini, Walter. *Beyond Pandemonium: From the New Hebrides to Vanuatu*. Wellington: Asia Pacific Books, 1980.

———. "Christians in Politics." In G. W. Trompf, ed., *The Gospel Is Not Western*, pp. 183-185. Maryknoll, NY: Orbis Books, 1987.

Linnekin, Jocelyn, and Lin Poyer. "Introduction." In Jocelyn Linnekin and Lin Poyer, eds., *Cultural Identity and Ethnicity in the Pacific*, pp. 1-16. Honolulu: University of Hawai'i Press, 1990.

Luhmann, Niklas. "The World Society as a Social System." *Journal of General Systems* 8 (1982): 131-138.

Lynch, Bohun, ed. *Isles of Illusion: Letters from the South Seas*. London: Century, 1986 (1923).

Lynch, C. J. "The Constitution of Vanuatu." *The Parliamentarian: Journal of the Parliaments of the Commonwealth* 62 (1981): 45-53.

MacClancy, James V. "Vanuatu since Independence: 1980-83." *The Journal of Pacific History* 19 (1984): 100-112.

———. "Kastom and Politics." *International Journal of Moral and Social Studies* 3 (1988): 95-110.

———. "Mana: An Anthropological Metaphor for Island Melanesia." *Oceania* 57 (1986): 142-152.

MacClancy, Jeremy. *To Kill a Bird with Two Stones: A Short History of Vanuatu.* Vila: Vanuatu Cultural Centre Publication No. 1.

———. "Vanuatu and Kastom: A Study of Cultural Symbols in the Inception of a Nation-State in the South Pacific." Ph.D. diss., Wolfson College, Oxford, 1983.

MacDonald, Barrie. "Current Developments in the Pacific: Self-Determination and Self-Government." *The Journal of Pacific History* 17 (1982): 51–61.

Macdonald-Milne, Brian, and Pamela Thomas, eds. *Yumi Stanap: Leaders and Leadership in a New Nation.* Pacific Churches Research Centre, 1981.

MacQueen, Norman. "Beyond Tok Win: The Papua New Guinea Intervention in Vanuatu, 1980." *Pacific Affairs* 6: (1988), pp. 235–252.

———. "Sharpening the Spearhead: Subregionalism in Melanesia." *Pacific Studies* 12 (1989): 33–52.

McGregor, Andrew, and Mark Sturton. *Vanuatu: Toward Economic Growth.* Honolulu: East–West Center, 1991.

Makharita, Ragaa, Mary O'Sullivan, and Marguerite Castello. "Rural Training in Vanuatu." *Public Administration and Development* 11 (1991): 211–214.

Mark, Gamali. "Post-Primary Education in the New Hebrides: Problems and Prospects." Masters thesis, University of Leeds, 1979.

Marshall, A. J. *The Black Musketeers: The Work and Adventures of a Scientist on a South Sea Island at War and in Peace.* London: William Heinemann, 1937.

Matas-Kalkot, Singoleo Hanson. "Silon Dan: A Movement on the Island of Pentecost (Raga) in Vanuatu." In Carl Loeliger and Gary Trompf, eds., *New Religious Movements in Melanesia,* pp. 149–162. Suva: University of the South Pacific, 1985.

Miles, William F. S. "Anachronistic Antagonisms: France versus Britain in the New Hebrides, 1966–1977." In James Pritchard, ed., *Proceedings of the Nineteenth Meeting of the French Colonial Historical Society Providence, R. I. May 1993,* pp. 200–215. Cleveland, OH: FHCS, 1994.

———. "Colonial Hausa Idioms: Toward a West African Ethno-Ethnohistory." *African Studies Review* 36 (1993): 11–30.

———. *Elections in Nigeria: A Grassroots Perspective.* Boulder, CO: Lynne Rienner Publishers, 1988.

———. "Francophonie in Post-Colonial Vanuatu." *The Journal of Pacific History* 29 (1994): 49–65.

———. *Hausaland Divided: Colonialism and Independence in Nigeria and Niger.* Ithaca, NY: Cornell University Press, 1994.

———. *Imperial Burdens: Countercolonialism in Former French India.* Boulder, CO: Lynne Rienner Publishers, 1995.

———. *International and Minoritarian Francophonie: Convergence and Contradiction.* Jerusalem: Truman Research Institute, 1995.

———. "Minoritarian Francophonie: The Case of Israel, with Special Reference to the Palestinian Territories." *International Migration Review* 29 (1995): 1023-1040.

———. "Pigs, Politics and Social Change in Vanuatu," *Society and Animals* 5 (1997): 155-167.

———. "*Retour au Paradis?* France and Vanuatu in the South Pacific." *French Politics and Society* 12 (1994): 58-71.

———. "Traditional Rulers and Development Administration: Chieftaincy in Niger, Nigeria and Vanuatu." *Studies in Comparative International Development* 28 (1993): 31-50.

Minghi, Julian V. "Boundary Studies in Political Geography." *Annals of American Geographers* (Association of American Geographers), 1963, pp. 407-428.

Mlinar, Zdravko, ed. *Globalization and Territorial Identities*. Aldershot: Avebury, 1992.

Molisa, Grace, Nikenike Vurobaravu, and Howard Van Trease. "Vanuatu: Overcoming Pandemonium." In *Politics in Melanesia*, pp. 83-115. Suva: University of the South Pacific, 1982.

Monnier, Paul. *One Hundred Years of Mission: The Catholic Church in Vanuatu 1887-1987*. Vila, 1987.

Nietschmann, Bernard. "The Fourth World: Nations versus States." In George Demko and William Wood, eds., *Reordering the World: Geopolitical Perspectives on the Twenty-first Century*. Boulder, CO: Westview Press, 1994.

Norton, Robert. "Culture and Identity in the South Pacific: A Comparative Analysis." *Man* 28 (1993): 741-759.

O'Connell, D. P. "The Condominium of the New Hebrides." *British Yearbook of International Law 1968-1969*, pp. 71-145. London: Oxford University Press, 1970.

O'Reilly, Patrick. *Hébridais: Répertoire bio-bibliographique des Nouvelles-Hébrides*. Paris: Publications de la Société des Océanistes, 1957.

———. "Prophétisme aux Nouvelles-Hébrides: Le Mouvement Jonfrum à Tanna (1940-1947)." *Le Monde Non-Chrétien* 10 (1949): 192-208.

Paden, John N. "Language Problems of National Integration in Nigeria: The Special Position of Hausa." In Joshua A. Fishman, Charles A. Ferguson, and Jyotirindra Das Gupta, eds. *Language Problems in Developing Countries*, pp. 199-213. New York: John Wiley and Sons, 1968.

Pagni, Lucien. "Vanuatu: An Economy Caught between Culture and Modernism." *The Courier*, January-February 1989, pp. 18-27.

Philibert, Jean-Marc. "Living under Two Flags: Selective Modernization in Erakor Village, Efate." In Michael Allen, ed., *Vanuatu: Politics, Economics, and Ritual in Island Melanesia*, pp. 315-336. Sydney: Academic Press, 1981.

———. "The Politics of Tradition: Toward a Generic Culture in Vanuatu." *Mankind* 16 (1986): 1-12.

————. "Social Change in Vanuatu." In Albert B. Robillard, ed., *Social Change in the Pacific Islands*, pp. 98-133. London: Kegan Paul, 1992.

————. "Vers une symbolique de la modernisation au Vanuatu." *Anthropologie et Sociétés* 6 (1982): 69-97.

————. "Will Success Spoil a Middleman? The Case of Etapang, Central Vanuatu." In William J. Rodman and Dorothy Ayers Counts, eds., *Middlemen and Brokers in Oceania*, pp. 187-207. Lanham, MD: University Press of America, 1983.

Popkin, Samuel L. *The Rational Peasant: The Political Economy of Rural Society in Vietnam*. Berkeley: University of California Press, 1979.

Premdas, Ralph R. "Melanesian Socialism: Vanuatu's Quest for Self-Definition." *Journal of Commonwealth and Comparative Politics* 25 (1987): 141-160.

————. "Secession and Decentralization in Political Change: the Case of Vanuatu." In Ralph R. Ramada and Jeffrey S. Steeves, eds., *Politics and Government in Vanuatu. From Colonial Unity to Post-Colonial Disunity*. James Cook University of North Queensland, 1989.

————. "Vanuatu: Melanesian Socialism and Political Change." *The Round Table* 304 (1987), pp. 497-505.

Premdas, Ralph R., and Jeffrey S. Steeves. "Political and Constitutional Crisis in Vanuatu." *The Round Table* 313 (1990): 43-64.

————. "Politics in Vanuatu: The 1991 Elections. Ethno-Linguistic Accommodation and Party Competition." *Journal de la Société des Océanistes* 100-101 (1995): 221-234.

————. "Vanuatu: The Evolution of the Administrative and Political Context of Decentralization." *Public Administration and Development* 4 (1988): 231-248.

————. "Vanuatu: The 1987 National Elections and Their Aftermath." *Journal of Pacific History* 24 (1989): 110-117.

————. "Vanuatu: The 1991 Elections and the Emergence of a New Order." *The Round Table* 323 (1992): 339-357.

————. "Vanuatu: The Politics of Anglo-French Cooperation in the Post-Lini Era." *Journal of Commonwealth and Comparative Politics* 32 (1994): 68-86.

————, eds. *Politics and Government in Vanuatu: From Colonial Unity to Post-Colonial Disunity*. North Queensland: James Cook University, 1989.

Prescott, J.R.V. *Political Geography*. New York: St. Martin's Press, 1972.

Pujol, René. "La Codification des coutumes indigènes aux Nouvelles-Hébrides." *Journal de la Société des Océanistes* 13 (1956): 336-339.

Raffestin, Claude. *Pour une géographie du pouvoir*. Paris: Librairies Techniques, 1980.

Republic of Vanuatu. *Second National Development Plan 1987-1991*.

————. *Vanuatu National Population Census: May 1989*. Vila: Statistics Office, 1991.

Rice, Edward. *John Frum He Come: A Polemic Work about a Black Tragedy.* Garden City, NY: Doubleday and Company, 1974.

Rivers, W. H. R. *The History of Melanesian Society.* Cambridge University Press, 1914.

Robertson, R. T. "Vanuatu: Fragile Foreign Policy Initiatives." *Development and Change* 19 (1988): 617-647.

Robertson, Roland. "Globalization Theory and Civilizational Analysis." *Comparative Civilizations Review* 17 (1987): 20-30.

———. "Social Theory, Culture Relativity and the Problem of Globality." In Anthony King, ed., *Culture, Globalization and The World-System: Contemporary Conditions for the Representation of Identity.* Binghamton: State University of New York Press, 1991.

Robertson, Roland, and Frank Lechner. "Modernization, Globalization and the Problem of Culture in World-Systems Theory." *Theory, Culture and Society* 2 (1985): 103-117.

Robie, David. *Blood on Their Banner: Nationalist Struggles in the South Pacific.* London: Zed Books, 1989.

Rodman, Margaret Critchlow. *Deep Water: Development and Change in Pacific Village Fisheries.* Boulder, CO: Westview Press, 1989.

———. "Keeping Options Open: Copra and Fish in Rural Vanuatu." In Victoria S. Lockwood, Thomas G. Harding, and Ben J. Wallace, eds., *Contemporary Pacific Societies: Studies in Development and Change,* pp. 171-184. Englewood Cliffs, NJ: Prentice-Hall, 1990.

Rodman, William L. "Gaps, Bridges and Levels of Law: Middlemen as Mediators in a Vanuatu Society." In William L. Rodman and Dorothy Ayers Counts, eds., *Middlemen and Brokers in Oceania.* Lanham, MD: University Press of America, 1983.

———. "'A Law unto Themselves': Legal Innovation in Ambae, Vanuatu." *American Ethnologist* 12 (1985): 603-624.

———. "The Law of the State and the State of the Law in Vanuatu." In V. Lockwood, T. Harding, and B. J. Wallace, eds., *Contemporary Pacific Studies,* pp. 55-66. Englewood Cliffs, NJ: Prentice-Hall, 1990.

———. "Sorcery and the Silencing of Chiefs: 'Words on the Wind' in Postindependence Ambae." *Journal of Anthropological Research* 49 (1993): 217-235.

———. "When Questions Are Answers: The Message of Anthropology, According to the People of Ambae." *American Anthropologist* 93 (1991): 421-434.

Rodman, William L., and Margaret Rodman. "Rethinking Kastom: On the Politics of Place Naming in Vanuatu." *Oceania* 55 (1985): 242-251.

Romaine, Suzanne. "Pidgins, Creoles, Immigrant, and Dying Languages." In Nancy C. Dorian, ed., *Investigating Obsolescence: Studies in Language Contraction and Death,* pp. 369-383. Cambridge University Press, 1989.

Roslyn, Norman. "Transition and History of Education and Current Status of Education Administration and System in Vanuatu." *Asian Culture Quarterly* 12 (1984): 81–83.

Rothwell, N. "Kava: A Pacific Ritual." *Pacific Islands Monthly,* February 1988, pp. 16–18.

Rubin, Joan, and Bjorn H. Jernudd, eds., *Can Language Be Planned?* Honolulu: University Press of Hawai'i, 1971.

Ruhumbika, Gabriel. "The African Language Policy of Development: African National Languages." *Research in African Literature* 23 (1992): 73–82.

Rumley, Dennis, and Julian V. Minghi, eds., *The Geography of Border Landscapes.* London: Routledge, 1991.

Sahlins, Peter. *Boundaries: The Making of France and Spain in the Pyrenees.* Berkeley: University of California Press, 1989.

Sanchez, Marc. *Un Lycée à Port Vila.* Centre Culturel de Port-Vila, 1979.

Santerre, Renaud. "Linguistique et politique au Cameroun." *Journal of African Languages* 8 (1969): 153–159.

Scarr, Deryck. *Fragments of Empire: A History of the Western Pacific High Commission 1877–1914.* Canberra: Australian National University Press, 1967.

Schelesinger, Philip. "On National Identity: Some Conceptions and Misconceptions Criticized." *Social Science Information* 26 (1987): 219–264.

Scott, James C. *The Moral Economy of the Peasant: Rebellion and Resistance in South East Asia.* New Haven and London: Yale University Press, 1976.

Shears, Richard. *The Coconut War: The Crisis on Espiritu Santo.* Melbourne: Cassell Australia, 1980.

Shineberg, Dorothy. *They Came for Sandalwood: A Study of the Sandalwood Trade in the South-West Pacific 1830–1865.* Melbourne: Melbourne University Press, 1967.

Slowe, Peter M. *Geography and Political Power: The Geography of Nations and States.* London: Routledge, 1990.

Smith, Anthony D., ed. *Ethnicity and Nationalism.* Leiden: E. J. Brill, 1992.

———. *National Identity.* Reno: University of Nevada Press, 1991.

———. *Theories of Nationalism.* 2d ed. New York: Holmes and Maier, 1983. 1st ed. New York: Harper and Row, 1971.

Spriggs, Mathew. "'A School in Every District.'" *The Journal of Pacific History* 20 (1985): 23–41.

Stein, Howard F., and William G. Niederland, eds. *Maps from the Mind: Readings in Psychogeography.* Norman: University of Oklahoma Press, 1989.

Sturton, Mark, and Andrew McGregor. *Vanuatu: Toward Economic Growth.* Honolulu: East-West Center, 1991.

Taylor, Peter. *Political Geography: World-Economy, Nation-State and Locality.* 3d ed. Essex: Longman Scientific and Technical, 1993.

Tétu, Michel. *La Francophonie: Histoire, problématique et perspectives.* Paris: Hachette, 1988.

Thérien, Jean-Philippe. "Co-operation and Conflict in la Francophonie." *International Journal* 48 (1993): 492-526.

Thomas, Bradford L. "International Boundaries: Lines in the Sand (and the Sea)." In George J. Demko and William B. Wood, eds., *Reordering the World. Geopolitical Perspectives on the Twenty-first Century,* pp. 87-99. Boulder, CO: Westview Press, 1994.

Tonkinson, Robert. "Church and Kastom in Southeast Ambrym." In Michael Allen, ed., *Vanuatu: Politics, Economics, and Ritual in Island Melanesia,* pp. 315-336. Sydney: Academic Press, 1981.

———. "Forever Ambrymese? Identity in a Relocated Community, Vanuatu." *Pacific Viewpoint* 25 (1984): 139-159.

———. "National Identity and the Problem of Kastom in Vanuatu." *Mankind* 13 (1982): 306-315.

———. "Sorcery and Social Change in Southeast Ambrym, Vanuatu." *Social Analysis* 8 (1981): 77-88.

———. "Vanuatu Values: A Changing Symbiosis." *Pacific Studies* 5 (1982): 44-63.

Trask, Haunani-Kay. "Natives and Anthropologists: The Colonial Struggle." *The Contemporary Pacific* 3 (1991): 159-166.

Tryon, Darrel. *Bislama: An Introduction to the National Language of Vanuatu.* Canberra: Australian National University, 1987.

Tryon, D. T., and J. M. Charpentier. "Linguistic Problems in Vanuatu." *Ethnies: Droits de l'homme et peuples autochtones* 4 (1989): 13-17.

Turner, James West. "'Owners of the Path': Cognatic Kinship Categories in Matailobau, Fiji." *Oceania* 56 (1986): 275-303.

Van Lierop, Robert F. "Statement on Behalf of the Member States of the South Pacific Forum to the Special Committee on Decolonization on the Question of New Caledonia." New York: United Nations, 1990.

———. "Statement to the 45th Session of the General Assembly on Agenda Item 18: Implementation of the Declaration on the Granting of Independence to Colonial Countries and Peoples." New York: United Nations, 1990.

Van Trease, Howard. *The Politics of Land in Vanuatu: From Colony to Independence.* Suva: University of the South Pacific, 1987.

Vanuatu: Twenti wan tingting long team blong independens. Suva: Institute of Pacific Studies, 1980.

Videau, Daniel. "L'Evolution récente des territoires français du Pacifique." *Académie des Sciences d'Outre-Mer* 42 (1982): 57-72.

Villacorta, Wilfrido V. "The Politics of Language in the Third World: Toward Theory Building." *International Journal of the Sociology of Language* 88 (1991): 33-44.

Vos, Edwin. "EEC-Vanuatu Cooperation." *The Courier,* January–February 1989, pp. 28-30.

Wallerstein, Immanuel. *Geopolitics and Geoculture: Essays on the Changing World-System.* Cambridge University Press, 1991.

———. "The National and the Universal: Can There Be Such a Thing as World Culture?" In Anthony King, ed., *Culture, Globalization and The World-System: Contemporary Conditions for the Representation of Identity.* Binghamton: State University of New York Press, 1991.

Waterman, Stanley. "Partitioned States." *Political Geography Quarterly* 6 (1987): 151-170.

Weinstein, Brian. *The Civic Tongue: Political Consequences of Language Choices.* New York: Longman, 1983.

———. "Francophonie: Language Planning and National Interests." In Cheris Kramarae, Muriel Schultz, and William M. O'Barr, eds., *Language and Power,* pp. 227-242. Beverly Hills, CA: Sage Publications, 1984.

———. "Francophonie: Purism at the International Level." In Bjorn H. Jernudd and Michael Shapiro, eds., *The Politics of Language Purism,* pp. 53-79. Berlin: Mouton de Gruyter, 1989.

———. "Language Planning in Francophone Africa." *Language Problems and Language Planning* 4 (1980): 55-77.

———. "Language Strategists: Redefining Political Frontiers on the Basis of Linguistic Choices." *World Politics* 31 (1979): 345-364.

———, ed. *Language Policy and Political Development.* Norwood, MA: Ablex Publishing Corporation, 1990.

Weisbrot, David. "Custom, Pluralism, and Realism in Vanuatu: Legal Development and the Role of Customary Law." *Pacific Studies* 13 (1989): 65-98.

Whitbeck, John V. "The Road to Peace Starts in Jerusalem: The Condominium Solution." *Middle East Policy* 3 (1994): 110-118.

Williams, Colin H. "Towards a New World Order: European and American Perspectives." In Colin H. Williams, ed., *The Political Geography of the New World Order,* pp. 1-19. London: Belhaven Press, 1993.

Williams, Colin, and Anthony D. Smith. "The National Construction of Social Space." *Progress in Human Geography,* 7:502-518. London: Eric Arnold, 1983.

Woodward, K. "Historical Summary of Constitutional Advance in the New Hebrides, 1954-1977." Vila: British Residency, 1978.

Wurm, Stephen. "Papua New Guinea Nationhood: The Problems of a National Language." In Joshua A. Fishman, Charles A. Ferguson, and Jyotirindra Das Gupta, eds., *Language Problems in Developing Countries.* New York: John Wiley and Sons, 1968.

Young, Michael. "Gone Native in Isles of Illusion: In search of Asterisk in Epi." In James G. Carrier, ed., *History and Tradition in Melanesian Anthropology,* pp. 193-223. Berkeley: University of California Press, 1992.

————. "Kava and Christianity in Central Vanuatu." *Canberra Anthropology* 18 (1995): 61–96.

Zorgbibe, Charles. "Les Nouvelles-Hébrides: Une indépendance difficile." *Revue politique et parlementaire* 39 (1980): 56–64.

————. *Vanuatu: Naissance d'un état.* Paris: Economica, 1981.

Young, Crawford. *The Politics of Cultural Pluralism.* Madison: University of Wisconsin Press, 1976.

INDEX

About the Author

WILLIAM F. S. MILES, a graduate of Vassar College and The Fletcher School of Law and Diplomacy, is presently professor of political science at Northeastern University. He has authored books on the French Antilles *(Elections and Ethnicity in French Martinique: A Paradox in Paradise)*, on West Africa *(Hausaland Divided: Colonialism and Independence in Nigeria and Niger; Elections in Nigeria: A Grassroots Perspective)*, and Pondicherry *(Imperial Burdens: Countercolonialism in Former French India)*. He is presently working on a book about Mauritius.